Corporate Philanthropy at the Crossroads

PHILANTHROPIC STUDIES

Robert L. Payton and Dwight F. Burlingame,
GENERAL EDITORS

Corporate Philanthropy at the Crossroads

EDITED BY
Dwight F. Burlingame
AND
Dennis R. Young

Indiana University Press

BLOOMINGTON AND INDIANAPOLIS

Publication of this book is made possible in part with the assistance of a Challenge Grant from the National Endowment for the Humanities, a federal agency that supports research, education, and public programming in the humanities.

The paper used in this publication meets the minimum requirements of American National Standard for Information Sciences—Permanence of Paper for Printed Library Materials, ANSI Z39.48-1984.

MANUFACTURED IN THE UNITED STATES OF AMERICA

Library of Congress Cataloging-in-Publication Data

Corporate philanthropy at the crossroads / edited by Dwight F. Burlingame and Dennis R. Young.
      p.   cm. — (Philanthropic studies)
   Includes bibliographical references and index.
   ISBN 0-253-33077-7 (cloth : alk. paper)
   1. Corporations—Charitable contributions—United States. 2. Downsizing of organizations—United States.   I. Burlingame, Dwight. II. Young, Dennis R., date.   III. Series.
HG4028.C6C665   1996
331.7'65'0973—dc20   96-3321

   2 3 4 5   01 00 99 98 97

For Lee and Sharon
Seth, Barry, Cheryl, and Mark

CONTENTS

FOREWORD

JAMES P. SHANNON

In the decade of the 1980s many American corporations were dramatically restructured. Whether this process occurred voluntarily or involuntarily on their part, it has put the current managers of corporate philanthropy on notice that henceforth their departments would be evaluated by management against the same standards of performance, efficiency, production, and achievement as all other departments in their companies. The problem posed by these new standards is that until now many corporate giving programs have had no clear mission statement, no regular documentation of their effectiveness and no systematic way of measuring whether or how their work products complemented the mission or the strategic plans of their parent companies.

In the same decade the number of graduate schools in this country offering advanced degrees in philanthropy (global and domestic), volunteerism, or nonprofit management has grown dramatically. Alert corporate managers now know that they need outside help to create new systems for tracking the efficacy of their giving programs; and academics working in the new nonprofit curricula now realize their acute need for realistic strategies and research methods to help corporate grantmakers survive and prosper in a dramatically altered corporate milieu.

In April 1994 the Mandel Center for Nonprofit Organizations at Case Western Reserve University and the Indiana University Center on Philanthropy convened a meeting of selected corporate grantmakers and academics active in research on corporate philanthropy to explore how these two groups might identify a mutually attractive research agenda for the decade of the 1990s and the twenty-first century. This book is the work product of that symposium. Its authors modestly admit that their collective efforts are a tentative beginning to what all parties hope will be an extended and fruitful discussion over time of the elements which make up the art form this text calls "corporate philanthropy."

To be successful this effort at cooperation will require goodwill, mutual respect, and continuing collegial dialogue between practitioners of the art of grant making and scholars in search of new and better ways to study and to report on how this art form can be measured, quantified, and evaluated.

Traditionally, some (not all) American business firms have set an admirable example for their global peers in their willingness to share voluntarily some of their profits with the various communities in which they have a significant presence. Unfortunately these magnanimous corporate citizens have done little since colonial days to document precisely why and how they have shared their largesse with the larger society beyond their corporate boundaries. The fact of their generosity is well documented. The reasons for it are not so clear. Hence the challenge for them now is to become more self-conscious about their giving and more willing to work with scholars interested in doing research and publications on why and how corporate philanthropy can best serve its sponsors and society at large.

Admittedly corporate grantmakers and would-be students of this art form have come belatedly to their mutual acceptance of corporate philanthropy as a legitimate subject for academic study. In this tardy recognition they follow the trail blazed by for-profit corporations which learned long ago their need for scholarly assistance to turn the art of corporate management into a quasi science.

In essence, the several authors of this book present a set of four paradigms for organizing an abundance of discrete data surrounding American philanthropy as it has developed historically. In the words of Dennis Young and Dwight Burlingame these four paradigms could be described as follows:

- (1). "The Neo-Classical/Corporate Productivity Model [is designed] to contribute to the ability of the firm to make profits. . . . [Its] ultimate measure of success is increased corporate productivity and enhancement of the financial bottom line." [Students of corporate economic theory will readily associate this paradigm with the early research and continuing influence of Milton Friedman, and the Chicago School of Economics.]
- (2). "The Ethical/Altruistic Model [is] . . . based on the assumption that corporations generate financial surpluses that are used by corporate leaders to do what is right for society. . . . [This model] conceives of corporations as citizens and corporate executives as societal leaders . . . [who] allocate some of their surpluses according to criteria of social value and ethical and moral precepts not tied to bottom line considerations."
- (3). "The Political Model [is rooted in a corporation's desire] to preserve corporate power and autonomy by building private initiatives [among nonprofit grantees] as an alternative to the growth of governmental authority and by limiting government interference in the free enterprise system. . . . In this view, corporate philanthropy is not driven by profits or by social good per se but by the desire of the

corporate giving community to bolster its position in the environments in which it operates."

- (4). "The Stakeholder Model posits that the corporation is a complex entity that affects, and is affected by, various significant groups— stockholders, managers, workers, customers, suppliers, community groups, and so on. . . . In this view managing a corporation is an exercise . . . guided by the desire of corporate leadership to steer a clear path through the shoals of stakeholder interests."

It is probably correct to say that no existing corporate grant-making program is a "pure" example of any one of these four paradigms. Hands-on corporate grantmakers, analyzing their own current programs, will undoubtedly find elements of some or even of all four paradigms in their current operations. Experienced corporate executives and corporate grants officers have long been aware that their giving programs differ from company to company and from time to time, depending on changes of CEOs, company history, product lines, profits, folklore, competition, legislation, regulation, taxes, and accidents.

The four paradigms offered in this text do not exhaust the categories for studying corporate philanthropy. Readers of this text are encouraged to suggest other paradigms, with suggestions for topics of research related to such new conceptual frameworks for organizing the abundance of data already available (and still to be discovered) about why and how and with what effect corporations continue to share their largesse with the larger society around them.

The concern of corporations about the health of the society in which they operate is not unique to the United States. But the positive role corporations have played historically in this country as active partners with governments (at all three levels) and with nonprofit voluntary agencies *is* unique. As we prepare for the twenty-first century all three sectors of our society are on notice that the rules governing their operation are changing and are likely to continue to change at a more rapid pace.

In the wise and prescient words of John W. Gardner, "A society whose maturing consists simply of acquiring more firmly established ways of doing things is headed for the graveyard. . . . In this ever-renewing society what matures is a system or framework within which continuous innovation, renewal and rebirth can occur. . . . The only way to conserve is by innovating. The only stability possible is stability in motion."

PREFACE

DWIGHT F. BURLINGAME AND DENNIS R. YOUNG

The last decade has witnessed a marked increase in the number of academic programs focusing on study of the nonprofit sector. A component of such study is the role of business in supporting charitable enterprise through corporate giving or philanthropy. Corporations' support of charitable organizations now represents roughly 5 percent of the $129.88 billion given annually (Giving USA, 1995). Corporations have always given to worthy causes. In return they have received tax exemptions as well as direct benefits such as happier or better educated employees, positive community relations, and the like. More enlightened companies have seen philanthropy as a social as well as an economic investment, with the two inextricably linked. In their view, good business is not possible without a healthy community in which to operate.

However, it is no longer clear that corporate management today accepts corporate social responsibility and corporate giving as simply the "right thing to do." Moreover, the downsizing of corporate contributions staff at a time when requests for gifts are increasing has put considerable pressure on the corporate contributions officer—both from within the company and from the outside. Questions by senior corporate management continue to focus on: How to evaluate social investment effectiveness? How does corporate giving contribute to the bottom line? How does one measure effectiveness? How to best organize and structure corporate giving? And so on.

How can research in the academy assist in answering such questions and provide understandings and needed information to corporate giving practitioners, their corporate colleagues, and the nonprofit beneficiaries of their programs? This question was the major focus of a conference held in Cleveland, jointly sponsored by the Mandel Center for Nonprofit Organizations at Case Western Reserve University and the Indiana University Center on Philanthropy in April 1994. This book follows from that successful conference, which brought researchers and practitioners to the same large table to frame a research agenda for corporate philanthropy in the next decade. *Corporate Philanthropy at the Crossroads* is intended to help researchers, nonprofit constituents, and corporate officials explore their mutual interests to understand and assist business's support of the nonprofit sector, and the role of philanthropy and volunteerism in the life of the corporation itself.

FOCUS AND CONTENTS

This work is most directly relevant to researchers and practitioners of corporate philanthropy. Nonprofit managers and development officers and students of nonprofit and corporate management will also find this work informative. Finally, the book will be of interest to all stakeholder groups of today's corporation.

In chapter 1 Craig Smith makes a strong case for connecting corporate giving directly to company strategy. He sees philanthropy as a powerful competitive resource which also plays a productive role in helping to solve society's social problems. Smith views corporate philanthropic effort comprehensively to include socially focused aspects of marketing, R & D, government affairs, and human resource management, as well as corporate giving per se. From this perspective, Smith calls for research to determine the economic value that corporate philanthropy adds to business. Viewing corporate social contributions in totality can help businesses assess the impact of their social contributions in light of the overall strategic position of their companies.

The second part of the book reviews current trends and emerging paradoxes in corporate philanthropy. In chapter 2 John A. Yankey examines the reason why nonprofits continue to seek corporate support even though it represents only a small proportion of the total giving to nonprofits. Focusing on corporate giving strategies, Yankey analyzes cause-related marketing, sponsorships, gifts-in-kind, employee volunteerism, and partnerships between nonprofits and government.

In chapter 3 Alice Korngold and Elizabeth Hosler Voudouris examine in greater detail the emerging important role that corporate volunteerism plays for the modern corporation, and they offer a model to evaluate its impact.

The third part focuses on the state of research on corporate philanthropy. In chapter 4 Donna Wood and Raymond Jones provide an extensive review that frames the question of business philanthropy within the broader context of corporate social performance (CSP). They argue that stakeholder theory and a stakeholder management framework are essential to understanding and evaluating how corporations fulfill their responsibilities in our society.

In chapter 5 Dwight Burlingame and Patricia Frishkoff provide the results of their research in Indiana and Oregon on how firm size affects corporate philanthropy. In chapter 6, David Lewin and J. M. Sabater report their research on how community involvement through volunteer programs affects employee morale and corporate performance.

Questions of ethics and power are examined in the fourth part. In chapter 7 Lance Buhl offers an ethical framework for understanding corporate philanthropy. He argues that a paradigm shift from "doing good for the community by doing well for the company" to "doing well for the company by doing good for the community" is in order. Buhl reasons that acting on such a paradigm shift will enliven the contributions function in the company as well as push the research agenda.

Based on his research on business executives, Jerome Himmelstein examines issues of power and corporate philanthropy, in chapter 8. He concludes that corporate giving is highly idiosyncratic, usually based on each individual corporation's "political" perspective. He finds that "politics" in the context of corporate philanthropy involves finding the areas where public interest and corporate interest overlap.

Appropriately, this work ends with a quest to articulate research questions that have been generated by authors and participants at the Cleveland conference. In a field where the paradigm is in flux, the need for more and better analysis is clear. Competing theories of corporate philanthropy provide the backdrop for a provocative research agenda aimed at assisting practitioners while it advances scholarly understanding.

ACKNOWLEDGMENTS

Any project of this kind requires the hard work and resources of many individuals and organizations. The authors and participants at the conference helped shape the debate and gave generously of their talent and time. And special thanks go to those major sponsors who provided financial resources including The Lilly Endowment, the George Gund Foundation and BP America, and to other corporate participants including IBM, TRW, NEC, Hewlett-Packard and SRP.

In addition, conference support was provided by Linda Serra and other staff of the Mandel Center as well as Tess Baker and other staff from the IU Center on Philanthropy.

REFERENCES

Carroll, Archie B. "Social Issues in Management Research: Experts' Views, Analysis, and Commentary," *Business and Society*, vol. 39, no. 1 (April 1994), 5–29.

Kaplan, Ann E., ed. *Giving USA 1995: The Annual Report on Philanthropy for the Year 1994*. New York: AAFRC Trust for Philanthropy, 1995.

1

Desperately Seeking Data

Why Research Is Crucial to the New Corporate Philanthropy

CRAIG SMITH

This book could not have come at a more opportune time. The matter of developing and fulfilling a research agenda for corporate philanthropy is not just academically interesting. It is also the issue around which the future of corporate philanthropy itself may pivot. If corporate philanthropy is to flourish or even survive, it will be at least in part because researchers have generated the theoretic framework, the methodologies, measurements, and data that show skeptical corporate executives how corporate philanthropy assists corporate competitive strategies.

Why do we need research now? I would like to address that question from the corporate practitioners' perspective—with my own twist added in, of course. I am not a corporate contributions officer myself. But as president of Corporate Citizen, I network with them on an almost daily basis. It has been clear to me that within the last few years interest in research has been building dramatically. But the number and quality of studies has not kept pace with the demand.

THE OLD PARADIGM FOR CORPORATE PHILANTHROPY

To understand why and what kind of research is needed, one must first understand the dramatic shift that has taken place in our field as we have moved from the industrial era to the information era. The old paradigm grew from a social compact peculiar to industrialism. There was general agreement that society is best served if a company's giving is kept at arm's length from business processes.

In the old paradigm, philanthropy research served only a small role.

It was confined largely to the development of standards for determining how much a company should "give back" to society as its "fair share." Most companies agreed that percentage of pretax profit was the accepted reference point. Others focused on percentage of sales or a percentage based on number of employees.

The new paradigm of philanthropy represents an entirely different social compact. This new paradigm began to emerge in the mid-80s and did not move into ascendancy until 1990. In the new view, corporate philanthropy serves the public interest best as a catalyst for integrating a company's products, personnel, financial power and management know-how on behalf of social change. In other words, the ideal philanthropy initiative is one that delivers the company as a whole as an instrument for the solution to a social problem. While serving society, such an initiative should also serve the donating company itself, helping it become more competitive.

THE NEW PARADIGM REQUIRES RESEARCH

In the emerging paradigm, corporate philanthropy is a business function that must prove its worth just like any other function. The CEO no longer shields it from challenge by other interests within the company. Stripped of this traditional protection, corporate philanthropy now is required to demonstrate how it can "add value" to business strategies while still advancing social causes. But to do this, corporate philanthropy practitioners need the results of good research.

However, this research has not been forthcoming. Academics are too far removed from the realities of corporate philanthropy practices to generate the necessary research. They simply are not privy to internal discussions within companies that could shed light on the complex motives and methods employed by corporate practitioners. Consultants, on the other hand, have been too close to companies to be able to step back and provide a framework that explains the role that corporate philanthropy plays for the firm.

Yet a consensus is emerging on the need for research—and the type of research that it needed. The consensus-building began in 1990, when the Keystone Project—the first national meeting on this topic—was convened in Colorado, under the sponsorship of the University of Denver, the Piton Foundation, and Corporate Philanthropy Report. Since then, a number of informal gatherings for further exploration and development have been held. IBM and American Express have played leadership roles, and the Boston College Center for Corporate Community Relations and the Public Affairs Councils have kept the candle

burning. The Council on Foundations has also increased its involvement in this topic in the past few years. The Indiana University Center
on Philanthropy and Case Western Reserve University also made an
important contribution with their symposium on a research agenda for
corporate philanthropy in the spring of 1994. Since that time a Corporate Citizenship Measurement Study was created out of a coalition of 15
major corporations with the purpose of developing new measures that
show the relationship between corporate citizenship and business performance. The Seattle-based think tank with which I am associated,
Corporate Citizen, is the fiscal agent for that study. Furthermore, the
Conference Board's Business and Society Program, under the direction
of Boston University Professor James Post, is conducting a number of
studies that link competitiveness to corporate citizenship both domes-
tically and internationally. Furthermore, organizations outside the
United States, such as Business in the Community in London and the
Canadian Centre on Philanthropy are thinking along the same lines and
providing the possibility for international comparative analysis.

DRAWING ON THE EXPERIENCE OF THE QUALITY MOVEMENT

What is this emerging consensus? From the perspective of
practitioners, it looks like this: To "sell" corporate philanthropy in the
current climate, our field must apply research in the same way the
quality gurus applied it in the 1980s and 1990s. Just as Deming and
Juran were convinced that quality was as much a competitive factor as
price—a counterintuitive notion at the time, today's internal advocates
for corporate philanthropy are convinced that corporate philanthropy
adds to the competitiveness of companies—another counterintuitive
proposition. We need to challenge prevailing beliefs with good research
just as Deming and Juran did with statistical techniques.

Maneuvering within the corporate world, Total Quality Management innovations quantitatively demonstrated that a given business
unit could achieve its ends more fully by upgrading quality than if it
continued the old ways. Each TQM intervention involved clarifying the
goals of each function, rethinking how to get there, and measuring the
impact once it arrived. It can be said that TQM puts research in the
driver's seat.

Just as the quality gurus had to contend with many obstacles, so do
we. We may be in the information age, but corporate culture is still
wedded to vestigial notions developed during industrialization. One of
these is that "hard" functions drive returns on investments, while "soft"
functions are peripheral. But thanks to TQM/reengineering, tools are

available to suggest how indirect activities like philanthropy can have a tangible effect on corporate performance.

TAPPING NEW RESEARCH INTO FUNCTIONAL AREAS

Consider the sponsorship field, for example. It has grown from $200 million a decade ago to $2 billion in 1994, while advertising budgets have risen hardly at all. Research suggests that while ad dollars might deliver more "visibility," sponsorship dollars actually have more "impact." Other research shows that the impact is greatest when a spectrum of marketing objectives are achieved indirectly through a single, sponsored event. Furthermore, the types of sponsorships that look most like philanthropy—cause marketing, arts marketing—seem to afford the greatest opportunity to assist the most complex mix of objectives.

Thus, by looking carefully at the ways that market research has been used to legitimate sponsorships, corporate giving officers can show how their function can boost marketing strategies indirectly, even while their direct aim is to achieve social ends. In fact, they may even be able to convince budget setters that corporate philanthropy is a better invest-ment than marketing, at least under certain conditions.

Our field can reap a similar benefit by becoming versed in the methods other functions use to show their own worth. For example, consider the fields of R & D and government affairs. The traditional assessment measures for each of these functions have been rather simplistic: Corporate lobbyists count wins and losses in regulatory warfare battle; R & D departments count patents. But when forced to show precisely how each of these departments creates strategic advan-tages for the company overall, they have been forced to look to new measures, for example, evaluating success in fostering research partner-ships or developing grassroots coalitions.

According to Peter Schafer of the Public Affairs Council, the most exciting breakthroughs in the field of government relations have to do with measuring relationships. Such measurements are intrinsically in-teresting to corporate philanthropy practitioners who, increasingly, are coming to understand that their own greatest contribution to business success comes from mobilizing important relationships that would never be possible without philanthropy.

But perhaps the most fruitful corporate realm from which our own field can draw useful insights is the field of human resources manage-ment. Thanks to professor David Lewin, we have some tantalizing hypotheses about the link between employee productivity, morale and corporate philanthropy. The more we know about research in the human resources field—how employees are evaluated, for example—the better we will be at explaining how employee-driven expressions of philanthropy such as matching gifts and workplace funding can reduce fringe benefits costs and promote creative teamwork and other aims of personnel management.

We should not stop there. An exploration of the research, methodologies, and measures of cross-functional roles and units of business is in order. These roles and units include business ethics, environmental management, quality control, and the executive leadership function of the CEO. What is common to all these areas is that they are charged with making the parts of a company add up to a larger whole. From these fields we extrapolate ways of describing how corporate philanthropy can add value to the cross-functional strategies that companies are striving to achieve these days.

In other words, if corporate philanthropy is to pull its own weight, practitioners need measures that can show what it can do. By looking over our shoulders to peer functions and departments we can gather the tools to clarify what is unique about our field and how it complements other divisions, units, and functions.

Once corporate philanthropy practitioners gain the research tools they need, the field itself is sure to change. Undoubtedly, corporate philanthropy initiatives will emerge from the bargaining between the in-house foundation executive and the managers who control marketing, human resources, and other functions. Increasingly, we will see hybrid projects simultaneously funded from business units and philanthropy. And more companies will find their own version of, say, Ronald McDonald House—projects that serve as an overall rallying point for all semiautonomous members of a disparate corporate family.

IS THE NEW PARADIGM A GOOD THING?

Is a revolution in corporate philanthropy, made possible by research, a good thing? This is hard to say. To be sure, empowered corporate philanthropy within information era firms will lead to more powerful corporations, or should we say, to a more subtle kind of corporate power. It will allow these companies to extend their reach beyond the economic realm directly and deeply into the hearts and minds of citizens. Some may find this prospect disquieting because it requires us to trust in the goodness of management values to a greater degree than ever before. Yet, are these values truly benign? We do not know. This new corporate power can be insidious or inspiring depending on the purposes for which it is used. It may trigger a further exploration of the underlying managerial values that drive these processes.

So we must conclude with a note about leadership. In the old paradigm, CEOs expressed their civic leadership by sitting on the de rigueur nonprofit boards, rallying their CEO peers on behalf of causes and defending philanthropy expenditures because it was "the right thing to do." In the new paradigm, the civic leader is the company itself once all its parts have been aligned toward a socially engaged course.

RESEARCH SHOULD ALSO FOCUS ON LEADERSHIP

But this does not mean the CEO can turn his or her back on the big questions of leadership. There is an ever greater need for vision. More than ever before, the corporations—particularly large global corporations—can be drivers of necessary global change. Just how this new leadership role should be expressed is another question to be pursued by researchers.

More than ever before, corporate practitioners seem to be reaching out and saying to researchers, "We need you." It remains to be seen whether they can really provide what is needed.

2

Corporate Support of Nonprofit Organizations
Partnerships across the Sectors

JOHN A. YANKEY

In 1992, corporate giving declined for the first time in more than two decades. It marked the fifth straight year business philanthropy failed to keep pace with inflation (Moore, 1993, p. 8). However, even when taking into account noncash support, corporate giving represents only a small portion (approximately 5 percent) of all charitable contributions. Why then, if corporate giving is growing neither in magnitude nor importance, are so many nonprofits seeking their support? And, why are so many companies changing the way they view support for nonprofit organizations?

The answers are to be found in the emerging trends in corporate philanthropy and philanthropically related activities that have developed during the past decade and the changes in the way government, business, and nonprofits must now work together to address the nation's greatest needs. Competition for corporate dollars will continue to intensify in the years ahead; and, while the actual dollar amount of corporate support may be waning, many businesses are working creatively with nonprofit organizations on initiatives that may serve society's needs even more effectively. The challenge is to be prepared for the changing corporate philanthropic agenda and to assist in the creation of new partnerships between the public, private, and nonprofit sectors of society.

This chapter will explore the why and how of corporate giving and philanthropically related activity. It will focus on corporate giving strategies, including the concepts of enlightened self-interest, strategic giving, and charitable investment. Practices and issues in corporate support of nonprofits as they relate to cause-related marketing, corporate sponsorship, gifts-in-kind, employee volunteerism, and partnerships between government and nonprofits will be outlined. Last, it will focus upon the best-known corporate giving mechanism—the United Way—and the role of corporations in the governance, funding, and success of this federated approach to fundraising.

ENLIGHTENED SELF-INTEREST, STRATEGIC GIVING, AND CHARITABLE INVESTMENT

Until the early 1950s, corporate giving was legally restricted to charities that were in some way connected to the activities of the business. The rationale was that management's primary responsibility was to shareholders and to their return on investment. As a result of legal challenges in the mid-1950s, the courts ruled that corporations were free to give to charities whether or not they were related to the products of the company. These rulings opened the door for corporate sponsorships of a variety of local and national charities. Corporate funding in support of the arts and education increased dramatically.

To understand the reason behind current trends in corporate support of nonprofits, one must first look to the changes in the 1980s and their effect on corporate America, government, and the nonprofit sector. The 1970s were a decade of diminishing productivity levels, high oil prices, and "stagflation." By 1979, inflation was at 12 percent annually and the prime rate stood at 21 percent. The nation's economy was weak, and America was underprepared for the accelerating challenge of corporate globalization. The American public was ready for a change. The "movie star" persona of Ronald Reagan, coupled with a radical supply-side economic agenda that many did not understand, proved an irresistible chorus favoring less government, lower taxes, and economic stability.

A key element of Reaganomics was a reduction in the growth of spending and the role of the federal government in health, human services, education, and other discretionary programs, along with an accompanying shift of responsibility to state, local, and nonprofit agencies to meet these needs. However, the agenda also included a reduction in personal income tax rates in order to stimulate the economy, an acceleration of depreciation for business investment in plant and equipment to create jobs, and a dramatic increase in national defense spending to balance the threat of the Soviet Union. From the onset, critics charged that to reduce taxes, increase defense spending, and provide economic stability would require unprecedented reductions in government spending.

Dramatic cuts in a wide array of social programs were the legacy of Reagan's first term in office. "Cut off from government funds . . . nonprofit organizations found themselves scrambling to fill a financial vacuum. Corporate America—supposed to benefit from Reagan's changes—seemed a logical place to go fundraising" (Zetlin, 1990, p. 10). But corporate America was going through its own dramatic changes. In the early 1980s, "the rash of leveraged buyouts and other kinds of merger and acquisition activity reduced the number and variety of major corporations, while placing some of them under severe financial constraints" (Murray, 1992, p. 12). By the time Reagan began his second term, many corporations were responding to numerous business challenges including foreign competition, emerging opportunities in international markets, changes in technology, and shareholder pressure to improve debt-to-equity positions and cut costs in order to remain competitive and profitable.

Thus, just as corporate America was finding it harder to keep up with the multitude of requests from the nonprofit sector, it was being asked to respond with unprecedented generosity. Companies—especially visible, profitable ones—were flooded with funding requests. Corporations were having to respond to questions concerning their decisions to fund one charity and not another. Answers such as "we've always done it that way" or "it seems like a good cause" were no longer satisfactory answers for competing nonprofits or shareholders. Corporate America was recognizing that many of today's most pressing social problems, most of which will negatively impact business for years to come, could not be solved by government or nonprofit organizations alone. Businesses began to think differently about their charitable giving and to evaluate why they give the way they do.

Today, with changes in government support levels and the increased competitive climate for business, corporate giving strategies have come full circle. Recognizing both the risks and opportunities corporate philanthropy presents, "an emerging strategy is to treat donations like investments and to expect some return from them" (Dienhart, 1988, p. 64). The problem for some is how investment, which is self-interest, can guide charity, which is altruistic. Noted management guru Peter Drucker (1984) argues that altruism cannot be the criterion by which corporate giving is evaluated. Business can discharge its "social responsibilities" by converting them into "self-interest," which, for Drucker, means "business opportunities."

The resulting approach, called "strategic giving" by Zetlin (1990), means giving with an eye on the business's eventual best interests. Whether the term "strategic giving" or "charitable investing" is used, the concept is the same. "A firm charitably invests when [it] believes donations will increase the ability to produce products in the future or yield consumer benefits in the future" (Dienhart, 1988, p. 67). It was argued this strategic approach could even be used to minimize risk, a key component of maximizing profits. An example of this type of enlightened self-interest can be found in B. Dalton Bookseller's support for literacy programs or Aetna Insurance's support for AIDS research.

In their book *Companies with a Conscience,* Mary Scott and Howard Rothman (1992) discuss the extent to which enlightened self-interest can serve corporate objectives. By studying 12 firms with extraordinary records of philanthropic support and profitability, they point out the issue often is one of short-term versus long-term strategies:

> these companies have made related decisions that had a negative impact on their bottom lines in the short-term. But the enduring nature of these businesses and the fact that every one of their products and services remains heavily in demand in an almost cultlike fashion, shows that their long-term vision was correct. (p. 209)

Ben and Jerry's Ice Cream, one of the 12 companies highlighted, operates as a profitable business; yet, what drives the company's success is an unwavering commitment to the community, its workers, and a wide array of social causes. Scott and Rothman argue it is this early commitment to quality and social responsibility that make these companies more profitable and philanthropic than others.

Evidence of the strength and longevity of strategic giving as a trend in corporate philanthropy is its ability to stand up, regardless of the condition of the economy or the company's financial strength. For example, despite record financial losses over the past several years, IBM continues to give away millions of dollars in computer equipment each year. In the ultracompetitive world of personal computers, this strategy is just good business. Whether sales are down or business is booming, "corporate grantmakers are becoming more focused on strategic giving, the art of meshing community needs with corporate interests and identifying the ways in which grants can make the most impact" (Fisch, 1992, p. 6).

THE WHY OF CORPORATE GIVING

Companies exist to make profits. Today, in order to achieve this goal, corporate America must be a "good neighbor," helping to solve society's problems. What are the specific objectives of this type of strategy? How do corporations and nonprofits benefit from partnerships with each other? To explore these questions, it is helpful to first discuss the challenges facing both corporate America and the non-profit sector.

Business today functions in an atmosphere of shrinking markets and intense domestic and international competition. Corporations must compete on several levels. Demographics are radically altering the makeup of the workforce and consumer populations. How to penetrate these shrinking markets, improve customer response, and develop new market niches and new products are major concerns for businesses today. The challenge of hiring and retaining skilled workers has never been more daunting. At the same time, society's problems have invaded the workplace as never before. Drug abuse, violence, illiteracy, and many other problems threaten corporate America's ability to compete and prosper. Corporate leaders "say they are worried their businesses will suffer if they can't put company time and money into solving America's deepening social problems" (Bailey, 1992, p. 10). Customers are demanding better service, higher quality and lower prices from products that are safe for the environment and from companies that give back to the community. "In many ways, with many voices, they are demanding that business play an active role in solving social problems, because without business participation, solutions may not be possible" (Steckel, 1992, p. 6).

For many nonprofit organizations, the major challenge is to do more with less. After more than a decade of government spending cuts, some nonprofits have been brought to the edge of extinction, and others have been left scrambling for alternative sources of income. At the same time, demand for services has exploded. In an environment of tenuous income, higher service demand, increasing expenses, and more competition for philanthropic donors and dollars, the climate—to many— seems more like war than charity.

BUSINESS AND NONPROFIT BENEFITS OF WORKING TOGETHER

Companies must find ways to further penetrate shrinking existing markets and to cost-effectively develop new markets. By partnering with a nonprofit, a business may be able to target just the right market. When Chanel wanted to reach wealthy, influential New Yorkers to launch a new perfume, it went to the Metropolitan Opera. By sponsoring an opening night fund-raising dinner and fashion show, both partners profited. The Met received $1.2 million in donations in a short period of time; and Chanel reached the audience it wanted (Steckel, 1992, p. 14). When Chrysler launched its new Eagle Vision in 1993, it gave the Museum of Science and Industry in Tampa, Florida, $20,000 for the museum to display the car and keep it clean for museum goers

(Sebastian, 1993, p. 1). Through such public purpose partnerships, businesses have the opportunity to stand out from the competition and to enhance their public image, while improving their ability to make a profit. Whether the goal is targeting a new market, launching a new product, or increasing sales, a partnership with a nonprofit organization can have multiple benefits.

Corporate America is challenged by more than just products and markets. Personnel issues often are the most difficult problems to solve. Here, too, a partnership with a charity may serve many needs. Recruiting and retaining good employees is difficult, but a recent study of 188 companies "found that employee morale was three times higher in companies with a strong degree of community involvement" (Steckel, 1992, p. 25). Companies are learning it is not enough to give financial support; rather, they must augment their efforts by contributing expert personnel, volunteers, materials, and equipment in addition to financial support. As Maita (1992) points up, many businesses are leveraging their monetary contributions by adding volunteers to the mix. Instead of writing a check and walking away, corporate America is becoming an integral part of solving society's problems. The combination of financial, capital, and human resources, if effectively utilized, provides a unique opportunity to attack even the most pressing and difficult problems. By being more closely involved, businesses can better understand the complexity and stubbornness of solutions and better appreciate the impact funding and other support have in their communities.

This type of partnership also benefits the charity. Increasing operating income is the most obvious benefit, but increased visibility also is important. The opportunity to educate the public about the organization's mission is critical to the ability to attract donors to the cause. By taking advantage of a money-making venture, an organization also develops valuable business skills with positive crossover effects on their problem-solving efforts.

THE HOW OF CORPORATE GIVING

CAUSE-RELATED MARKETING

Cause-related marketing (CRM) has existed for more than 20 years, but in today's highly competitive world both businesses and nonprofits are fueling a resurgence in its use. CRM is, basically, a joint venture between a corporation and a nonprofit group to market products or services through a public association. For example, consumers may be encouraged to purchase a company's products, knowing that the company has agreed to donate a portion of each sale to the nonprofit. While there are more elaborate strategies, most are modifications of this simple concept. As Garrison (1990) notes about CRMs, they

> . . . offer new sources of financial support and increased public exposure. Both are important in a fund-raising arena that grows more and more competitive. For corporate partners, cause-related marketing provides an opportunity to increase product sales, gain public recognition and, at the same time, support the causes they care about. (p. 40)

Critics charge that the basic concept of cause-related marketing is essentially flawed and that a charitable contribution should not provide the donor with a profit. While supporters agree that CRM is not traditional philanthropy, they argue that neither does it substitute for corporate social responsibility. Opponents further charge that CRM efforts frequently help causes which likely need such funding the least (Gurin, 1987, p. 49). Despite this criticism, CRM has proved to be an effective way to raise money for a variety of different causes, including some outside the mainstream. For example, Steckel (1992) highlighted Johnson & Johnson's 1987 CRM activity called Shelter Aid, which raised more than $1.5 million for battered women's shelters. The campaign was the company's most successful promotion ever. In another CRM activity, the magazine Mirabella told its advertisers that for every ad page in its first anniversary issue, $1,000 would go to one of four charities, including an AIDS foundation. The magazine raisied $82,000 for the nonprofits—and upped the number of ad pages in that issue.

For corporations, CRM is a valuable tool in a company's effort to increase sales or target new markets. While consumer loyalty, price, and quality continue as the primary drivers in buyer decisions, corporate social responsibility is now an important second-tier criterion. As reported by Elliott (1993), a recent survey conducted by the Roper Starch Worldwide market research company in New York found that approximately two-thirds of study participants indicated they were somewhat or very likely to switch brands "based on a good cause," providing price and quality were the same. CRM is one approach in the process of changing the way which corporations and nonprofits help each other address pressing social needs. CRM, used effectively, creates win-win outcomes and should be viewed as one element or component of better corporate and nonprofit relationships.

CORPORATE SPONSORSHIP

What began as hometown businesses' support for the local Little League team has now grown into a $2.9 billion-a-year industry which includes big-time sporting events and a variety of local and national advertising campaigns. As more and more businesses use their philanthropy to improve customer and employee relations, corporate sponsorship continues to grow in popularity (Maita, 1992).

For nonprofits there are many benefits. Whether a national event, a traveling exhibit, or a local fund-raiser, corporate sponsorship programs help charities to move many people to action—collecting pledges or encouraging volunteer efforts. Sponsorship programs also offer nonprofits a great way to get their messages out and, with the help of corporate marketing departments, a chance to put on an event larger than what might otherwise be possible.

Corporate sponsorship programs can be very costly, however, and may present significant organizational challenges. Most require large numbers of paid or volunteer workers that stretch the resources of even the most heavily fortified organizations. More recently, IRS challenges to some corporate-sponsored sporting events have caused some charities to become cautious. In the main, these concerns are unnecessary since almost all purely charitable events have so far gone unchallenged. Therefore, as corporations and nonprofits continue to search for ways to increase income and to effectively communicate with large numbers of customers/donors, it is expected corporate sponsorship programs will continue to grow in magnitude and frequency.

GIFTS-IN-KIND

In-kind contributions of products or services is one of the most effective corporate giving strategies. Product donations save time, energy, and money. Free services help to create new business opportunities while giving back to the community. Further, gifts-in-kind receive favorable treatment under current tax law and may even allow a firm to recoup a portion of the actual production cost for obsolete inventory. Making this even more attractive is the potential cost savings afforded by reduced inventory levels and carrying costs. But most compelling is the opportunity to turn a potential public relations liability into a useful public image asset.

The two most common ways to dispose of excess inventory are by selling to a liquidator or by dumping it. Companies often lose money by selling to liquidators, and it may even be better for tax purposes to dump obsolete products rather than to sell them. However, dumping perfectly useful products can turn into a public relations nightmare for the company. For example, teenage mothers are barely getting by and ABC Company dumps 1,000 cases of disposable diapers because they have slight imperfections; or, inner-city children are freezing and the XYZ Company has deposited some 500 coats at the local dump. These scenarios present major public relations challenges (Smith, 1989, p. 43).

But inventory gifts are just part of the picture. Services also provide positive benefits to both nonprofit organizations and corporations. Livingston & Company, a Seattle-based advertising agency, does pro bono work for many local charities, including the Seattle zoo, aquarium, and others. Why this interest in donating services when this same time could just as well be spent on paying customers? First, as suggested by Steckel, the agency wants to give something back to the community. Second, it gets a very direct return. By doing high-visibility ads for local nonprofits, Livingston generates increased interest from paying customers in the community. Working with community charities to produce creative and innovative advertisements allows this business to get noticed by potential customers who might otherwise not be aware of the firm's work.

EMPLOYEE VOLUNTEERISM

Money isn't the only necessary element in short supply at most nonprofit organizations. Many nonprofits serving community needs lack the personnel to implement their most promising programs. Corporate America is responding to this challenge as increasing numbers of corporations have established programs to encourage employees to volunteer. Some companies have gone so far as to institute "sophisticated volunteerism departments—complete with their own budgets and staffs" (Miller, 1989, p. 38). Target Stores has an annual budget of $250,000, and corporate volunteers focus their efforts on community-based programs selected for support by the employees themselves (Steckel, 1992, p. 127).

While most companies do not allow for volunteer efforts on company time some, like IBM, actually encourage paid release time for volunteers. What does the company get out of it? In addition to an improved public image and positive community relations, noted management expert Peter Drucker says company volunteer programs are effective management training opportunities for employees to hone their skills in managing and motivating people (Steckel, 1992, p. 126).

The most successful employee volunteer programs have several elements in common. Employees drive the effort, and those doing the volunteering are allowed to select the causes they support. Also, successful programs are vigorously supported by the company with volunteers being featured in the corporate newsletter and being recognized in other ways by management. In an era of increasing demand for services, a good corps of volunteers can be as important as cash to many nonprofits.

BUSINESS, EDUCATION, AND GOVERNMENT PARTNERSHIPS

In 1983, the National Commission on Excellence in Education began its report titled "A Nation at Risk" with these words:

> Our nation is at risk; our once unchallenged pre-eminence in commerce, industry, science, and technical innovation is being overtaken by competitors throughout the world . . . the educational foundations of our society are presently being eroded by a rising tide of mediocrity that threatens our very future as a Nation and a people. (Lund and Wild, 1993, p. 7)

This bold report helped spark an aggressive effort to create partnerships between business, education, and government. Some of corporate America's biggest names, recognizing the risk to their own survival, have joined with government and nonprofit organizations to address this growing concern. Fortune 500 companies, including Eastman Kodak, American Express, and Ford Motor Company are working with local businesses, as well as government and nonprofit agencies, to develop innovative programs to educate America's children (Brothers, 1992, p. 7).

Now, more than ten years later, the partnerships that are helping America improve its education system are beginning to respond to other social needs. In Denver, Colorado, a partnership between a local community college, state government, and a coalition of businesses, provides job retraining for disabled workers. "The state pays most of the tuition; the college provides space, instructors, and support staff. IBM and other companies donate computers and Martin Marietta, with other firms, provides volunteers and leadership" (Armbrister, 1989, p. 25). Why are companies so willing to participate? Once again, enlightened self-interest and social responsibility are the keys to corporate involvement. McKesson, a distributor of pharmaceuticals, established a partnership with a local high school more than ten years ago to provide academic and work experience to "at risk" students. McKesson's program coordinator views the company's involvement pragmatically: "If employers don't get involved now, we can hardly complain ten years from now about a work force that can't read or write" (Armbrister, 1989, p. 29).

These new partnerships with nonprofits have placed corporate America in an emerging role as advocate for change. For many years, corporations have tried to exert influence in matters of tax and trade policy, but now there is an increasing awareness that companies must do the same in the area of social policy. Corporate officials have reported their undertaking advocacy at the request of nonprofits (Bailey, 1992, p. 7).

Although growth in overall corporate giving is flat, many companies are providing larger grants to fewer causes with an eye toward meaningful and measurable results. At the same time, corporate advocacy efforts are focused on:

- pressing government at all levels to become more effective.
- combining grant dollars and company investment capital with corporate expertise and government funds.
- supporting advocacy groups and coalitions whose goals include sweeping changes in the way government provides services.
- supporting efforts to bring disparate groups together to solve complex community problems. (Bailey, 1992, p. 6)

Corporate America's advocacy and focus on measurable results will be an essential part of nonprofit competition for a limited pool of business resources in the future. The greater the number of effective nonprofit partners and the more measurable the results, the more likely that corporate America will support the effort with dollars and other philanthropic assistance.

EVALUATING SUCCESS

Given that effectiveness is a must for the continuation of these partnerships, how do corporations and nonprofits evaluate their respective successes? Steckel and Simons (1992) offer a number of potential evaluation foci. For corporations, they suggest the following:

- Impact upon Sales
- Target Market Results
- Retailer and Distributor Activity and Response
- Scope and Timing of Publicity
- Employee Involvement and Attitudes
- Management Support and Attitudes
- Public Reaction to Partnership Choice
- Revenue and Expense Results
- Working Relationships with Partner(s)

Suggested foci for nonprofits' evaluation include:

- Money and Other Support Received
- Exposure and Media Coverage
- Public Response to Partnership
- Increased Awareness of the Cause

Sylvia Clark (1994) persuasively argues that corporate support for nonprofits must take into account all philanthropic and philanthropically related activity in measuring impact and determining added value to corporations. She suggests specific categories for corporate community involvement for which data should be sought and presented to senior management. These categories, where appropriate, include both cash and noncash sub-categories. Among the categories suggested are:

- Grants and Community Relations
- Employee Related Support
- Memberships
- Sales and Promotion
- Product or Asset Donation

Donna Wood and Raymond Jones (1994) provide an excellent review of research in corporate social performance, examining—among other things—the concept and models of corporate social performance and whether it can be measured. Referencing a number of measurement indices, for example, *Fortune* magazine's Corporate Reputation Survey, Arthur Andersen's Sullivan Principles, and the KLD Social Investment Scale, Wood and Jones identify a number of variables which have been used by corporations at different times to measure their social performance.

THE UNITED WAY

For more than one hundred years the United Way of America (UWA) has served the human services needs of communities across America. At the community level, corporations interact with local United Ways through involvement with their employees, through internal decisions about gifts or corporate funding to United Ways, and through United Way fund-raising campaigns. For many years, most companies have met the bulk of their local obligations to human service needs through their United Ways (Brilliant, 1990; Troy, 1986). However, recent scandals and a long-standing argument over "donor choice" have raised questions about corporate America's continuing role with this philanthropic giant. At issue is whether the United Way should continue to be the primary vehicle for corporate participation in community social welfare activities or whether companies should allow other nonprofit organizations to conduct workplace solicitation and establish payroll deduction arrangements. Also at issue, as a direct result of the 1992 UWA scandal, is the role of corporate leadership in the governance of both UWA and local United Ways.

As early as the 1970s, and increasingly so in the decade of the 1980s, the UWA was under pressure to allow donors a choice of designations for giving. The argument made was, and is, that due to the controversial nature of some agencies funded or not funded, donors should be offered an opportunity to restrict their contributions to those agencies whose missions are consistent with donors' values. While this individualistic approach to choice seems reasonable to many, others view it as highly problematic in that it "strikes at the basic core of United Ways' mandate to unify community fund raising and to distribute funds based on need" (Glaser, 1994, p. 66). By 1990, the trend toward donor choice was in full swing and the UWA could do no more than attempt to control the form donor-designated giving would take. The UWA selected a strategy of educating donors in an attempt to maximize giving within the scope of United Way–supported agencies.

United Ways' fear that should donor choice become *the* mode of operation "there could by extension be more of a move away from a United Way donor option plan to a company donor option which allows for giving to alternative funds" (Brilliant, 1990, p. 207). It appears this fear may be well founded. During the past two years, non–United Way workplace giving has increased while United Way giving has experienced a decrease. As anticipated by United Way leadership, employees' demands for greater choice and accountability have resulted in a number of corporations expanding their workplace charity options. Such companies as Levi Strauss, Gannett, USA Today, Mattel, Citibank, Turner Broadcasting—and many others—now allow non-UW charities to solicit their employees. The consequences of this erosion of United Ways' historical monopoly on workplace solicitation are yet to be determined. However, John Glaser (1994) in writing about the UW scandal, argues that the issue of donor choice is by far the most significant external issue which will determine the direction of the movement in the future. Glaser suggests that the manner in which the United Way balances its service to community needs and people's interest in giving to the charity of their choice is a fundamental management and marketing challenge which must be met.

The UWA and local United Ways are further challenged by the lingering aftermath of the 1992 scandal. While significant effort has been made nationally and locally to deal with negative consequences, there remains—for many people—a loss of public trust.

> People trust nonprofits. It's almost as simple as that. We tend to believe in what they do, and almost more importantly, in how they do it. They are tackling some of the most pressing problems of our time

for reasons other than personal gain. For this, we grant them respect. We acknowledge their integrity. We give them our trust. (Steckel, 1992, p. 13)

These words, written in an unrelated context, speak well to the tragedy of United Way's fall from grace. Many of America's corporate leaders served on the UWA Board. Why, then, did this happen? What went wrong with the governance of the organization?

While determining the exact cause of this leadership crisis is somewhat difficult, pointing out significant shortcomings within the exercise of accountability is less so. As Glaser (1994) states, "The entire United Way movement simply failed to recognize the problems of its professional leadership until it was too late. . . . As for the Board of Governors, it must bear the lion's share of responsibility for these events for their failure to understand the different perceptions people have of organizations which make profit their measure of success as opposed to those whose bottom line is serving people" (pp. 204–205).

So, what of accountability—how should future United Way Boards conduct themselves? Glaser, who has written the most exhaustive "insider's account" of what went wrong and why, identified 13 lessons learned. Most of these related to the Board of Governors and their role in guiding the UWA. The lessons include the need to set clear, precise, and unambiguous goals for staff and the evaluation of staff based on these goals and the organization's mission. Still others focus on conflict of interest statements and the establishment of acceptable salary ranges. But the most telling lessons relate to the need for outside oversight by competent experts and evaluators. This one lesson, according to Glaser, could have avoided this scandal by providing an avenue for independent assessment and oversight. While nonprofits are entitled to execute their mission without unnecessary or undue obstacles, they must be accountable to the public at large, to those whose needs they serve, and to those whose support they seek. Corporate leaders who provide much of the leadership for the UWA and local United Ways must assume key roles in re-establishing public trust.

CONCLUSION

One cannot ignore the pressures facing corporations today. In an environment of slow growth, tight credit, and government deficit spending it will be increasingly difficult for businesses to expand. Yet, history has demonstrated that astute business people find ways to expand even during difficult times. One avenue for expanding may be as a result of partnerships with nonprofit organizations. However, research related to these potential partnerships could prove fruitful for both corporations and nonprofit organizations. While such research could encompass a variety of issues, the following questions are among those to which answers would help positively shape the future nature of the partnerships:

- How do corporations measure the full range of their corporate support of nonprofits, including financial contributions, in-kind gifts, volunteer hours, and so on?
- What measures demonstrate the value of corporate support of nonprofits on financial performance?
- How should corporate philanthropy fit with other corporate functions, for example, governmental affairs, marketing, or human resources?
- How does corporate volunteerism contribute to better employee morale?
- What is the impact of a corporate partnership upon the nonprofit organization's mission?
- Do nonprofit organizations lose their autonomy in partnerships with corporations?
- Are management skills of corporate and nonprofit partners honed as a result of the partnership?
- What social policy advocacy roles can corporations assume in assisting nonprofit organizations pursue their missions?

Corporate partnerships with nonprofit organizations represent a vital element of growth and expansion for both corporate America and the nonprofit sector. The trends clearly indicate the need and opportunity for these partnerships to exist. These new alliances hold the promise for creative solutions to pressing social problems and present new opportunities for win-win outcomes for corporations' shareholders and nonprofits' stakeholders.

REFERENCES

Armbrister, T. "When Companies Care." *Reader's Digest* (April 1989), 25–32.
Bailey, A. L. "Corporations' New Social Advocacy." *Chronicle of Philanthropy* (April 7, 1992), 6–13.
Brilliant, E. *United Way: Dilemma of Organized Charities.* New York: Columbia University Press, 1990.
Brothers, T., ed. "School Reform: Business, Education and Government as Partners." *The Conference Board,* no. 1011 (1992), 7.

Clark, S. "It All Adds Up." *Foundation News* (March-April 1994), 47–49.

Dienhart, J. W. "Charitable Investments: A Strategy for Improving the Business Environment." *Journal of Business Ethics* 7, no. 1–2, (1988), 63.

Drucker, P. "The New Meaning of Corporate Social Responsibility." *California Management Review* 26 (Winter 1984), 59.

Elliott, S. "A Survey Says that Cause-Oriented Campaigns Don't Just Make People Feel Good, They Work Too." *New York Times*, December 6, 1993.

Fisch, J. "Recession Hits Corporate Funders Hardest of All Grantmakers." *Nonprofit Times* (June 1992), 1, 6.

Garrison, J. R. "A New Twist to Cause Marketing." *FundRaising Management* (February 1990), 40.

Glaser, J. *The United Way Scandal: An Insider's Account of What Went Wrong and Why*. New York: Wiley, 1994.

Gurin, M. "Don't Rush into Cause-Related Marketing." *NSFRE Journal* (1987), 49.

Lund, L., and C. Wild. "Ten Years after a Nation at Risk." *The Conference Board*, no. 1041 (1993), 7.

Maita, S. "Corporate Philanthropy: Getting Down to Business." *Grassroots Fundraising Journal* (September 1992), 6–7.

Miller, A. "Doing Well by Doing Good." *Newsweek*, vol. 114, no. 2 (1989), 38.

Moore, J. "Corporate Giving to Charities Dropped in 1992, First Decrease in 20 Years." *Chronicle of Philanthropy* (September 21, 1993), 8.

Murray, V. "Understanding Corporate Philanthropy." *Grantsmanship Center News* (Spring 1992), 12.

Sebastian, P. "With Coffers Less Full, Big Companies Alter Their Gifts to Charities." *Wall Street Journal*, November 26, 1993, 1, 8.

Scott, M., and H. Rothman. *Companies with a Conscience: Intimate Portraits of Twelve Firms that Make a Difference*. New Jersey: Carol Publishing Group, 1992.

Smith, G. "Corporations Turning Charity into Cash." *Business and Society Review* 69 (Spring 1989), 42–45.

Steckel, R., and R. Simons. *Doing Best by Doing Good: How to Use Public Purpose Partnerships to Boost Corporate Profits and Benefit Your Community*. New York: Dutton, 1992.

Troy, K. "Meeting Human Needs: Corporate Programs and Partnerships." *The Conference Board* (1986), 1–55.

Wood, D., and R. Jones. "Research in Corporate Social Performance: What Have We Learned?" Paper presented at the National Conference on Corporate Philanthropy: A Time of Challenge and Opportunity, Cleveland, April 28, 1994.

Zetlin, M. "Companies Find Profit in Corporate." *Management Review* 79, no. 12 (1990), 10.

3

Corporate Volunteerism

Strategic Community Involvement

ALICE KORNGOLD AND ELIZABETH HOSLER VOUDOURIS

Economic tensions that are forcing businesses to reexamine corporate structures, systems and activities, are also pushing community involvement to a higher place on the corporate agenda. In fact, businesses are recognizing that strategic involvement in the community presents unique opportunities to the company to enhance its position in the market and to develop and instill vision, teamwork, and leadership skills among personnel. An additional factor that propels companies toward active participation in the community is a heightened awareness of the imperative to create work environments where learning is fostered as a strategy to strengthen leadership (Senge, 1990, pp. 7–22). Volunteer involvement promotes leadership development and learning.

Businesses have suffered from the devastating impact of urban blight on the education and preparation of the workforce and the buying capability of consumers. Companies realize that the health and welfare of the communities where their employees and customers live and work are critical to the success of business. The recent popularity of management systems thinking further underscores these notions of dependency and interdependency between systems (Senge, 1990, pp. 4–16). Businesses understand that they are not islands in society, but vital forces that can help shape the community and benefit from the enhanced welfare.

Although companies are increasingly aware that their businesses depend on the well-being of the community at large, due to heightened competitive pressures, they are, ironically, unable to extend philanthropic generosity. Consequently, businesses are recognizing the extraordinary and multiple benefits of a community involvement strategy that emphasizes volunteerism among employees throughout the company.

This chapter will show that business volunteerism has unique potential to benefit the company, employees, and the community. Moreover, there are three key factors that will maximize the impact of the company program. First, corporate community involvement strategy must be aligned with the corporate mission and goals just like any other company initiative or department. Second, when companies integrate and coordinate their philanthropy, senior-level involvement on non-profit boards, and volunteerism among the broader ranks of employees, these valuable contributions complement each other and maximize impact in addressing community needs. Third, the community involvement strategy should be designed to serve company goals in the areas of human resources, marketing, public relations, and community affairs. In addition, many companies find that their impact in serving the community is greater when they focus their philanthropy and volunteerism in addressing one, two or three critical issues.

It will also be shown in this chapter that impact evaluation is essential to the effectiveness and viability of corporate community involvement. While many companies accept the premise that volunteerism is good for business, it is important to establish mechanisms to document and measure the benefits to the company, employees, and the community. After all, in other corporate endeavors, top management expects consistent reporting from all departments in order to determine where resources should be allocated, which programs are effective, and which initiatives should be continued. Furthermore, a carefully documented evaluation of the program's impact provides information that is needed in order to enhance opportunities to serve corporate and community interests. Finally, a report of the program's impact reinforces volunteers, inspires others to join in the effort, increases the program's visibility, strengthens support for the program both internally and externally, and maximizes the public relations benefits to the company.

TRENDS IN CORPORATE VOLUNTEERISM

A few studies and numerous articles demonstrate a rapidly increasing trend in support of corporate volunteerism. According to a study conducted by the Points of Light Foundation and the Conference Board (1993), 92 percent of the 452 corporations that responded to a national survey indicated that they encourage their employees to become involved in volunteer activities. In addition, 72 percent of top corporate executives affirmed the success of corporate volunteer programs in helping companies meet strategic goals and community needs. Most importantly, the study documented rapid and substantial increase in corporate volunteerism.

> In over 70 independent Corporate Volunteerism Councils nationwide, 1,048 companies share their volunteer experiences. New programs are added every day. The growth from 600 such member companies in 1985 represents a recognition that volunteer programs are one of the best ways for corporations to support their involvement in the community. Forty five percent of contributions/community relations managers in 100 Fortune 500 companies anticipated expanding their employee volunteer programs over the next two to five years, in spite of down sizing. (Wild, 1993, p. 9)

According to the survey findings, top executives indicated that volunteer involvement made workers more productive. Ninety percent affirmed that volunteerism programs helped the company recruit better employees. Seventy-seven percent indicated that volunteer programs increased retention rates among employees. Finally, 80 percent "strongly agreed" that the company's volunteerism program helped improve the company's public image.

These findings are borne out by studies of the experiences of various companies. Federal Express (Solomon, Ragland, Wilson, and Plost, 1991) surveyed employees to determine the benefits they derived from volunteering. Survey results confirmed that employees perceived that participation contributed to career development and job productivity. Respondents also identified the following eight job skills that were enhanced through volunteer involvement: teamwork, ability to motivate others, organization, leadership, listening, decision making, speaking, and writing. Moreover, according to an evaluation of General Mills' volunteerism program (1994), 56 percent of employees who volunteered indicated that they learned new leadership skills, and 36 percent indicated an opportunity to improve work skills.

Other studies reflect the corporate endorsement of volunteerism. In "The New Corporate Philanthropy" (1994, p. 105), Craig Smith argued that "for the first time, businesses are backing philanthropic initiatives with real corporate muscle. In addition to cash, they are providing nonprofits with managerial advice, technological and communications support, and teams of employee volunteers." Additionally, a Cone/Roper Study stressed the value of community involvement as a marketing tool: "Consumers express greater support for companies addressing issues at the local level" (1994, p. 4).

In addition to these formal studies, recent trends in corporate volunteerism are documented throughout the media. A number of articles attest to the value of volunteerism in supporting company goals for personnel development, including enhanced employee morale, professional development, and leadership training. *Newsweek* (Annetta Miller, 1989) reported that volunteerism programs are effective in rebuilding employee morale in a climate that is otherwise undermined by corporate restructuring and downsizing. Moreover, volunteerism is an effective way to engage retirees in the continuing life of the company.

The Wall Street Journal reported that volunteerism "raises employee morale and boosts productivity. Corporate volunteer programs cause workers to take pride in their jobs and work more closely with colleagues" ("Labor Letter," Nov. 23, 1993) In another article, *The Wall Street Journal* (Isenberg, 1993) reported that corporate volunteerism is a valuable vehicle for professional management development:

> Carefully selected volunteer experience is a new fast track for high-potential managers. It can be both a training ground and a proving ground for a company's best people. Three to five years of volunteer work can provide management experience most corporations couldn't provide over 20 years, if it can at all. (p. 5)

The Chronicle of Philanthropy ("Tapping Companies," August 1994) reported that corporate volunteer programs are a great benefit to participants, the corporation, and the nonprofit organizations that they serve. Volunteer programs demonstrate that the company seeks to improve employee morale and foster teamwork, and to sharpen skills of individual employees: "[Volunteer work] is a cost effective way to improve [employee] performance." In the article, Susan Smith, manager of corporate contributions and community relations at EDS headquarters in Dallas, asserted that volunteerism is an effective tool for employee training and leadership development: "Not only is it cheaper, but it is taking the training out into the community. It helps the community and the company." The *Chronicle* also reported that employees are often invited to include family members and friends in the company-sponsored volunteer project, allowing employees an opportunity to become involved in the community without taking time away from their families.

New York Newsday (Schmidt, 1990) reported that corporate volunteerism not only helps the community, but "helps the firm reap profits that range from improved work force morale to a better educated labor pool." Taiga Ermansons, manager of corporate community relations for Time Warner, explained that "the return on investment is that the company has a stronger base to work from in the community." *Industry Week* (Caudron, 1994) reported on the benefit to companies in the areas of recruitment and retention: "It's easier to retain employees when they feel good about the company they work for, and it's easier to recruit employees when they realize a company is concerned about more than its bottom line." Volunteerism can bring additional benefits. "Maintaining an impact as a socially responsible business is also important to socially aware consumers who make product choices based on deeply held personal values. Furthermore . . . community activities can enhance a company's relationship with local government."

Other media articles also attest to the trend of businesses integrating volunteerism with philanthropy in order to maximize the company's impact in addressing a critical community issue. *Foundation News* (Hiquera, 1992) reported that corporations are realizing that volunteers can enhance the impact of grant dollars at a nonprofit organization. *Crain's New York Business* (Bayless, 1992) called corporate volunteers a "low-cost contribution to the community in tough economic times—a way to look good for less." *American Demographics* (O'Hare, 1991) explained that while corporate philanthropy is intended to create better employee and customer relations, it must focus on certain issues that reflect the mission of the business.

Importantly, companies are recognizing the strategic implications of volunteerism programs that are aligned with the corporate mission and goals. For example, Peter C. Hutchinson, formerly chair of Dayton Hudson Foundation and vice president, external relations, Dayton Hudson Corporation, explained that businesses have a responsibility to play a leadership role in the nonprofit sector: "A company should work on issues or concerns that are of direct and important strategic value to the company itself. . . . Concern about that issue must also be manifest in the business leaders themselves . . . the combination of strategic linkage and personal concern is almost unbeatable" (Hutchinson, 1991).

There is tremendous potential for business volunteers to have a real impact on society. According to Peter Drucker (1994, p. 76), "it is becoming increasingly clear that through the social sector a modern developed society can again create responsible and achieving citizenship, and can again give individuals—especially knowledge workers—a sphere in which they can make a difference in society and recreate community."

A SUCCESSFUL CORPORATE VOLUNTEERISM PROGRAM

In the past two years, the Business Volunteerism Council of Cleveland, Ohio, has assisted a total of 70 companies in developing and implementing strategies for community involvement. BVC was established in January 1993 as an initiative of the corporate community. The Cleveland business leaders who formed BVC were motivated by their concern about rapidly increasing needs in the community coupled with diminishing funding available from the small number of companies that had traditionally supported nonprofit efforts in the community. These business leaders had a vision of an organization that would involve a broad base of businesses in addressing community issues by involving employees in contributing their time and talents as volunteers. BVC was designed to provide comprehensive services in linking individuals from companies who have a broad variety of interests and skills together with hundreds of nonprofits seeking volunteer assistance.

BVC's primary service is to provide information and consulting services to assist businesses in establishing community involvement strategies that integrate philanthropy with executive involvement on nonprofit boards of trustees, and volunteerism among employees, retirees, and families. In response to corporate interests, BVC is developing and testing a model to evaluate the impact of corporate volunteerism on the company, employees, and the community.

Although BVC is unique in its mission and services, there are more than 70 Corporate Volunteer Councils (CVCs) nationally that serve 1,048 companies with volunteerism programs. These CVCs are coalitions of corporations with active employee volunteer programs. CVCs are usually managed by volunteers from the membership and sometimes receive some degree of staff assistance from the local Volunteer Center. There are Volunteer Centers, or Voluntary Action Centers, in more than 450 communities nationwide. Volunteer Centers recruit and refer individuals to volunteer activities in the community (Wild, 1993). In addition, the Points of Light Foundation is a national organization that lends support to companies with employee volunteerism programs. The factors that distinguish BVC from CVCs and Volunteer Centers are the following: a corporate board that drives the mission and the organization, substantial corporate funding, and a paid staff of eight individuals who provide fee-based consulting and volunteer training and referral services to businesses and nonprofit organizations. In addition, BVC has developed innovative products and services that are purchased and used by companies throughout the country.

BVC's experience with 70 businesses has led it to identify various critical factors for a strong company volunteer program. BVC has found that successful corporate volunteerism programs are aligned with the corporate mission and integrated with corporate philanthropy and that they address the company's marketing and human resource objectives. Strategically based corporate volunteer programs are no longer viewed as superfluous "warm fuzzy" features of a company's community service agenda, but are designed for maximum impact in benefiting employees, the company, and the community.

DEFINING THE MISSION

The first step in establishing a successful volunteer program is for the company to determine what it seeks to accomplish from the program and the benefits it seeks to derive. Each company has particular and unique reasons for establishing and supporting a volunteerism program. Program goals need to be identified and articulated at the beginning of the process in order to ultimately determine the success of the program as well as ways in which the program can be enhanced.

The following factors are essential to consider when developing goals for the company's volunteerism program: corporate mission; business goals; demographics of local market; client development and corporate marketing; corporate philanthropy; demographics of workforce; and human resource objectives.

Implementation: Once the company establishes its reasons for promoting business volunteerism, strategies that are effective in ensuring the success of the program include the following:

- **An audit, and a strategy:** Strategic involvement begins with an audit of the company's existing relationships with nonprofit organizations and the development of a strategy for enhanced involvement that serves the interests of the employees, the company, and the community. Often, a company can strengthen its impact by focusing its contribution in addressing one or two critical community issues.
- **An advisory committee:** Broad-based employee involvement is assured by establishing an advisory committee made up of a cross-section of employees who play the leadership role in coordinating short- and long-term volunteer projects. Committees choose the projects, recruit friends and colleagues to participate, and develop program policies and procedures. Employee ownership of the program is critical to the program's success.

- **Senior-level support and recognition for volunteerism:** The CEO plays an instrumental role in creating a climate that is conducive to volunteering, serving as a role model through his or her own community involvement, and thanking and recognizing volunteers in a visible and meaningful way.
- **Involvement of senior managers on nonprofit boards of trustees in the communities where the company does business:** Serving on a nonprofit board of trustees not only provides good networking and public relations opportunities for the company, but it provides the individual with the opportunity to develop professional and leadership skills. Importantly, if a company is channeling human and financial resources to a nonprofit, it is helpful to have a representative on the board of trustees to help guide the successful deployment of those resources.
- **Ongoing assessment and reporting on all activities of the volunteerism program:** By collecting and reporting information about volunteer activities, the company ensures that stakeholders will recognize the impact of the volunteerism program. This is discussed further in a later section of this chapter.

There is sometimes a tension between two key themes. While a company volunteer program must serve the corporation's key goals as articulated by senior management, the program must be driven and shaped by those employees who are enthusiastic about community service. After all, the program's very viability depends upon the interest, participation, and peer leadership of employees. With mutual understanding, sensitivity, and collaboration, a successful program meeting corporate and individual needs can emerge.

A number of companies have succeeded in developing successful volunteerism programs in a fairly short time. The following case study illustrates the importance of the factors described above.

Case Study: McDonald & Company C.A.R.E.S. Eighteen months ago, eight employees from McDonald & Company approached BVC for assistance in establishing a volunteerism program. Within ten months, 162 employees had participated in at least one of 17 projects. Additionally, several senior vice presidents who were not already serving on nonprofit boards joined boards that met their interests and that welcomed their skills. As developed below, McDonald & Company developed an integrated community service strategy that is aligned with the corporate mission, meets corporate objectives, serves employee interests, and addresses needs in the community. This case demonstrated the importance of the success factors noted above.

McDonald & Company Investments, Inc. operates a full-service, regional investment banking, investment advisory, and brokerage business through its principal subsidiary, McDonald & Company Securities Inc. and through the Gradison Division and S. J. Wolfe Division of McDonald Securities. McDonald Securities has 34 offices in nine states, including headquarters in Cleveland.

Volunteerism is consistent with McDonald & Company's goals. The corporate ethos at McDonald & Company is defined by five enduring values: "Integrity; The trust of our clients; Our reputation; The well-being and happiness of our employees"; and "The betterment of our community through our service and support" (Summers, 1994). Consequently, the company's commitment to community service is a direct reflection of the company's enduring values. In addition, volunteerism serves corporate objectives for public relations, marketing, and human resource development.

Senior management recognizes the importance of supporting employee initiatives for community involvement. "Early last year, it came to my attention that employees and their families wanted to get involved in something meaningful," explains William Summers, President and CEO of McDonald & Company Securities. "We fostered the development of an employee driven volunteerism program, McDonald C.A.R.E.S., as a vehicle to involve employees and their family members in addressing critical needs in our community. Through this program, we have learned that when the workplace provides employees with opportunities beyond the scope of their work, employees are happier and more productive; this has contributed to the overall betterment of the company."

In this supportive environment, an employee-driven volunteer program began to develop. Early in 1993, eight McDonald & Company employees formed an advisory committee and utilized BVC's services to identify needs in the community that would lend themselves to volunteer activity. The committee worked with senior management to develop a name—McDonald & Company C.A.R.E.S. (Community Action Rewards Everyone who Serves)—and a mission—to organize and coordinate events and activities through which McDonald & Company employees could donate their time to the community.

The results of an employee survey, conducted by the advisory committee, indicated that many employees were interested in participating in group volunteer activities where teams of employees could make a large impact in a short time. Employees expressed interest in issues related to children, education, homelessness, and hunger. The C.A.R.E.S. Committee sought BVC's help to identify worthwhile projects that lent themselves to team building and enhanced morale. Between February and December, 1993, McDonald C.A.R.E.S. recruited almost half of all employees in the Cleveland office to participate in 17 events. Employees and family members from McDonald & Company volunteered for various activities: They held a baby shower for the abused women and children in residence at Providence House; helped build homes for Habitat for Humanity; collected food for Harvest for Hunger; tutored illiterate adults; mentored children; served food to homeless families; planted trees; built a split-rail fence around a playground at the Cleveland Sight Center; and distributed winter clothing to the homeless.

After participating in many shorter-term volunteer activities, several McDonald & Company volunteers sought longer-term involvement. The employee surveys indicated a particular interest in education. With assistance from BVC, the Committee identified Project: LEARN, a nonprofit that works to improve basic reading and writing skills of adults in Greater Cleveland. Project: LEARN developed a special series of tutor-training sessions that were offered on-site at McDonald & Company. Project: LEARN and the company collaborated to arrange for the students to receive their training on-site at McDonald & Company. To date, 25 McDonald & Company employees have committed themselves to tutor illiterate adults for three hours a week for the next year.

Project: LEARN recently recognized McDonald & Company at its Annual Meeting for the company's outstanding commitment to the cause of improving adult literacy. Richard Peterson, Executive Director, Project: LEARN, lauds the commitment of McDonald & Company: "Because of their efforts and commitment, we have been able to cut down on our student waiting list by 20 percent."

William Summers and other senior managers support the efforts of the C.A.R.E.S. Committee by participating in company-sponsored volunteer activities; sending thank you notes to volunteers after each volunteer event; inviting volunteers to lunch to thank them for their efforts; and listing the names of all volunteers in the daily sales sheets that are circulated company-wide. The C.A.R.E.S. Committee recognized every employee who volunteered in 1993 with a McDonald & Company T-shirt and a lapel pin featuring the McDonald & Company C.A.R.E.S. logo.

In addition, William Summers encourages the company's senior managers to become involved in leadership on nonprofit boards in the community. Through the Business Volunteerism Council's (BVC) Volunteer Trustee Institute, senior managers at McDonald & Company receive training about the role and responsibilities of nonprofit board members and are referred for positions on nonprofit boards according to the candidates' skills and the needs of the organization.

Employees and management at McDonald & Company recognize that volunteering benefits employees and the company as well as the community. Participation in volunteer activities sponsored by McDonald C.A.R.E.S. improves employee morale and promotes better teamwork, both of which impact employee productivity. Community service also lends itself to networking and public relations opportunities, both of which are critical to individuals involved in the professional services industry. William Summers confirms the link between volunteerism and business goals: "In a relationship driven business, volunteerism benefits how we do business."

In January 1994, the C.A.R.E.S. Committee developed an Annual Report to share their community service achievements with McDonald & Company's internal and external stakeholders. McDonald & Company is currently in the process of documenting all group and individual volunteer initiatives and storing the information in a database in order to facilitate the process of impact evaluation and to enhance the 1994 Annual Report.

Overall, McDonald & Company's commitment to community service is a win-win-win situation for the community, employees, and the company.

OBSTACLES

While studies and articles noted earlier in this chapter document the motivating forces and benefits that are driving the trend to increased corporate community involvement, there are also obstacles that have been observed among BVC's 70 member companies. First, in today's work and social environment, employees are often overtaxed at work and in their personal lives; this certainly diminishes their capacity and interest in adding responsibilities such as volunteering. Second, tensions in the work environment, often exacerbated by internal problems (such as lay-offs) and external factors (such as competition in the marketplace), further undermine interest in devotion to community issues. Third, while corporate volunteerism is often a strategy to break down barriers in a hierarchical company, it is sometimes most difficult for hierarchical companies to foster volunteer programs that are driven and managed by employees.

Finally, and ironically, it is sometimes the nonprofits that will receive corporate volunteer assistance that create obstacles to successful partnerships. That is, in some cases nonprofits are ill prepared to harness and channel the corporate volunteer talent that is offered to them.

However, increasingly nonprofits are recognizing the value of corporate community involvement and are thereby seeking assistance—often from Volunteer Centers—to understand how to develop new opportunities that effectively utilize important volunteer time.

The Conference Board (1993), cites the following obstacles to expanding employee volunteer programs at the 454 companies that were surveyed: lack of employee time to participate (51 percent of respondents); administrative costs (35 percent); lack of middle management support (28 percent); lack of coordination of activities/programs (26 percent); lack of written policy (24 percent): employee apathy (19 percent); and lack of CEO support (8 percent).

The Conference Board (1993) also reports that the estimated cost of programs excluding staff time is less than $10,000 for 51 percent of the 454 companies that responded to the survey; $10,000 to $24,999 for 27 percent; $50,000 to $99,999 for 6 percent; and $100,000 or more for 16 percent. In addition, the report notes that the median amount of time spent managing employee volunteer programs by the person responsible is reported as 20 percent. The other major job responsibilities of that person are reported variously as: community relations (45 percent); contributions (36 percent); communications/public relations (32 percent); and personnel/human resources (11 percent).

LIFE CYCLES

Employee volunteerism programs at companies in Cleveland appear to follow the life cycle progression usually followed by most programs and project developments (Levitt, 1965). Typically, program life cycles manifest three or four distinct stages to include development, growth, maturity, and, at times, decline but hopefully renewal. Programs are often launched with a great deal of entrepreneurial and altruistic energy; that initial enthusiasm is a forceful driver in the first stage that seems to last for at least a year, and sometimes several years. However, a number of the most successful programs seem to reach a plateau at which the challenge is to reinvigorate the program. Two new factors that become obstacles to future program success include exhaustion on the part of the individuals who have dedicated their services to program leadership, and politics among the program leadership. Further study of the life cycles of corporate volunteerism programs will help companies to prepare for various stages and to build in mechanisms to ensure the program's ongoing success.

COMPANIES CONDUCIVE TO VOLUNTEERISM PROGRAMS

BVC has recognized that corporate volunteerism programs succeed more readily at professional service companies and at companies where employees are expected to develop relationships in the community. However, additional study is merited to identify the factors that make a particular company more conducive to a successful volunteerism program. BVC's experience has shown that given a certain degree of support in the form of consulting services and information, the volunteerism programs at some companies emerge quite forcefully in a brief time, while others never move forward at all. If the degree of success can be predicted based on certain internal and external factors, this would be useful to companies and their consultants in determining whether a volunteerism effort is worthwhile and whether certain factors can be addressed in order to ensure the program's success.

IMPACT EVALUATION: FIVE PHASES

While it is widely believed that benefits accrue to companies involved in the community, and the literature begins to support these assumptions, businesses are pressing for information to document and measure the impact of their community involvement in benefiting the company, employees, and the community. The 1993 survey conducted by the Conference Board and the Points of Light Foundation (Wild) indicates this trend: "As volunteer programs mature, the need for more record keeping also becomes apparent. The growing interest in assessment will also bring greater record management into volunteer programs" (p. 32). Impact evaluation studies are limited at this stage. However, companies that are leading the way in documenting and measuring the benefits of their programs are able to make the case for continued corporate support for volunteerism. Federal Express reported that while their survey results were not surprising, "they did help the professional staff in securing increased budgets and use of other company resources for community involvement projects" (Solomon, Raglan, Wilson, and Plost, 1991, p. 320). The study also demonstrated to Federal Express that beyond doing good, "volunteer managers need to operate their programs with a business perspective."

By establishing an ongoing process to evaluate the effectiveness of the program, the company can measure the value that is being derived from the program. To address this interest on behalf of its corporate clients, BVC developed an impact evaluation model and accompanying survey instruments. Although this material was designed for BVC members, companies throughout the U.S.A. and Canada have learned of BVC and requested copies of the impact evaluation model. Impact evaluation is important for several reasons:

- Top management expects consistent reporting from all departments in order to determine where resources should be allocated, which programs are effective, and what programs to continue;
- Evaluating the volunteer program's past and present will help enhance the program for the future (continuous quality improvement);
- Reporting on the program's impact will increase visibility and enhance support in the company—among employees and senior management; and
- Reporting on the program's impact expands public relations opportunities for the company.

There are four fundamental steps in documenting and measuring impact at a company:

- Identifying and articulating company goals for the volunteerism program;
- Determining what to measure in order to demonstrate goals achieved;
- Developing a method for gathering the data;
- Determining how the data will be used.

BVC's impact evaluation model adheres to current principles of program evaluation. The key objective in designing the model was to provide guidance to companies seeking to produce convincing evidence to demonstrate the value of the corporate volunteerism program, make recommendations for the future, and reinforce and further enhance support for the program (Newcomer, Hatry, and Wholey, 1994). The most fundamental first step is for the company to determine and articulate its goals for the volunteerism program; these goals will form the basis for developing the performance indicators by which the program will be evaluated and for identifying the data sources to be used for the measurements and analysis (Wholey, 1994). BVC's impact evaluation model includes a phase for process evaluation to reveal the realities of the day-to-day program delivery and identify opportunities for the most efficient program implementation (Scheirer, 1994). The model also includes survey instruments to measure the extent to which the employee volunteerism program meets employee interests (Miller, 1994). Finally, the model is designed to provide information for continuous quality improvement (Newcomer, Hatry, and Wholey, 1994; and Sonnichsen, 1994).

BVC has identified five phases of impact evaluation. While Phase I on record keeping is essential in all cases, the other four phases may have differing relevance to companies depending on corporate goals and needs. It is important for companies to inform stakeholders about the efforts and the impact of the company's involvement in the community. An annual report that summarizes the benefits derived by the company, employees, and the community will impress the board of directors, shareholders, and community leaders regarding the company's investment in the welfare of the community. In addition, an annual report will reinforce the enthusiasm of the volunteers who can see their contribution quantified and heralded.

PHASE I—RECORD KEEPING

Data collection and management becomes more complex depending on the goals the company seeks to measure. However, a number of goals can be measured with a straightforward record-keeping system. All companies should track the volunteer activities of employees and the company. Volunteer advisory committees and volunteer coordinators can help record activity with all of the pertinent volunteer information, but ideally, each company should identify an individual who has primary responsibility for record keeping (including maintaining the database) and any paperwork associated with the company's volunteerism program.

A simple record-keeping system may be used to track the number of volunteers, their volunteer activities, aggregated volunteer hours, and value of time contributed.

PHASE II—PROCESS EVALUATION

By conducting a process evaluation, companies can assess the effectiveness of the structure, policies, and administration of the company's volunteerism program (CQI—continuous quality improvement) to ensure that employees have access to information and volunteer opportunities. The volunteer advisory committee can examine the key features of a volunteerism program, and determine which features have been successfully implemented and which features are desirable for the future.

PHASE III—IMPACT ON EMPLOYEES

To determine the impact on employees, the company needs to understand the benefits that employees seek to derive through participation in the company's volunteerism program. This can be discovered through a survey that BVC developed. The second step is measuring the extent to which these benefits were in fact derived. This can also be determined by surveys.

PHASE IV—IMPACT ON THE COMPANY

To measure the impact on the company, the first step is to identify the benefits the company seeks to achieve. Then tools and methods can be developed to measure the extent to which benefits are derived.

The company can benefit from volunteerism in many ways. There may be a direct impact on the company's key business goals, by improving productivity, increasing income generated per employee, and addressing social issues. There may be human resource benefits such as enhancing morale, professional development, increased productivity, attendance, and retention, and improving team building. There may be marketing benefits, because of an improved perception of the company in the community, public relations and marketing opportunities, and an expanded business network.

PHASE V—IMPACT ON COMMUNITY

Finally, companies seek to measure their impact on critical social issues. Where nonprofit organizations are already measuring the impact of their efforts on the community, the company must only determine its contribution to the accomplishment of the nonprofit organization's overall effort. The measurement task is more complicated in the case of companies supporting efforts by nonprofits that are not themselves documenting their impact on the community.

SUMMARY

The momentum for corporate volunteerism is rapidly gaining. However, there is a risk that this trend will be a mere flash in the pan. It is incumbent upon those who advocate business volunteerism to develop and conduct studies to document and measure the benefits that accrue to companies, employees, and the community. Ultimately, rigorous impact evaluation is essential to the institutionalization of business volunteerism. Proof is needed to show the value to corporations that invest in volunteerism as a vehicle for enhancing the quality of life for citizens in the community.

REFERENCES

Aupperle, Kenneth E. "An Empirical Measure of Corporate Social Orientation." Vol. 6 in *Research on Corporate Social Performance Policy*, ed. L. E. Preston. Greenwich CT: JAI Press, 1984. Pp. 27–54.

Bailey, Anne Lowrey. "Corporations New Social Advocacy." (Ports) *Chronicle of Philanthropy* (April 7, 1992), 6.

———. "Prudential: Collaborating to Strengthen Communities." *Chronicle of Philanthropy* (April 7, 1992), 12.

Bayless, Pamela. "Business Tapping Volunteer Impulse: Low-Cost Way to Fulfill Obligations." *Crain's New York Business* (October 19, 1992), 3.

"Building a current profile of socially responsible firms." *International Association for Business Society*, 1990. Pp. 297–303.

Caudron, Shari. "Volunteerism and the Bottom Line." *Industry Week* (Feb. 21, 1994), 13.

Cone/Roper Study. "A Benchmark Survey of Consumer Awareness and Attitudes Towards Cause-Related Marketing" (May 1994), 4.

Cox, Craig, and Sally Power. "Executives of the World Unit." *Business Ethics* (September-October 1992), 17.

Cuseuza, John Sebastian. "The Beauty of Social Action." *Business Ethics* (November-December 1992), 13.

Drucker, Peter F. "The Age of Social Transformation." *Atlantic Monthly* (November 1994), 53–80.

Fine, Tracy A. "Most Companies Encourage Volunteerism." *Chronicle of Philanthropy* (May 4, 1993), 16.

Flaherty, Susan. "The Voluntary Sector: Corporate Citizenship in the U.S. and Japan." *Voluntas* (May 1991), 58–77.

General Mills. *"Corporations in the Community."* 1994.

Hall, Holly, and Jennifer Moore. "Company's Garden Benefits Soup Kitchen." *Chronicle of Philanthropy* (June 30, 1992), 26.

Hiquera, Jonathan J. "Value-Added Volunteers." *Foundation News* (March-April 1992), 44.

Hutchinson, Peter C. "Providing Effective Leadership in the Community." In James P. Shannon, ed., *The Corporate Contributions Handbook*. San Francisco: Jossey-Bass, 1991.

Independent Sector. *A Vision of Evaluation: A Report on Learning from Independent Sector's Work on Evaluation*, ed. Sandra Trice Gray. Washington, D.C., 1993.

Isenberg, Howard. "Nonprofit Training for Profitable Careers." *Wall Street Journal* (Aug. 23, 1993), 5.

Korngold, Alice. "Education: Interest and Impact." *Trustee*, American Hospital Association (July 1994), 21.

Korngold, A., and P. Dube. "An Assessment Model for Cooperative Education Program Planning, Management and Marketing." *Journal of Cooperative Education*, (1982), 29-37.

———. "Documenting Benefits and Developing Campus and Community Support." In Ryder, Kenneth G., and James W. Wilson and Associates, eds., *Cooperative Education in a New Era*. San Francisco: Jossey-Bass, 1987. 47–57.

Korngold, A., and J. Pastore. "The Evolution of a Comprehensive Experiential Learning Program: A Case Study." *Journal of Cooperative Education* (Winter 1987), 47–57.

"Labor Letter: A Special News Report." *Wall Street Journal* (Nov. 23, 1993), 1.

Lamb, William B. "Measuring Corporate Social Performance." IABS Proceedings, 1994.

Levitt, Theodore. "Exploit the Product Life Cycle." *Harvard Business Review* 43 (November-December 1965), 81–94.

Miller, Annetta. "Doing Well by Doing Good." *Newsweek* (June 10, 1989), 36.

Miller, Thomas I. "Designing and Conducting Surveys." In Wholey, Joseph S.,

Harry P. Hatry, and Kathryn E. Newcomer, eds., *Handbook of Practical Program Evaluation*. San Francisco: Jossey-Bass, 1994.

Minton-Eversole, Theresa. "Companies as Community Citizens." *Training and Development* (November 1991), 21–30.

Moore, Jennifer "92% of Big Companies Encourage Volunteer Efforts, Survey Finds." *Chronicle of Philanthropy* (June 30, 1992), 13.

Newcomer, Kathryn E., Harry P. Hatry, and Joseph S. Wholey, "Meeting the Need for Practical Evaluation Approaches: An Introduction." In Wholey, Joseph S., Harry P. Hatry, and Kathryn E. Newcomer, eds., *Handbook of Practical Program Evaluation*. San Francisco: Jossey-Bass, 1994.

O'Hare, Barb Clark. "Good Deeds Are Good Business." *American Demographics* (September 1991), 38–42.

Peterson, Richard. Oral communication, Feb. 11, 1994.

The Points of Light Foundation. *Learning from Leaders*. Washington, D.C., 1993.

Scheirer, Mary Ann. "Designing and Using Process Evaluation." In Wholey, Joseph S., Harry P. Hatry, and Kathryn E. Newcomer, eds., *Handbook of Practical Program Evaluation*. San Francisco: Jossey-Bass, 1994.

Schmidt, Josephine. "They Gave at the Office, Companies Finding Volunteerism Brings Good Return on Investments." *New York Newsday* (March 19, 1990), 10.

Seltzer, Michael, and Michael Cunningham. "General Support vs. Project Support: A 77 Year Old Debate Revisited." *Nonprofit World* (July-August 1991), 16–20.

Senge, Peter M. "The Leader's New Work: Building Learning Organizations." *Sloan Management Review* 32, no. 1 (Fall 1990), 27–36.

"75% of Accountants Do Charity Work." *Chronicle of Philanthropy* (January 14, 1992), 12.

Shannon, James, ed. *The Corporate Contributions Handbook*. San Francisco: Jossey-Bass, 1991.

Smith, Craig. "The New Corporate Philanthropy." *Harvard Business Review* (May-June 1994), 105.

Solomon, Sheryl W., et al. "Encouraging Company Employees to Volunteer." In James P. Shannon, ed., *The Corporate Contributions Handbook*. San Francisco: Jossey-Bass, 1991.

Sonnichsen, Richard C. "Evaluations as Change Agents." In Wholey, Joseph S., Harry P. Hatry, and Kathryn E. Newcomer, eds., *Handbook of Practical Program Evaluation*. San Francisco: Jossey-Bass, 1994.

Summers, William. Interview with Alice Korngold. Jan. 10, 1994.

"Tapping Companies for Volunteers." *Chronicle of Philanthropy* (August 9, 1994), 41.

Wild, Cathleen. *Corporate Volunteer Programs: Benefits to Business*. New York: Conference Board, 1993.

Wholey, Joseph S. "Assessing the Feasibility and Likely Usefulness of Evaluation." In Wholey, Joseph S., Harry P. Hatry, and Kathryn E. Newcomer, eds., *Handbook of Practical Program Evaluation*. San Francisco: Jossey-Bass, 1994.

4

Research in Corporate Social Performance
What Have We Learned?

DONNA J. WOOD AND RAYMOND E. JONES

From a scholarly perspective, the literature on business philanthropy is like *dim sum*, interesting and enjoyable, but not very filling. It gives insight into the management aspects of corporate philanthropy but does not offer a complete or accurate picture of what corporate philanthropy is and should be. Instead there is a set of arguments about why companies should or should not give money away, and if they do, advice on how to do it. This view tends to be focused on practical concerns such as:

- how much money a company should give;
- what gifts (other than money) are welcome and useful;
- how shareholders react to charitable giving;
- what stakeholders will be mollified or angered by certain gifts;
- how one organizes a charitable giving program;
- how a giving program can be sustained through economic hard times;
- how charitable giving can pay off for the company.

Instead of viewing philanthropy in such a completely practical manner, we need to frame questions of business philanthropy within the broader context of corporate social performance (CSP). This will get us further along in our scholarly task of understanding the roles corporations play in society and the responsibilities they have to members of society. Our task in this chapter is to survey the literature in corporate social performance to see what we have learned about these roles and responsibilities, how they are fulfilled, and how they can be measured. Examining the broad CSP context gives us a framework for better understanding what business philanthropy is and should be.

Another (but related) stream of literature—stakeholder theory and management—is critically involved in any assessment of what we know about corporate social performance. Stakeholders—groups and organizations that are affected by or can affect a company's operations (Freeman, 1984)—are the source of expectations for corporate performance and the recipients of corporate output. In regard to CSP, they are the answer to the question, "To whom should the firm be responsible?" Much of the research in CSP is oriented toward finding how well firms are meeting the needs, demands, and expectations of particular stakeholders. A new theory is needed that can absorb the best of existing theories of the firm (especially the neoclassical "self-interested" and the behavioral "satisficing" theories) and can also accommodate the realities of business's intricate societal interconnections. Eventually business philanthropy will be understood within such a theoretical perspective—not as just another self-interested "strategic" act, or as a way of muddling through complexities, but as a way for firms to engage more fully in their societal relationships and duties. We will frame the paper around these questions:

- 1. What is corporate social performance (CSP)?
- 2. Can we measure CSP?
- 3. Does CSP make a difference?
- 4. What is missing in our understanding of CSP? (answer: stakeholders)
- 5. How can we better understand corporate philanthropy, given what we know about CSP and stakeholders?
- 6. How can we summarize what we know about CSP and stakeholder concepts and apply these conclusions toward a new theory of the firm?

WHAT IS CORPORATE SOCIAL PERFORMANCE?

U.S. scholars have argued this question concerning the roles and obligations of business in a capitalist-democratic society for decades. The neoclassical economic view is represented by Friedman's (1962, 1970) contention that "the social responsibility of business is to make a profit." The CSR/CSP view, represented by scholars in the field of business and society (or social issues in management, SIM), has focused on business's interdependencies with other elements of society and the responsibilities that arise because of those interrelationships. Early scholars attempted to remain within the neoclassical paradigm, although arguing to broaden its parameters. Lately, however, scholars have begun to move toward a new theory of the firm—probably a stakeholder theory—that would permit a more complex analysis and understanding of company-society relationships. It is this new theoretical wave that intrigues us.

EARLY DEFINITIONS: CORPORATE SOCIAL RESPONSIBILITY

Early writers in business and society (e.g., Bowen, 1953; Elbing and Elbing, 1964; Heald, 1970) were concerned with what they saw as an excessive autonomy and degree of power for business, apparently unconnected to any responsibility for the negative consequences of business activities. But early definitions were vague and ambiguous:

> [CSR is] the firm's consideration of, and response to, issues beyond the narrow economic, technical, and legal requirements of the firm . . . [to] accomplish social benefits along with the traditional economic gains which the firm seeks. (Davis, 1973)

> The fundamental idea of "corporate social responsibility" is that business corporations have an obligation to work for social betterment. (Frederick, 1978)

In the 1960s and 1970s, there were many unsuccessful attempts to specify CSR more precisely (see Dalton and Cosier, 1982; Jones, 1980; Keim, 1978a, b; Tuzzolino and Armandi, 1981). Three models from the 1970s proved appealing and useful to SIM scholars. In the absence of critical analysis and attempts at synthesis, however, these works were used for years as independent and implicitly competing models of corporate social responsibility:

- 1. Preston and Post's (1975) concept of public responsibility, embedded in the idea that business and society are separate but "interpenetrating systems" rather than business being a subsystem of the larger societal system;
- 2. Carroll's (1979) four-part categorization of corporate social responsibility, set in a "three-dimensional" context that included management philosophy and particular social issues as additional axes; and
- 3. the conceptual shift away from "responsibility" toward the more action-oriented "responsiveness," represented by Ackerman's (1975) and Sethi's (1979) work on corporate social responsiveness.

Wartick and Cochran (1985) made an initial effort to synthesize all the competing and dissonant conceptual threads of SIM thinking into a comprehensive model. Wood (1991a, 1991b) built upon their work to construct the model that currently organizes much of the research and thinking about corporate social performance today. Critical challenges to Wood's CSP model are now beginning to arise, as seen in the work of Freeman and Liedtka (1991), Swanson (1994), Mitnick (1993), and Calton (1992).

CSR-DEFINING RESEARCH USING PRESTON AND POST'S INTERPENETRATING SYSTEMS AND PUBLIC RESPONSIBILITY

Preston and Post's (1975) concept of public responsibility refers to "the functions of organizational management within the specific context of public policy" (p. 10). Public responsibility is included with a manager's other responsibilities for planning, supervising, and so on. Public policy, defined as "the principles that guide action relating to society as a whole" (p. 11), is broader than law, narrower than public opinion or belief. Two areas of managerial involvement with the social system are defined: (1) the area of *primary involvement*, behaviors and transactions "that arise directly from [the firm's] specialized functional role.... Without them, the organization cannot be what it is" (p. 11), and (2) the area of *secondary involvement*, including "impacts and effects not intrinsic to the character of the organization but generated by its primary involvement activities" (p. 10). Managerial responsibility, according to Preston and Post (p. 97), includes *only* the primary and secondary impacts of the firm. A chemical company, for example, is rightly concerned with consumer safety and water pollution, both deriving from its primary function. Such a firm might have trouble justifying involvement with low-income housing or voting rights. In practice, however, the reciprocal influences of business and society are so broad ranging that companies may be able to justify social involvements far afield from their obvious primary or secondary responsibilities.

The idea of public responsibility being defined by a company's primary and secondary involvements with society is very closely linked to the notion of companies existing within a stakeholder network. "Involvements" are relationships, and the idea that stakeholders define and evaluate many of a company's responsibilities is consistent with the view of firms as members of a complex network of relationships in society. Further, the "interpenetrating systems" idea, which at first glance appears to be just a way of granting some academic credibility to managers' desire for autonomy, turns out to be an accurate (and prescient) view of how business actually functions globally—as a system unto itself, overlapping with (or "interpenetrating") other social systems, but not fully contained within or controlled by any dominant social system.

Virtually no research actually *uses* Preston and Post as a theoretical framework, although almost all CSR/CSP research *cites* the interpenetrating systems concept (see Mahon and Andrews, 1987). However, there is some evidence in the early empirical work on CSR that supports their notion of business responsibility in the area of primary involvement. Holmes (1977, 1978), using data gathered from 192 large companies, found that charitable contributions, support for education, minority hiring and development, and community affairs were considered the most pressing social issues by executives at that time. More importantly, she also discovered a relationship between industry type and social involvement type. For example, extractive and manufacturing industries were most aware of their pollution abatement responsibilities; extractive industries were most concerned with resource conservation; wholesale-retail sales and financial service industries were most involved in community affairs; only the financial services and real estate industries showed any interest in minority enterprise assistance or urban redevelopment; and consumer protection was a concern only for wholesale and retail sales companies. These data reflect companies' primary involvements with society.

For years the idea of business and society as interpenetrating systems has seemed foreign, although somehow attractive, to many SIM scholars who prefer to think of business as a subordinate subsystem within a larger, and dominant, society, that is, U.S. society. On the field of international business, this dominant-subordinate relationship of society to business clearly does not apply. We would predict that Preston and Post's idea of interpenetrating systems will gain theoretical credibility as scholars begin to unravel the complexities of international business-society relationships.

CSR-DEFINING RESEARCH USING CARROLL'S FOUR DOMAINS

Carroll (1979, p. 500) defined corporate social responsibility as encompassing "the economic, legal, ethical, and discretionary expectations that society has of organizations at a given point in time." In his CSP model, Carroll constructs a three-dimensional box, bounded by "economic, legal, ethical, and discretionary expectations" on one axis, management philosophies on the second axis, and particular social issues on the third axis. This large model, although intuitively appealing, has proved to be less than helpful in guiding empirical research. There are something like 90 conceptual boxes in Carroll's own depiction, and it is not clear what exactly is supposed to be found within them. However, Carroll's idea that businesses have *economic, legal, ethical*, and *discretionary* responsibilities has been easier to handle in empirical research and has enjoyed wide popularity among SIM scholars.

This categorization of social responsibilities has generated research seeking to validate Carroll's contention that managers consider economic responsibilities to be fundamental, followed in order of magnitude by legal and ethical responsibilities, and then (if resources permit) discretionary responsibilities, which Carroll later defined as corporate philanthropy. Aupperle (1984) attempted to validate this framework by constructing a survey instrument consisting of 20 items, each containing four statements (one for each of Carroll's four dimensions of CSR). Respondents (192 CEOs) were asked to allocate as many as ten points across the statements for each item. Mean scores showed that CEOs did weight the dimensions as Carroll had proposed. Factor analysis, however, showed that the economic and ethical dimensions appeared to be opposing ends of a single factor rather than two distinct factors. Aupperle reported this finding but did not follow through in interpreting it, choosing instead to emphasize the mean-score distribution across the four dimensions of CSR and lending weight to Carroll's assertion that economic factors come first, then legal, ethical, and discretionary factors. Correlation analysis showed that the economic factor was negatively related to each of the other factors, which showed weak positive relationships among themselves.

Aupperle, Carroll, and Hatfield (1985) were unable to find a relationship between CEOs' "social orientation," using Aupperle's questionnaire described above (1984), and financial performance or profitability measures. Likewise, Pinkston and Carroll (1993) found no relationships between managers' CSR orientation (using the Aupperle scale) and organizational size. Attitudinal research using Aupperle's scaling of Carroll's four categories of social responsibility has produced little in the way of empirical results.

Despite disclaimers to the contrary, Carroll's model does emphasize that the *fundamental* responsibility of business is economic. While his work is an attempt to extend the neoclassical paradigm to accommodate societal relationships and the effects of business operations, Carroll's main emphasis is that "the business of business is business." In practice, unfortunately, this structural-functional view of business as a social institution can mean that legal, ethical, and especially discretionary (charitable) responsibilities might be "put on hold" if business is bad or times are tough.

CSR-DEFINING RESEARCH USING SOCIAL RESPONSIVENESS

Early definitions of CSR were tied more to society's interests than to those of the firm. Preston and Post (1975) moved social responsibility closer to firm self-interest and opened the door to a new action-oriented way of thinking that came to be called "corporate social responsiveness" or, in Frederick's (1978:6) shorthand—CSR_2—defined as "the capacity of a corporation to respond to social pressures."

The idea of social responsibility as a function of firm self-interest has its roots in the work of Berle and Means (1932), who documented a separation of control from ownership in large corporations. The purpose of the organization—the control function of the firm—was to maximize the firm's self-interest, which was ostensibly the interests of owners, but in practice overlapped to a large extent with the interests of managers. This approach was adopted by Preston and Post and others who built on the notion that social responsibility was a function of firm financial performance.

Ackerman (1975) was also an early proponent of the self-interested/public affairs approach to corporate social responsiveness. He argued that for a company to increase financial performance it must act "responsibly" in meeting societal expectations about how a business should perform. The corollary was that a company might not improve financial performance by meeting "discretionary" responsibilities (those that went beyond what was expected of business by society). Ackerman's social responsiveness approach was similar to Preston and Post's public policy approach, in that "social performance" was seen as guided solely by the firm's self-interest. Morality, ethics, and "discretionary" or voluntaristic behaviors were not necessarily part of responsiveness.

Ackerman articulated a three-step social response process: (1) CEO attention to a set of external issues that affect the corporation, (2) prioritization of issues and development of structures for managing responses, and (3) institutionalization of response patterns within the firm. Ackerman claimed that an effective social response process would meet four criteria: (1) commitment and leadership of the highest executives, (2) a match between a firm's social policy and its organizational constraints, (3) stakeholder support and participation, and (4) managed implementation of social response processes.

Some research has shown that corporate responsiveness need not be CEO driven. In a comparative study of corporate responses to youth unemployment in (former) West Germany and Great Britain, Antal (1992) discovered that responsive innovations happen at many corporate levels and can be communicated and supported in several directions, including middle-up, lateral, and middle-out, not just top-down. Nevertheless, there is widespread support for the idea that top management support for a company's charitable giving program is essential.

According to Ackerman (1975), a socially responsive firm monitors and assesses environmental conditions, attends to the many stake-holder demands placed upon it, and designs plans and policies to respond to changing conditions. These behaviors correspond to three key management functions: environmental assessment, stakeholder management, and issues/public affairs management. There is now a vast literature on environmental assessment as it is incorporated into strategic planning processes, stakeholder management (including busi-ness-government relations and corporate political action, community affairs, and charitable giving), and public affairs/issues management. Wood (1991a, b) surveys this literature, and several years' worth of newer research can be found in the *IABS Proceedings* dating from 1990.

Miles (1987) took the view of responsiveness as a result of self-interest even further by emphasizing the "external affairs function" of business, claiming that business needed to *appear* responsible, in addi-tion to undertaking activities in society's best interests, in order to achieve greater profits. The external affairs function was viewed as an outcome of top management philosophy and business exposure (or industry variables). To Miles, responsibility was a means to the end of increasing the firm's financial performance.

This self-interested view of social responsibility and social perfor-mance in some ways is stronger than ever in SIM literature. Observe, for example, the attention paid to cause-related marketing and strategic philanthropy (Burke et al., 1986; Smith and Alcorn, 1991). In this litera-ture, philanthropic activity by firms is presented as a means of produc-ing some benefit (financial or otherwise) for the firm as well as provid-ing some benefit to society. The belief is strong that the economists are right about self-interest as the "prime mover" in human and organiza-tional affairs, even as business and society scholars strive to introduce other motives and incentives into the picture.

The development of this literature from the early days of Preston and Post (1975) up through the recent work on cause-related marketing and strategic philanthropy can be characterized by the simple idea that CSR/CSP would be supported by managers and their decision-making processes if only it could be shown that companies can "do good and do well," or even better, that they can "do well by doing good." This literature, however, has provided little explanation of why companies undertake "discretionary" activities that may or may not produce benefits, which may or may not be measurable, for themselves. Further-more, this simplistic connection between "social" and "financial" per-formance has rarely been seriously challenged. What it means, how-ever, is that *only owners are seen as having the right to evaluate corporate performance.* This assumption is in clear violation of a stakeholder model of the firm, which would suggest that all stakeholders have certain rights in evaluating firm performance.

WARTICK AND COCHRAN'S CSP MODEL

Wartick and Cochran (1985) correctly claimed that a corporate social performance model could move the SIM field beyond pro-and-con debates on social responsibility, or economic versus social responsibility, or responsibility versus responsiveness. Toward this objective, they deftly incorporated three major "challenges" to corporate social responsibility (which they identify as economic responsibility, public responsibility, and social responsiveness) into their CSP model, which consisted of three segments: (1) principles of corporate social responsibility (economic, legal, ethical, and discretionary), (2) processes of corporate social responsiveness (reactive, defensive, accommodative, and interactive), and (3) issues management. They emphasized that CSP can *integrate* the various concerns of business and society thinking (for example, the social, economic, and public responsibilities of firms), thus promoting more rigorous theory development in the field. They stopped just short, however, of formally defining CSP when they wrote of the "integration" of three basic threads in business and society. The term "performance" should speak of action, deeds, and outcomes that can be identified and evaluated.

Extensive research to test the ideas of the Wartick and Cochran CSP model has been conducted by Clarkson and his colleagues, using a case database gathered on Canadian companies over a ten-year period. In early publications, Clarkson praised the Wartick and Cochran model for its ability to incorporate economic performance as the primary responsibility of business, without excluding legal, ethical, and descretionary responsibilities. He saw the model as a means of connecting social responsibility and ethics with profitability. Clarkson attempted to measure Wartick and Cochran's concept of social responsiveness by identifying companies that exemplified "best practices" in responding to changing values, issues, and conditions in the management of specific social issues (such as human relations, natural environment, community relations, and ethics policies). He analyzed the social responsiveness of 32 Canadian firms and found that the data confirmed Aupperle's (1984) study on the relationship between economic and social performance. He provided some empirical evidence for the contention that the more economically motivated a firm is, the less emphasis it will place on legal, ethical, and discretionary issues and responsibilities (Clarkson, 1988).

In his most recent work, however, Clarkson (1994) has declared that the Wartick and Cochran CSP model is *not effective* in guiding research on corporate social performance. He now believes that "the fundamental problem was, and remains, that there is no definition of social responsiveness that provides a framework for the systematic collection, organization and analysis of corporate data." This shift in Clarkson's opinion of the construct validity of social responsiveness, as defined by Wartick and Cochran, came as a result of his increased exposure to and subsequent acceptance of stakeholder theory as a means of understanding CSP. Instead of focusing on the processes by which social responsiveness occurs, Clarkson is now interested in the relationship between stakeholder theory and ethical management in the workplace ("Toronto," 1994). Clarkson believes that the construct "social responsiveness" cannot effectively deal with multiple stakeholder interests. The Wartick and Cochran CSP model cannot push the theory of the firm away from its neoclassical roots toward a stakeholder approach.

WOOD'S CSP MODEL

Wood (1991a, 1991b) built on Wartick and Cochran (1985) to articulate structural principles of social responsibility, to show how processes of social responsiveness have defined much of the research in SIM, and to focus on outcomes of corporate behavior as the indicators of "performance." In this model, corporate social performance is defined as "a business organization's configuration of principles of social responsibility, processes of social responsiveness, and observable outcomes as they relate to the firm's societal relationships" (Wood, 1991a: 693). These three facets of CSP are interlinked and consist of subdimensions, as shown in Figure 1, which is a slight revision of Wood's original model. The difference is in the third box, "outcomes," which were listed as "programs, policies, and outcomes" and now are shown as stakeholder effects inside and outside the firm as well as institutional or systemic effects of business operations.

RESEARCH AND FOLLOW-UPS TO WOOD'S MODEL

Carroll (1994), in his expert panel research, found that Wood's CSP model, among recently published papers, was widely believed to be the most influential for the future of SIM research over the next decade. In her 1992 presidential address to the SIM division of the Academy of Management, Wood called for critical analyses of CSP ideas, empirical research using the CSP framework, and better integration of CSP with the stakeholder perspective and other potentially powerful theoretical constructs. The challenge is beginning to be answered, as seen in current research (most of it as yet unpublished except in conference proceedings).

Figure 1
The Corporate Social Performance Model

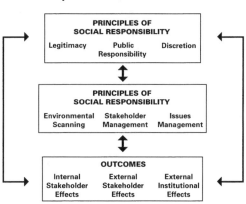

Collins (1992) attempted an explicit link between Wood's CSP model and stakeholder theory. Arguing that CSP could be defined only in relation to specific stakeholders, he constructed a matrix with Wood's CSP dimensions down the column and various critical stakeholder categories (customers, owners, employees, etc.) across the rows. In the cells of the matrix were to be ratings of corporate performance on each CSP dimension with respect to each stakeholder group, but Collins has not yet been able to work out a satisfactory rating system, and so this work remains as potentially fruitful.

Mallott's (1993) dissertation research, attempting to test both Carroll's CSR hierarchy and Wood's CSR principles, involved interviews with middle-level and senior managers who related stories they considered to reflect corporate social responsibility and irresponsibility. She found that managers did not distinguish between legal and economic CSR very readily, that ethical issues were seen as both personal and organizational in nature, and that discretionary CSR was a poorly understood concept. She found also that managers related well to the principle of public responsibility (Preston and Post), but did not grasp the macrolevel principle of legitimacy or the microlevel principle of discretion. Mallott correctly observed that managers' failure to see these principles does not mean that they do not exist; but research to substantiate their existence still remains to be done.

Mitnick (1993, 1994) has applied general systems theory to Wood's CSP model to show how the various concepts involved in CSP— Carroll's social responsibility categories, Wood's social responsibility structural principles, Ackerman's responsive processes, Sethi's social responsiveness types, Preston and Post's interpenetrating systems, Freeman's stakeholders, Wartick and Cochran's issues management, and more—can be systematized and sorted according to their contribution to the guidance, implementation, or evaluation of a CSP "system." Although Mitnick does not go so far as to derive a theoretical logic for CSP, he does show how to use systems theory as a "sorting logic" for the various competitive concepts in CSP.

CAN CORPORATE SOCIAL PERFORMANCE BE MEASURED?

A vast array of measures have been used in empirical research on corporate social performance. Some measures indicate the results of company *responses* to particular social issues, such as minority or female workers or pollution abatement. Some measures merely indicate the company's *intent* to address social problems, for example, the existence of written policy statements on minority hiring or pollution control. *Events* such as factory explosions, plane crashes, oil spills, or product recalls have been used as negative indicators, or measures of corporate social irresponsibility (CSI). A company's record of criminal convictions or regulatory fines has been similarly used to indicate CSI. Some measures, such as the *Fortune* "most admired" ratings, are based on executives' own assessments of their and others' performance. The percent of pretax earnings donated to charity has been used as a CSP measure. Newer indices, such as 1980s Sullivan Principles compliance scale or the 1990s KLD social investment scale, are crude rankings of company performance on several dimensions believed to be part of overall CSP. Because both the *Fortune* and KLD ratings are composite indices and are in current use, we will describe each of them briefly.

Every year *Fortune* magazine publishes its Corporate Reputation Survey, a list of America's most admired corporations. These "reputation" rankings are based on an opinion poll which measures the perceptions of large corporations among over 8,000 senior executives, outside directors, and financial analysts. More than 300 companies in 32 industries are included in the list. The *Fortune* index measures such subjective attributes as management quality, product quality, innovativeness, long-term investment value, financial soundness, ability to attract and retain talented people, responsibility to the community and environment, and wise use of corporate assets. Multiple regression analysis is applied to the data to obtain a reputation rating from 1 (low) to 10 (high). Not surprisingly, given the nature of the respondents, "quality of management" is typically considered the most important attribute of corporate reputation by those polled.

Although it is an interesting example of how various corporate managements are perceived by peers and "intimates," the *Fortune* ranking has questionable value and validity as a measure of CSP. Are companies "admired" simply because they have good financial performance? Perhaps good financial performance plus a strong public affairs focus gets a company to the top of the list (witness Philip Morris's top five position for several years). More importantly, a firm can achieve a high score on "reputation," but still be very deficient in certain areas. Whose reputation is better: a firm with mediocre scores on all the measures or a firm with widely varying scores (say, very high financial performance and very low community performance)? Those who use these rankings as a CSP measure justify it with an "everybody thinks so" defense, which skirts the core CSP issue of what a company is actually doing and what its actual impacts are. There is no conceptual or theoretical basis for using the *Fortune* scale as a measure of social performance.

The KLD scale is a new composite indicator of corporate performance on a number of socially relevant dimensions. Kinder, Lydenberg, and Domini (1993) is a social investment firm that specializes in "social choice" investing. Although the KLD ratings have been available for only a few years, they are already gaining wide acceptance as "social screens" among investors and investment analysts. The firm produces a social performance rating (KLD rating) on more than 800 publicly held firms based on performance on the following variables: product liability, community relations, South African involvement, nuclear power involvement, employee relations, environmental protection (pollution), women and minority issues, military contracting, and other CSP-relevant dimensions.

The Domini 400 Social Index (DSI) is an index of 400 common stocks of companies based on their performance on multiple applications of the KLD social performance screens and, aside from the social screens, this index mirrors the Standard and Poor's 500. The DSI is predicated on the belief that customers and investors will choose products and companies that have favorable social performance ratings. Firms that have an adequate score on these various screens, therefore, are portrayed in the investment community as "socially responsible firms" that are worthy candidates for social investing.

There are a number of challenges that can be brought against the KLD ratings and the DSI. First, as a measure of corporate social performance, the numerical ratings are very crude (normally a 1–3 scale, and sometimes a 0–1 scale to indicate presence or absence of some trait) and are based on qualitative judgments about company performance taken from typically inadequate information. Second, scores on the various screens are added to achieve a rating score for a company, even though there is no conceptual basis for believing that all screens carry equal importance. Third, and perhaps most conceptually limiting, no explanation is offered as to why these categories of activity are included and not others, or why these categories are considered to indicate "social performance." There is an unfortunate "political correctness" factor in the KLD ratings, in that they are based on such high-profile issues as South Africa and environmental protection. Other measures of CSP, such as the extent to which a company employs child labor, or presence in repressive countries other than South Africa, are not considered. Nevertheless, *the Domini 400 has outperformed other lists* in terms of financial returns. In 1993, for example, the Domini 400 stocks had a total return of 56.38 percent compared to the S&P 500's return of 46.54 percent (Brill and Reder, 1993). This does not prove the validity of the KLD rating or the Domini index (but see Sharfman, 1993), but it does suggest that the idea of "doing well by doing good" may have some empirical basis. The KLD scale is not perfect, but it is the nearest thing to a comprehensive CSP measure that currently exists.

Overall, the disparity of CSP measures used has made it very difficult for research to accumulate. Measures are developed for certain purposes—say, to test for a statistical link between corporate crime and accounting measures such as ROI (see Baucus, 1989)—and may not be readily transferrable to other purposes such as the development of a general theory of corporate social performance. In the remainder of this paper, we examine the empirical research in CSP, represented by 65 separate studies, to see what we can learn about CSP and the emerging stakeholder theory of the firm.

DOES CORPORATE SOCIAL PERFORMANCE
MAKE A DIFFERENCE?
TOWARD A STAKEHOLDER THEORY OF THE FIRM

To answer the title question, one must extend it a bit: *To whom* does corporate social performance make a difference? For neoclassical economists, only stockholders/owners matter. For stakeholder/CSP theorists, many other groups and organizations matter.

In the neoclassical economic theory of the firm, CSP would be a viable concept only if it increased shareholder value; Friedman (1970) objected to the idea of corporate social responsibility (assuming that CSR was costly) on the grounds that managers had no right to spend owners' money on unprofitable aims and interests. So, the search has been on for many years to link CSP with firm financial performance and to show that CSP is not unprofitable. At worst, such a theory would show that CSP was benign; at best, CSP would be shown to be in the firm's best economic interests.

Arlow and Gannon's (1982) review of research in CSP drew no conclusions. Ullmann (1985) surveyed the literature on social and financial performance and reported very mixed results. There were no consistent or accepted measures of CSR or CSP, and even worse, there was no sound theoretical reason why CSR/CSP *should* be related to financial performance. Although the idea of stakeholder theory was in the literature, it was too undeveloped to be a candidate for supplanting the neoclassical economic view.

Frooman (1994) has updated and gone beyond Ullmann's work to produce the most comprehensive and interesting analysis of social-financial performance links currently in existence. Frooman groups studies according to the type of measure used to indicate economic performance. He finds that, regardless of the CSP measure used, mixed and ambiguous results are obtained in the aggregate from studies that use accounting measures, market share or sales measures, investor return measures, or risk measures as indicators of economic performance. However, of the nine event studies that correlated abnormal stock returns with the announcement of a socially irresponsible event, eight of them showed significant negative returns following the event announcement. In addition, we discovered two more studies showing negative stock price results following announcement of corporate criminal involvement (Randall and Neuman, 1979; Weir, 1983), bringing the consistency finding to ten of eleven studies. That is, *it appears that the market does indeed punish firms for socially irresponsible behavior.* Among the studies showing negative returns, CSP indicators included product recalls, accusations of criminal misconduct, and the publication of pollution indices. (The one insignificant finding used airplane crashes as the CSI indicator, suggesting that crashes may be seen as uncontrollable tragedies rather than corporate irresponsibility.)

The question "To whom does corporate social performance make a difference?" necessarily involves stakeholders. These groups and organizations in the firm's environment that can affect or are affected by the firm's operations are the missing link in empirical studies of CSP and in our theoretical understanding of the firm in society. There is no theory to explain why stockholders would or would not prefer a company that gives 1 percent of pretax earnings to charity, or that hires and develops minority or women workers, or that ranks higher in pollution control indices. Yet most CSP research assumes that such preferences will exist, and that stockholders are the most (or only) appropriate stakeholder group for assessing the results of CSP, regardless of how it has been measured. Ullmann (1985: 541) pointed out that a positive relationship between the two "could indicate that a company's management is dealing effectively with the firm's external stakeholders and their multiple demands."

McGuire et al. (1988) do not propose a coherent theory that would explain a relationship between social and financial performance, but they do briefly review a number of theoretical perspectives on such a relationship. In this context, they explain "stakeholder theory" and its relevance to corporate social performance as follows:

> . . . modern corporate stakeholder theory (Cornell and Shapiro, 1987) contends that the value of the firm depends on the cost not only of explicit claims but also of implicit claims. From this viewpoint, the set of claimants on a firm's resources goes beyond the stockholders and bondholders to include stakeholders who have explicit claims on the firm like wage contracts and others with whom the firm has made implicit contracts, involving, for instance, quality service and social responsibility. If a firm does not act in a socially responsible manner, parties to implicit contracts concerning the social responsibility of the firm may attempt to transform those implicit agreements into explicit agreement that will be more costly to it. For example, if a firm fails to meet promises to government officials in regard to actions that affect the environment (dumping, etc.), government agencies may find it necessary to pass more stringent regulations, constituting explicit contracts, to force the firm to act in a socially responsible manner. Moreover, socially, irresponsible actions may spill over to other implicit stakeholders, who may doubt whether the firm would honor their claims. Thus, firms with an image of high corporate social responsibility may find that they have more low-cost implicit claims than other firms and thus have higher financial performance (Cornell and Shapiro, 1987).

It should not be difficult to see, through all this economic talk of contracts implicit and explicit, that the key variable is the degree of *trust* in the stakeholder relationship (see Calton and Lad, 1994; Calton and Ring, 1994). Boal and Peery (1985), in their research on the "cognitive structure" of CSR, claim that a "stakeholder perspective" is not supported by their data, yet they did find that their subjects differentiated the interests of owners, employees, customers, and society at large and appeared to understand that balancing of these interests was a necessary management task. Based on their findings, they offer these guidelines for socially responsible management decision making: "an acceptable decision outcome should be economically worthwhile, should justly affect stakeholders, and should either protect or promote the rights of those affected" (1985: 80).

In a stakeholder theory, the question "Does CSP make a difference?" would be broadened to include *stakeholders* in addition to stockholders. Understanding the empirical literature on CSP in a stakeholder context would require a better grasp of what dimensions of corporate-stakeholder relationships are most salient and how they are represented in empirical measures. Based upon their particular interests and levels of involvement in a company, stakeholders may:

- **establish expectations** (which may be explicit or implicit, and may or may not be communicated) about corporate performance,
- **experience the effects** of corporate behaviors (with or without awareness of their source),
- **evaluate the effects** or potential effects of corporate behaviors on their interests, or the fit of corporate behaviors with their expectations,
- **act** upon their interests, expectations, experiences, and/or evaluations.

Empirical research in CSP and stakeholder relationships needs to be concerned with (1) which stakeholder is setting the expectations that are relevant to the CSP measure being used, (2) which stakeholder experiences the effects of company behavior, (3) which stakeholder is evaluating the company's performance (and on what basis does the stakeholder evaluate performance), and (4) which stakeholder(s) are acting.

For example, consider a study that attempts to relate corporate charitable giving with stockholder returns. Expectations are set by industry (as in the 5 or 2 Percent Clubs), by government (which sets tax-deductible limits on corporate charitable giving), and by community groups themselves. The stakeholders experiencing the effects of corporate giving would include communities, agencies, and their clients. However, the evaluative stakeholder in such a study is the owner group; neither the stakeholders setting expectations nor those experiencing effects are judging the outcomes of corporate performance. And, it is conceivable that no stakeholder is acting. Thus, in order for all these variables to be related, there would have to be a theory about how owners would evaluate information about charitable giving with respect to *their own* interests.

In order to push toward a stakeholder theory of corporate social performance, we conducted a meta-analysis of empirical studies of CSP. We assumed that CSP measures could be said to represent the interests and/or expectations of one or more stakeholder groups, and we grouped the studies according to the stakeholder(s) represented in the CSP measure. Space limitations prevent a full exposition here, but some of the data tables are shown below.

COMMUNITY/CHARITY STUDIES

Table 1 shows a summary of CSP studies that use community involvement or charitable giving as a measure of CSP. Two findings shown in this figure confirm what we already know about corporate charitable giving from regular Conference Board reports: larger firms give more money (Levy and Shatto, 1980), and larger firms give a lower proportion of their pretax earnings (Kedia and Kuntz, 1981). Also, Wokutch and Spencer (1987) tell us that companies giving a larger amount to charity are more likely to be highly ranked on this dimension in the *Fortune* reputation ratings.

Many of the findings concerning community involvement or charitable giving as a measure of CSP are ambiguous. Virtually all studies of CSP defined as community involvement or charitable giving present only descriptive statistics or correlations with company or industry structural characteristics. The implicit assumption seems to be that it is something about the company itself—its size, its product base, its ownership structure—that drives the company's community relations patterns. However, these results are very difficult to interpret. What do we know, for example, when we have seen that firms with highly concentrated ownership give a lower proportion of their earnings to charity?

In Figure 2, the correlational results of studies included in Table 1 are shown graphically in a relational model. It is apparent that different

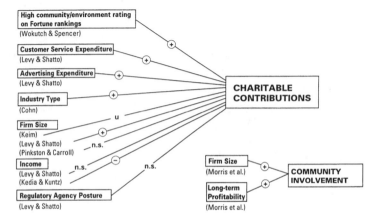

Figure 2
Graphic Depiction of Relationships in Table 1

theoretical perspectives—resource dependence, classical organization theory, and even microeconomics—are informing these studies one by one, with no attempt to consolidate across studies, resulting in a very mixed picture on what the observed relationships mean.

Employee studies. When employees are used as the relevant stakeholder group for measuring CSP, very few results have been obtained. From Pinkston and Carroll (1993) we get the descriptive information that managers consider employees to be important stakeholders and employee health and safety issues to be important to the firm. The limited statistical findings available show that larger firms are more likely to have a mandatory retirement policy (considered to be negative CSP; Copperman, 1981), companies with an employee newsletter have better long-term profitability (Morris et al., 1990), and diversified firms are more likely to have OSHA violations (Hill, Kelley, and Agle, 1990). Roman and Blum (1987) show that companies with managers that have more socially responsible attitudes are more likely to have Employee Assistance Programs (but one might wonder why employees of those companies are so overstressed as to need EAPs).

We suggest that this poverty of findings results from a mismatch of stakeholder measures. We would like to see a study that correlates data on treatment of employees (e.g., the existence of employee-friendly programs and policies) and variables such as placement on "the 100 best companies to work for" list, union organization, strike data, average wage and benefits rates compared to industry averages, and health and safety records. Such a study would not accept the idea that it is right for only owners to evaluate how a company treats employees, as is the case with studies correlating employee variables with profits or stock price.

Social justice studies. Seven studies were categorized as relating to social justice, using some measure of the treatment of minorities and women by corporations (Cohn, 1970; Eilbirt and Parket, 1973; Corson and Steiner, 1974; Buehler and Shetty, 1975; Holmes, 1977; Ingram, 1978; Kedia and Kuntz, 1981). Most of these studies have to do with minorities and women as employees; a very few are concerned with minorities as customers. Kedia and Kuntz (1981) provide the best descriptive findings, showing that companies with larger proportions of minority employees tend to be larger, have more market share, and have facilities in neighborhoods with large minority populations. The same study found that the proportion of women officers was *negatively* related to these same organizational variables.

Customer/consumer studies. When customers or consumers are the relevant affected CSP stakeholder and evaluation of CSP is being conducted by either customers or owners, a great many statistical relationships appear. Voluntary disclosure of product safety information

Figure 3
Graphic Depiction of Results in Table 2

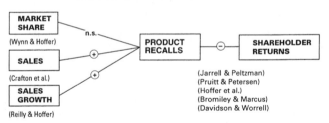

yielded no interpretable results in Ingram's (1978) study, but most other studies display statistically significant findings, as we see in Table 2.

Interestingly, two studies show *positive* relationships between product recalls and sales. Sales data are often used as a surrogate for organizational size, which would suggest that larger companies experience more product recalls. This result could be interpreted as merely a descriptive relationship; large companies sell more things and so would be expected to have more product recalls by the laws of probability. *Proportionally*, however, we do not know if larger (or higher sales) companies have more problems with product recalls; this would be interesting information about CSP.

The remainder of the studies using customers as a relevant stakeholder group are event studies that display an astonishing consistency in results, consistent with Frooman's (1994) finding regarding this methodology. Product recall announcements result in negative and permanent abnormal stock returns; investors calculate the future costs of bad product decisions and take this into account in the price they are willing to pay for a stock.

Finance and economics scholars have asserted for many years that their models work, that they can explain large amounts of variance in the variables they use, that their relationships are highly significant statistically, and that their theories are predictive. The problem is, from a CSP perspective, *they appear to be right*—given their theory, data, methods, and interpretive models. But in the context of broad intertwining stakeholder relationships and responsibilities, *they cannot be right*. Figure 3, showing results of studies using customers as the affected stakeholder of CSP and owners as the evaluative stakeholder, demonstrates this dilemma and also points to a hopeful interpretation for CSP scholars.

Consider that the 25-year search for a relationship between corporate social and financial performance has met with practically no success *except* when variables are chosen that represent stakeholders acting within *market* mechanisms. Markets are taking notice of irresponsible

Figure 4
Graphic Depiction of Results in Table 3

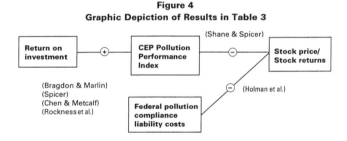

firm behavior because such behavior results in additional costs for the firm and, by extension, its owners. This finding should not be taken to mean that the economic model of the firm is correct after all, but that CSP scholars can learn something from the power of this model—when applied by its own rules—and then go beyond it toward a stakeholder theory of the firm in society.

Natural environment studies. To illustrate how this might proceed, Table 3 and Figure 4 show results of CSP studies using the natural environment as the primary stakeholder affected by corporate behavior.

Market-based studies are the only ones to show significant results. Spicer (1978a) found positive relationships between better pollution performance and several accounting measures of profitability, and in a second study (1978b) showed that higher risk factors correlated with worse pollution performance. Holman, New, and Singer (1985) correlate two accounting measures and find a negative relationship between federal pollution compliance liability costs and total rate of return. Higher costs, lower return—a simple market relationship, not muddied by involvement of other stakeholders. Shane and Spicer (1983), similarly, correlate the CEP pollution performance index with stock price and find negative abnormal returns for poor pollution performance (that is, a positive relationship between the variables but only demonstrated in a downward direction). Owners, apparently, take into account that poor pollution performance may result in future fines, clean-up costs, and additional costly regulation, and adjust polluting stocks downward accordingly.

Most other studies concerning pollution performance, however, show no significant relationships among the variables used. We suggest again that stakeholder mismatches are responsible. Why would one expect pollution rankings to be correlated with financial performance (an indicator of customer evaluations of the firm), unless there were some organized, large-scale, systematic effort to boycott high-polluting firms and purchase from cleaner ones? Why would a company's disclo-

62 | DONNA J. WOOD AND RAYMOND E. JONES

sure of its pollution performance in the annual report (used largely by
owners or potential investors) have any effect on profitability (again, an
indicator of customer expectations, effects, and evaluations)? One wants
to see studies correlating pollution performance and ratings of companies by *environmental interest groups.* Also, studies relating pollution
performance to corporate political action on environmental matters, as
well as differential regulatory rule making and compliance efforts of the
government, would be very interesting and would provide a much
better match of stakeholder involvements.

Corporate reputation studies. Reputational indices include the ones
produced in the early 1970s by Milton Moskowitz (1972) and published
in *Business and Society Review,* the annual reputation rankings by *Fortune*
magazine, and more recently the KLD (Kinder Lydenberg Domini)
scale. These indices have occasionally been used as a measure (better, a
surrogate) for corporate social performance on the assumption that
companies with better reputations would be better social performers.
Table 4 and Figure 5 summarize studies using these CSP indicators.

The stakeholder groups represented by reputational ratings are
somewhat ambiguous. The Moskowitz ratings, for example, represent
one person's judgment about how well a company is or is not meeting
its social responsibilities. The *Fortune* ratings, given the nature of respondents, could be seen as similar to asking the foxes how well they
keep guard over the henhouses. The KLD ratings, although more
specifically targeted than the others at corporate social involvements,
and ranging across a broader field of behaviors, are still crude and
subjective indicators of company performance on a small set of social
responsibility dimensions. Are these measures good surrogates for
overall societal views of firms? The answer is probably "no," although
better measures are not yet available.

Figure 5
Graphic Depiction of Results in Table 4

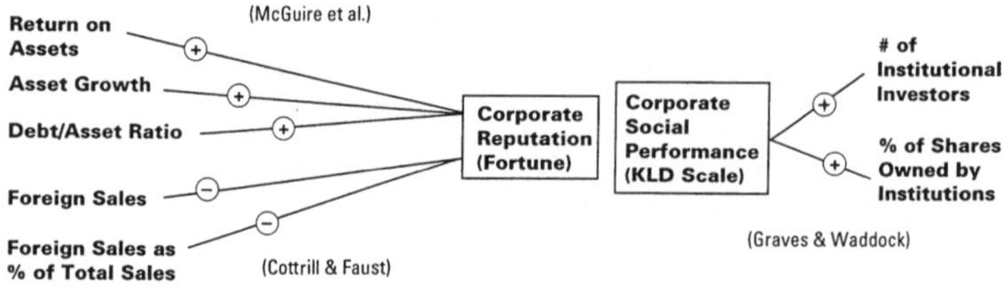

However, it can be argued that the ratings are a somewhat accurate representation of "corporate image" (and it can be argued that to some extent this is true—especially for the *Fortune* ratings). McGuire et al. (1988) purported to show a significant relationship between CSP and financial performance. But in fact, what they showed was a relationship between financial performance and companies' reputations in the eyes of peers—other executives and financial analysts. Finally, the KLD database is new and will require further study before conclusions can be drawn about it as a CSP measure.

Information disclosure studies. Twelve studies used some measure of CSP information disclosure and related this disclosure to company financial performance. Many of these studies use the Social Involvement Disclosure Scale developed by Ernst and Ernst, a scale of the number of social involvement disclosures in company annual reports. A few studies did independent content analysis of annual reports for their CSP disclosure measure. One study (Kohls, 1985) used a process-oriented scale rather than a disclosure-oriented one.

Some studies find positive relationships between disclosure and earnings (Fry and Hock, 1976; Preston, 1978; Bowman, 1978; Anderson and Frankle, 1980); two find negative relationships (Ingram and Frazier, 1983; Holman, New, and Singer, 1985); one study reports a U-shaped curve (Bowman and Haire, 1972); and others find no relationship at all (Abbott and Monsen, 1979; Freedman and Jaggi, 1982). Kohls (1985) reports positive relationships between CSR disclosure in annual reports and the existence of responsive processes in the firm.

In this set of studies, the theoretical problem of stakeholder mismatching is apparent. Disclosure of information in annual reports could be assumed to have some effect on stock prices if owners or potential owners actually evaluate such information as they make investment decisions. But why would disclosure have any impact on, or any relationship with, accounting measures of financial performance? What stakeholders are involved here in setting expectations, experiencing effects, or evaluating results? These unclear research findings reflect a lack of theoretical clarity.

Responsiveness studies. It is easier to make a theoretical argument about why a company's social responsiveness structures and processes might have an impact on profitability or stock price than it is to make the same argument about social responsibility. Seven studies of CSP using indicators of responsiveness were included in our analysis. The results, however, do not tell us very much. Not surprisingly, some studies show that the existence of responsive mechanisms such as integrating social issues into strategic planning (Aupperle, 1984) or the existence of a public affairs unit (Sonnenfeld, 1982) correlates with a greater awareness of social problems. Newgren et al. (1985) found a positive relationship between a company's use of environmental analysis and one measure of financial performance—the price/earnings ratio, and Morris et al. (1990) show a relationship between the existence of a public affairs office and long-term profitability. Otherwise, relationships between responsive structures and financial performance have been statistically insignificant (Mitchell, 1983; Aupperle, Carroll, and Hatfield, 1985) or uninterpretable (Holmes, 1978).

Governance studies. Very little quantitative research has been conducted on the governance aspects of CSP. Aupperle, Carroll, and Hatfield (1985) found no relationship between the existence of a social responsibility committee on the board of directors and firm financial performance. Kohls (1985) found that companies with a higher proportion of outside directors scored *lower* on his responsive process scale (a negative relationship), but the existence of a public policy or CSR committee of the board of directors was positively correlated with the existence of responsive processes. Since no other studies were discovered in this category, little can be said regarding the validity of corporate governance indicators as measures of CSP.

A stakeholder theory of CSP might suggest that CSP-supporting governance structures might serve as moderating variables in a relationship between, say, top management values and behaviors, and firm financial performance, because of the board's responsibility to oversee and direct basic management policy and direction. This hypothesis remains to be tested empirically.

Studies of managers' values. Miles (1987) suggested that the philosophy of the top management team was a critical factor in the degree to which a company exhibited social responsiveness, and Carroll (1979) emphasized this factor as well in his model of corporate social performance. The studies that have attempted to use managers' values as a CSP indicator have all been based upon Carroll's four categories of CSR (economic, legal, ethical, and discretionary/philanthropic responsibilities), and use some variant of Aupperle's forced-choice measurement instrument. Aupperle (1984) found a positive relationship between his measure of "concern for economic performance" (versus "concern for society") and a firm's total risk, but did not obtain significant results when correlating his "concern" measure with any financial performance variables, firm size, or industrial sector. Aupperle, Carroll, and Hatfield (1985) obtained similar results but showed in addition that total risk was negatively correlated with "concern for society." Pinkston and Carroll (1993) found no relationship between organizational size

Figure 6
Graphic Depiction of Results in Table 5

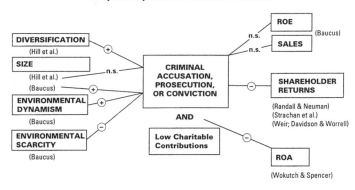

and managers' social responsibility orientation (e.g., economic, legal, ethical, or philanthropic). Results have not been impressive, but this is likely because the studies have not drawn explicit empirical links between managers' expressed values (or more accurately, preferences among four CSR categories) and their behaviors. In addition, they have not considered the interests and involvements of the stakeholders who are setting expectations, receiving impacts, and evaluating results.

Legal/regulatory studies. Finally, in Table 5 and Figure 6, studies examining CSP from a legal or regulatory compliance aspect are summarized. The event studies, showing that investors negatively evaluate the announcement of criminal accusation or conviction, are consistent in their findings of negative abnormal returns to stock prices following news of criminal conduct—alleged or demonstrated. Wokutch and Spencer (1987) show that companies with criminal convictions and low rates of charitable giving tend to have lower financial performance as measured by return on assets and return on sales.

The other studies, however, are either impossible to interpret or report no significant findings. Again, as has been the case in so many other studies, a theoretical mismatch of stakeholder involvements may be to blame for these inconclusive results. For example, imagine if Baucus were to extend her data into a longitudinal study of corporate crime and its effects, showing eventually that criminal companies are more closely monitored by government, are less likely to get what they want from the public policy process, and over time have much higher regulatory compliance and legal defense costs than do noncriminal companies. Such a study would examine the consequences of law breaking from the point of view of a stakeholder—government—that is more intimately involved than owners. Or, imagine if Hill, Kelley, and

Agle correlated OSHA violations with long-term OSHA compliance requirements (suggesting, perhaps, government is a legitimate evaluator of regulatory compliance behavior, and that companies might choose not to violate the law because of the higher future transaction costs incurred), and with unionization and union activity such as strikes or slowdowns, or even more relevant, contract negotiation demands concerning health and safety conditions (representing employees as evaluators of a CSP factor that affects them directly).

Summary. Some interesting findings appear upon studying these tables of empirical work in CSP, grouped by the stakeholders of interest. First, it is apparent that Preston and Post's (1975) idea of corporate public responsibility existing in the areas of primary involvement with society is confirmed again and again. Companies commit to different kinds of social programs, policies, projects, and involvements, depending on the nature of their industry and their business exposure.

Second, it appears that consistent findings arise when *market measures* and market-oriented stakeholders are matched in the same study. Frooman's (1974) finding that event studies produce a consistent relationship between irresponsible acts and negative stock returns reflects a good theoretical match between measures. It makes sense, in market terms, that owners would evaluate the long-term financial implications (liability payouts and litigation costs, future cost of insurance, additional regulatory constraints, possible consumer boycotts, etc.) and adjust the price of the stock accordingly.

Third, a great many of the empirical studies we have reviewed exhibit a *mismatch of variables* when seen within the context of stakeholder theory. For example, ROE, ROI, and similar profitability accounting measures of profitability *do not indicate owners' evaluation of a firm's social performance.* Although they provide information that can then be used in decision making by anyone with an interest in buying, selling, or retaining stock, they are too narrowly focused to tell us much about how a company's stakeholder set is evaluating, and consequently acting upon, the firm's social performance. In fact, we could suggest that these studies use these measures not because *owners* use them, but because *managers* do. Managers represent the great hidden stakeholder in corporate life and in corporate social performance.

Neoclassical economic theory insists that managers are agents of owners and are obliged to act as fiduciaries for owner's limited financial interests in the firm's performance. Berle and Means (1932) told us, however, that managers of large publicly owned companies are subject to very little actual influence by owners. Agency theory and transactions costs theory tell us a great deal about the problems of controlling agents who are far removed from principals, or who exhibit behavior that is very costly for principals to monitor and correct. In the field of business and society, we have already seen the effects of the dramatic conceptual shift in the 1970s from responsibility (which put managers too much in the spotlight and on the hook) to responsiveness (which allowed aggressive corporate political action to supplant the moral component of responsibility). Does anyone wonder why Philip Morris consistently makes Fortune's top-five most admired companies list, even though that company appears to have developed the most aggressive campaign ever seen against mortally ill cancer, emphysema, and heart disease victims who smoked and then participated in litigation against the company?

Mismatching of variables in CSP studies reflects our general scholarly confusion about what companies are about and who should be evaluating them. Our contention is simple, although the theoretical implications are complex: Expectations, effects, and evaluations need to be better matched in terms of the stakeholder(s) involved. Some examples of how one might think about matching appropriate stakeholders with events or CSP measures are shown in Figure 7.

Figure 7
Stakeholder and Corporate Social Performance

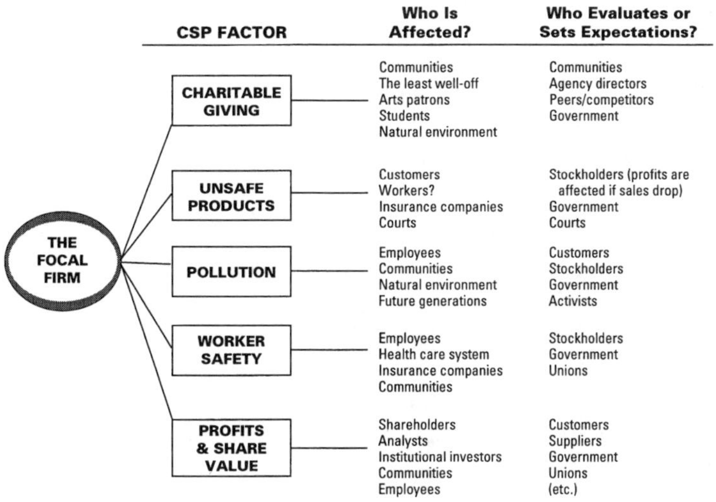

CSP FACTOR	Who Is Affected?	Who Evaluates or Sets Expectations?
CHARITABLE GIVING	Communities The least well-off Arts patrons Students Natural environment	Communities Agency directors Peers/competitors Government
UNSAFE PRODUCTS	Customers Workers? Insurance companies Courts	Stockholders (profits are affected if sales drop) Government Courts
POLLUTION	Employees Communities Natural environment Future generations	Customers Stockholders Government Activists
WORKER SAFETY	Employees Health care system Insurance companies Communities	Stockholders Government Unions
PROFITS & SHARE VALUE	Shareholders Analysts Institutional investors Communities Employees	Customers Suppliers Government Unions (etc.)

THE FOCAL FIRM

After we have begun to conceptualize complex stakeholder networks, we can then think in more depth about how relationships between stakeholders and a firm (and among stakeholders themselves) arise, are nurtured (or not), change, and die. We can think more systematically about how to theoretically characterize the relationships a company has with its stakeholders, by examining such issues as:

- the type of power over resources that each stakeholder has with respect to the firm (e.g., symbolic, material, or coercive power);
- the nature (number, complexity, type) of the issues involved in the relationship;
- the ways in which stakeholders express their expectations and evaluations;
- the ways in which the company receives and interprets those expectations and evaluations, and acts upon them.

REVISITING BUSINESS PHILANTHROPY

There are a large number of ways that one can view corporate philanthropy. Consider, for example, this list of ideas about what corporate philanthropy is:

- Discretionary social responsibility, as Carroll sees it.
- Inexpensive training for employees in leadership, teamwork, and other skills.
- Do-gooding to help the "underprivileged."
- Community relations, tit-for-tat mutual support for various projects, variances, requests, and so on.
- Social ladder climbing for top executives.
- Compliance with blackmail demands of nonprofit groups.
- Strategic investment in target markets.

These views vary greatly in the degree to which they express philanthropy or charitable giving as an expression of the firm's (or managers') self-interest, and they differ in the "good faith" aspects of attempts to solve serious social problems or enhance the quality of community life. However, they all depend on a bilateral relationship—the firm and the charitable organization—in which something is exchanged between the transacting parties. There is little acknowledgment in any of these views of the firm's existence in a dense web of stakeholder relationships, or of the nature of philanthropy as a long-term problem-solving effort.

If one views "stakeholder theory" from the traditional perspective of a firm at the center of a bicycle wheel (with stakeholders at the ends of the spokes and particular management problems and opportunities arising from each stakeholder relationship), then philanthropy can easily be cast simply as a means by which the firm can achieve some self-interested end. Philanthropy would be seen in terms of its fit with the company's strategic direction or as a tool the company could use to address some especially problematic issue for its industry. Wood ("Toronto," 1994) has pointed out the difference between the bicycle wheel model of stakeholder management (viewing stakeholders as a thing to be managed), and an interactive model of stakeholders in the environment (viewing stakeholders as members of relationships that are mutually driven). In any case, the bicycle wheel approach results in a self-interested view of firm philanthropy; this approach pays little attention to firm philanthropy as a means of bettering society.

An interesting example of a business charity project which takes this "bicycle wheel" approach to CSP is the TAP Project, described by Carroll and Horton (1994). The five-year project was launched in the spring of 1992 to address such problems as poverty, crime, and poor living conditions in the inner city of Atlanta. TAP received private-sector contributions of over $32 million as well as a $33 million grant from the U.S. Department of Housing and Urban Development. While the intent of the program was to empower poor communities through interactions with corporate leaders, it has become evident that the program is going to have minimal long-term impact on the quality of life of inner-city Atlanta. The program's major focus will simply be to ensure that the program is carried through over the five-year period, resulting in a polishing of corporate image but little real social change. This is short-term charity, not long-term philanthropy. No one will be taught how to fish, although many fishes will be given out.

But, if one views "stakeholder theory" in terms of a complex net-work of interorganizational relationships, then philanthropy is seen in terms of its intent to better the human condition and its effectiveness at solving social problems. Business philanthropy would not be seen as very different from individual or foundation philanthropy, but as part of a business's responsibility to contribute to solving social problems. Note that this view swings us back to the language of the 1960s and 1970s! The difference is, that three decades of research and events have shown that the idea of business organizations existing in such a com-plex societal web is reality, not platitude.

For example, if the TAP project had been viewed as an opportunity to use the Atlanta social web to solve a major social problem, the focus would have been on providing long-term benefits to the community and not simply on making sure the project ran for five years. Imagine how the $65 million might have been allocated to solve, say, the high dropout rate among high school students. Imagine that the entire 6th- and 7th-grade classes of the Atlanta public school system were targeted and a specific goal was set of 95 percent high school graduation and 70 percent enrollment in advanced education. Now, each corporation would adopt a classroom (a popular model developed in many cities) and invest philanthropic and volunteer resources in providing incentives and encouragement for the long-term education, self-esteem, and opportunities of these 35 students. The project would have to involve families, schools, churches, community groups, intramural sports leagues, local government, and a host of other stakeholders in addition to the corporate sponsors. The five-year frame of the project would be sufficient to measure how well the specific objective was accomplished. Even more important, such a five-year commitment to education would create new patterns of social interaction that would not end when the five years was over, and thousands of children would be nudged along the road to higher education and life success because of these new patterns.

One cannot imagine this kind of project in a "corporation-to-community" bicycle spoke model. Thinking solely about how and why sponsors must be able to conduct a five-year program will not produce long-term benefits for the community. The needs and interests of all the various stakeholders who will affect and be affected by the program must be considered. The bicycle spoke approach simply does not have the capability to look beyond corporate self-interest in "managing" this troublesome relationship. If philanthropy is taken to mean long term efforts to better the human condition, then multiple interests must be taken into account and multiple stakeholders must participate in the decisions and actions of the philanthropic projects.

CONCLUSION: WHAT DO WE KNOW, AND WHAT'S NEXT?

So, what does the empirical literature in corporate social performance tell us? We acknowledge that this meta-analysis has not examined the quality of the studies considered, and indeed the quality varies wildly. We have tried not to draw conclusions from, say, the studies using the Moskowitz ratings (one man's vision of CSP), or from the purely descriptive studies of relatively small samples (who knows what their relevance might be?), but challenges could still be made, quite rightly, to the validity and generalizability of most of these studies. Nevertheless, a benefit of having a large body of empirical research available for review is that some findings are confirmed (as in the event studies showing market attention to corporate irresponsibility), some findings suggest directions for replication or extension, and some point to entirely new areas for research. We feel that these few tentative conclusions can be made:

- 1. The performance of a business firm has no simple set of antecedents, and no simple consequences. Causality is complex.
- 2. Businesses do involve themselves, as Preston and Post had predicted, in CSR activities related to their primary areas of involvement with society.
- 3. The relationship between corporate social performance and financial/economic performance is still ambiguous because (a) there is still no theory to clarify how these two should be related, although we are moving closer to such a theory by considering the importance of stakeholders to CSP, (b) there is no comprehensive, valid measure of CSP, (c) most studies are lacking in methodological rigor and are therefore of uncertain validity, reliability, and generalizability, and (d) there is confusion about which stakeholders are represented by which measures.
- 4. Event studies show consistently a relationship between news of social irresponsibility and abnormal negative stock returns. This is the only methodology that has produced such consistent results. Market measures, used within market-based theory and illustrating market processes, *do show a relationship between social and financial performance*. However, the demonstrated relationship is negative— bad performance costs—whereas we would prefer to have a theory deriving a positive relationship.
- 5. An extrapolated finding, not directly addressed in any of these studies but implicit in the "grand view" of them as a body of literature, is this: The social control of business occurs through business's relationships with stakeholders. *Public policy controls* (law, regulation, litigation, public agendas), *market controls* (consumer, owner, employee, supplier, and competitor expectations and behaviors), and *normative controls* (moral suasion, symbols, references to values, or reputation) do exist. This is a fruitful area for future research.

How corporate social performance is viewed is often a matter of what measurement is selected. Although the measures that have been used so far have focused on particular areas of CSP, and although many of them have value, they have limited use in depicting how and why specific stakeholder relationships occur and develop. Many of these measures have no underlying logic that serves to explain why the variables being measured are supposed to produce meaningful results.

The empirical rigor and mathematics of CSP theory are still not just underdeveloped, but missing. CSP theory at present is not integrated with stakeholder theory, although it needs to be. Many scholars in the field are working toward such an integration, and great progress is being made. We hope to have contributed to these advances with this paper, and we look forward with excitement to continued developments in this area.

TABLE 1
CSP Studies Relating to the Community

Source	Year	CSP Measure	Findings*
Cohn	1970	donations	pos. w/ industry type (financial or industrial)
Eilbirt & Parket	1973	alphabetical list of 15 socially responsive behaviors	descriptive statistics show educational donations, minority employment, and pollution as high-involvement issues.
Corson & Steiner	1974	modified Eilbirt & Parket scale of corporate involvement using CED issues list[†]	descriptive statistics show minority employment, donations, and pollution control as high-involvement issues.
Buehler & Shetty	1975	modified Eilbirt & Parket scale of corporate involvement in 15 social issues	descriptive statistics show minority employment, urban renewal, and donations as high-involvement issues.
Holmes	1977	modified CED issues list	descriptive statistics show charitable contributions, education assistance, minority hiring/development, & community affairs as top five social issues.
Ingram	1978	community donations & involvement disclosure	uninterpretable relationships.

Keim	1978b	"social effort" (philanthropy)	pos. w/ increasing smaller size, neg. w/increasing larger size
Levy & Shatto	1980	charitable contributions	pos. w/size of customer service expenditure pos. w/ size of advertising expenditure pos. w/ firm size (book value of equity) n.s. w/ firm income n.s. w/ regulatory agency posture on charitable giving
Kedia & Kuntz	1981	% charitable contributions	neg. w/ firm charter (state or federal regulation) neg. w/ ownership concentration neg. w/corporate market share neg. w/ firm size neg. w/ firm income
Wokutch & Spencer	1987	philanthropic donations	pos. w/ high rating on "responsiveness to community and environment" on *Fortune* "most admired" ratings
Morris, Rehbein, Hosseini, & Armacost	1990	sponsorship of community activities	pos. w/ organizational size pos. w/ long-term profitability
Pinkston & Carroll	1993	importance ranking of organizational stakeholders	n.s. w/size, but owners, consumers, & employees were ranked higher than communities and government

*Correlation results are reported as + (positive relationship), - (negative relationship). or n.s. (nonsignificant relationship) in this and subsequent tables.
†Issue list varies by industry.

TABLE 2
CSP Studies Relating to Customers/Consumers

Source	Year	CSP Measure	Findings
Wynn & Hoffer	1976	product recalls	n.s. w/ market share
Ingram	1978	product safety/ improvement	uninterpretable relationships disclosure
Crafton, Hoffer, & Reilly	1981	product recalls	pos. w/sales
Reilly & Hoffer	1983	product recalls	pos. w/ sales growth
Jarrell & Peltzman	1985	product recalls	negative returns (event study)
Pruitt & Peterson	1986	product recalls	negative returns (event study)
Davidson, Chandy, & Cross	1987	airplane crashes	no significant abnormal returns (event study)
Hoffer, Pruitt, & Reilly	1988	product recalls	negative returns (event study)
Bromiley & Marcus	1989	product recalls	negative returns (event study)
Davidson & Worrell	1992	product recalls	negative returns (event study)
Pinkston & Carroll	1993	importance ranking of organizational stakeholders	n.s. w/size, but owners, consumers, & employees were ranked higher than communities and government

TABLE 3
CSP Studies Relating to the Natural Environment

Source	Year	CSP Measure	Findings
Bragdon & Marlin	1972	CEP pollution index	pos. w/ ROE
Eilbirt & Parket	1973	alphabetical list of 15 socially responsive behaviors	descriptive statistics show educational donations, minority employment, and pollution as high-involvement issues.
Corson & Steiner	1974	modified Eilbirt & Parket scale of descriptive statistics using CED issues list	show corporate involvement, minority employment, donations, pollution control as high-involvement issues.
Fogler & Nutt	1975	government pollution indexes	n.s. w/ price/earnings ratio n.s. w/ mutual fund purchases n.s. w/ common stock price
Belkaoui	1976	pollution disclosure in annual reports	pos. w/ monthly average residuals (but result was temporary)
Ingram	1978	environmental disclosure in relationships.	uninterpretable annual report
Spicer	1978a	CEP pollution performance index	pos. w/ ROE, P/E ratio, total risk, beta for three periods, 1968-1973

Spicer	1978b	CEP pollution performance index	neg. w/ risk
Ingram & Frazier	1980	CEP pollution performance index	n.s. w/pollution disclosure in annual reports
Chen & Metcalf	1980	CEP pollution performance index	pos. w/ financial return variables, but this relationship is spurious and due to size.
Freedman & Jaggi	1982	CEP pollution performance index	n.s. w/ social disclosure in annual report
Wiseman	1982	CEP pollution performance index	n.s. w/ social disclosure in annual report
Shane & Spicer	1983	CEP pollution performance index	pos. with stock price (CAPS) (negative returns with poor performance)
Holman, New, & Singer	1985	federal pollution compliance liability	neg. w/ total rate of return costs
Rockness, Schlachter, & Rockness	1986	pollution performance	mixed results w/ 12 acctg. ratios
Pinkston & Carroll	1993	prioritization of social issues	n.s. w/size, but employee health & safety, regulatory compliance, & environmental protection rated high across all organizational sizes

TABLE 4
CSP Studies Relating to Corporate Reputation

Source	Year	CSP Measure	Findings
Moskowitz	1972	apparently, author's perception of CSR (social responsibility)	socially responsible firms outperform the Dow-Jones
Parket & Eilbirt	1975	response to their earlier survey = CSR	pos. w/profit margin pos. w/ ROE pos. w/earnings per share

Vance	1975	CSR company list from *Business & Society Review* (Moskowitz reputational scale)	neg. w/ stock price increases
Fry & Hock	1976	Students' evaluation of industry reputation	neg. w/CSP disclosure in annual report (worse reputation, more disclosure)
Heinz	1976	CSR company list from *Business & Society Review* (Moskowitz reputational scale)	pos. w/ ROE
Sturdivant & Ginter	1977	28 high-CSR firms from *Business & Society Review*	pos. w/10-year growth in earnings per share
Alexander & Buchholz	1978	high-CSR firms from *B&SRev.*	n.s. w/2-year & 5-year stock price increases
Preston	1978	Moskowitz reputational scales	n.s. w/ Ernst & Ernst social disclosure scale
Cochran & Wood	1984	Moskowitz ratings: best, honorable mention, worst CSP	pos. w/ operating earnings/sales n.s. w/oper. earnings/ assets pos. w/ asset age (a measure of inefficiency)
McGuire, Sundgren, and Schneeweis	1988	*Fortune* reputation ratings	pos. w/ ROA pos. w/ asset growth, one period neg. w/debt/asset ratio n.s. w/total assets n.s. w/ income n.s. w/ sales growth n.s. w/ total return
Cottrill & Faust	1991	*Fortune* reputation ratings	neg. w/foreign sales neg.w/foreign sales as % of total sales

Graves & Waddock	1993	KLD scale/smart management	pos. w/ number of institutional investors pos. w/ percent of shares owned by institutional investors

TABLE 5
CSP Studies Relating to Legal/Illegal or Regulatory Behaviors

Source	Year	CSP Measure	Findings
Randall & Neuman	1979	prosecution for antitrust violations	result: decline in stock prices in the week following announcement
Strachan, Smith, & Beedles	1983	accusations of criminal misconduct	negative returns (event study)
Weir	1983	conviction for illegal acquisition or merger	negative returns (event study)
Wokutch & Spencer	1987	criminal behavior	n.s. w/ *Fortune* rating on "community/ environment" criminal behavior + low charitable neg. w/ ROA and ROE contributions
Davidson & Worrell	1988	accusations of criminal misconduct	negative returns (event study)
Baucus	1989	conviction for illegal behavior (antitrust, product liability, discrimi- nation, other)	pos. w/ environmental dynamism pos. w/organizational size neg. w/ environmental scarcity n.s. with organizational slack n.s. with declining financial performance n.s. w/ ROE (as a consequence) n.s. w/sales (as a consequence)

Hill, Kelley, & Agle	1990	OSHA violations	n.s. w/ organizational size pos. w/degree of diversification n.s. w/ decentralization n.s. w/poor financial performance
Pinkston & Carroll	1993	importance ranking of organizational stakeholders	n.s. w /size, but owners, consumers, & employees were ranked higher than communities and government
Pinkston & Carroll	1993	prioritization of social issues	n.s. w/size, but employee health & safety, regulatory compliance, & environmental protection rated high across all organizational sizes

REFERENCES

Abbott, Walter F., and Joseph R. Monsen. 1979. "On the Measurement of Corporate Social Responsibility." *Academy of Management Journal* 22:3 (September), 501–15.

Ackerman, Robert W. 1975. *The Social Challenge to Business.* Cambridge, MA: Harvard University Press.

Alexander, Gordon J., and Rogene A. Buchholz. 1978. "Corporate Social Responsibility and Stock Market Performance." *Academy of Management Journal* 21:3 (September), 479–86.

Anderson, J. C., and A. W. Frankle. 1980. "Voluntary Social Reporting: An Iso-Beta Portfolio Analysis." *The Accounting Review* 55:3, 467–79.

Antal, Ariane Berthoin. 1992. *Corporate Social Performance: Rediscovering Actors in Their Organizational Contexts.* Frankfurt am Main: Campus Verlag.

Arlow, Peter, and Martin J. Gannon. 1982. "Social Responsiveness, Corporate Structure, and Economic Performance." *Academy of Management Review* 7:2 (April), 235–41.

Aupperle, Kenneth E. 1984. "An Empirical Measure of Corporate Social Orientation." In *Research in Corporate Social Performance and Policy,* ed. L. E. Preston. Vol. 6. Greenwich, CT: JAI Press. Pp. 27–54.

Aupperle, Kenneth E., Archie B. Carroll, and J. D. Hatfield. 1985. "An Empirical Examination of the Relationship between Corporate Social Responsibility and Profitability." *Academy of Management Journal,* 28, 446–63.

Baucus, Melissa S. 1989. "Why Firms Do It and What Happens to Them: A Reexamination of the Theory of Illegal Corporate Behavior." In *Research in*

Corporate Social Performance and Policy, ed. James E. Post. Vol. 11. Green-wich, CT: JAI Press. Pp. 93–118.

Belkaoui, A. 1976. "The Impact of the Disclosure of the Environmental Effects of Organizational Behavior on the Market." *Financial Management* 5:4, 26–31.

Berle, Adolph A., and Gardiner C. Means. 1932. *The Modern Corporation and Private Property*. New York: Macmillan.

Boal, Kimberly B., and N. Peery. 1985. "The Cognitive Structure of Corporate Social Responsibility." *Journal of Management* 11, 71–82.

Bowen, Howard R. 1953. *Social Responsibilities of the Businessman*. New York: Harper.

Bowman, Edward H. 1978. "Strategy, Annual Reports, and Alchemy." *California Management Review* 20:3, 64–71.

Bowman, Edward H., and Mason Haire. 1975. "A Strategic Posture toward Corporate Social Responsibility." *California Management Review* 18:2, 49–58.

Bragdon, Joseph H., and John T. Marlin. 1972. "Is Pollution Profitable?" *Risk Management* 19:4 (April), 9–18.

Brill, Jack, and Alan Reder. 1993. "Profit from Your Principles." *Financial Executive* 9:6 (November-December), 54–56.

Bromiley, Philip, and Alfred A. Marcus. 1989. "The Deterrent to Dubious Corporate Behavior: Profitability, Probability, and Safety Recalls." *Strategic Management Journal* 10, 233–50.

Buehler, V. M., and Y. K. Shetty. 1975. "Managing Corporate Social Responsibility." *Management Review* (August), 4–17.

Burke, Lee, Jeanne M. Logsdon, Will Mitchell, Martha Reiner, and David Vogel. 1986. "Corporate Community Involvement in the San Francisco Bay Area." *California Management Review* 28, 122–41.

Calton, Jerry M. 1992. "What Is at Stake in the Stakeholder Model?" *IABS Proceedings 1992*, 205–14.

Calton, Jerry M., and Lawrence J. Lad. 1994. "Social Contracting as a Trust-Building Process of Network Governance." *Business Ethics Quarterly* (forthcoming).

Calton, Jerry M., and Peter S. Ring. 1994. "Symposium: Trust and Trust Building Processes." *IABS Proceedings*.

Carroll, Archie B. 1979. "A Three-Dimensional Conceptual Model of Corporate Social Performance." *Academy of Management Review* 4, 497–505.

———. 1994. "Social Issues in Management Research: Experts' Views, Analysis, and Commentary." *Business and Society* 33:1 (April), 5–29.

Carroll, Archie B., and Gerald T. Horton. 1994. "The Atlanta Project: Corporate Social Responsibility on a Mega-Scale." *IABS Proceedings 1994*.

Chen, K. H., and R. W. Metcalf. 1980. "The Relationship between Pollution Control Record and Financial Indicators Revisited." *Accounting Review* 55, 168–77.

Clarkson, Max B. E. 1988. "Corporate Social Performance in Canada, 1976-86." In *Research in Corporate Social Performance and Policy*, ed. L. E. Preston. Vol. 10. Greenwich, CT: JAI Press. Pp. 241–65.

———. 1994. "A Stakeholder Framework for Analysing and Evaluating Corporate Social Performance." *Academy of Management Review* (forthcoming).

Cochran, Philip L., and Robert A. Wood. 1984. "Corporate Social Responsibility and Financial Performance." *Academy of Management Journal* 27, 42–56.

Cohn, J. 1970. "Is Business Meeting the Challenge of Urban Affairs?" *Harvard Business Review* 48 (2), 68–82.

Collins, Denis. 1992. "An Organization Performance Matrix: A Framework for Broad-Based Performance Measurements." Paper presented at the Academy of Management annual meeting, Las Vegas. August.

Copperman, L. F. 1981. "Employer Policies and the Older Worker." In *Research in Corporate Social Performance and Policy,* ed. L. E. Preston. Vol. 3. Greenwich, CT: JAI Press. Pp. 175–201.

Cornell, B., and A. Shapiro. 1987. "Corporate Stakeholders and Corporate Finance." *Financial Management* 16, 5–14.

Corson, John J., and George A. Steiner. 1974. *Measuring Business' Social Performance: The Corporate Social Audit.* New York: Committee for Economic Development.

Cottrill, M., and B. Faust. 1991. "Corporate Social Performance and Foreign Sales Exposure." *IABS Proceedings.*

Council on Economic Priorities. 1977. *The Pollution Audit.* New York: CEP.

Crafton, Steven M., George E. Hoffer, and Robert J. Reilly. 1981. "Testing the Impact of Recalls on the Demand for Automobiles." *Economic Inquiry* 19, 694–703.

Dalton, Dan A., and R. A. Cosier. 1982. "The Four Faces of Social Responsibility." *Business Horizons* 25, 19–27.

Davidson, Wallace N. III, P. R. Chandy, and Mark Cross. 1987. "Large Losses, Risk Management and Stock Returns in the Airline Industry." *Journal of Risk and Insurance* 57, 162–72.

Davidson, Wallace N. III, and Dan L. Worrell. 1988. "The Impact of Announcements of Corporate Illegalities on Shareholder Returns." *Academy of Management Journal* 31:1, 195–200.

———. 1992. "Research Notes and Communications: The Effect of Product Recall Announcements on Shareholder Wealth." *Strategic Management Journal* 3, 467–73.

Davis, Keith. 1973. "The Case for and against Business Assumption of Social Responsibilities." *Academy of Management Journal* 16, 312–22.

Eilbirt, Henry, and Robert I. Parket. 1973. "The Practice of Business: The Current Status of Corporate Social Responsibility." *Business Horizons* 16:4 (August), 5–14.

Elbing, Albert O., and Carol J. Elbing. 1964. *The Value Issue in Business.* New York: McGraw-Hill.

Ernst and Ernst. 1978. *Social Responsibility Disclosure—1978 Survey.* Cleveland, OH: Ernst and Ernst.

Fogler, H. Russell, and Fred Nutt. 1975. "A Note on Social Responsibility and Stock Valuation." *Academy of Management Journal* 18, 155–60.

Frederick, William C. 1978. "From CSR1 to CSR2: The Maturing of Business-and-Society Thought." Pittsburgh, PA: Working Paper, Katz Graduate School of Business, University of Pittsburgh. Reprinted in *Business and Society* 33:2 (1994).

———. 1987. "Theories of Corporate Social Performance." In *Business and Society,* ed. S. Prakash Sethi and Cecilia M. Falbe. Lexington, MA: Lexington Books. Pp. 142–61.

Freedman, Martin, and Bikki Jaggi. 1982. "Pollution Disclosures, Pollution Performance and Economic Performance." *Omega* 10, 167–76.

———. 1986. "An Analysis of the Impact of Corporate Pollution Disclosures Included in Annual Financial Statements on Investors' Decisions." *Advances in Public Interest Accounting* 1, 193–212.

Freeman, R. Edward. 1984. *Strategic Management: A Stakeholder Approach.* Boston: Pitman/Ballinger–Harper and Row.

Freeman, R. Edward, and Jeanne Liedtka. 1991. "Corporate Social Responsibility: A Critical Approach." *Business Horizons* 34:4 (July-August), 92–98.

Friedman, Milton. 1962. *Capitalism and Freedom.* Chicago: University of Chicago Press.

———. 1970. "The Social Responsibility of Business Is to Increase Its Profits." *New York Times Magazine* (September 13), 32–33, 122–26.

Frooman, Jeffrey S. 1994. "Does the Market Penalize Firms for Socially Irresponsible Behavior?" *IABS Proceedings 1994.*

Fry, Fred, and R. J. Hock. 1976. "Who Claims Corporate Responsibility? The Biggest and the Worst." *Business and Society Review/Innovation* 18, 62–65.

Graves, Samuel B., and Sandra A. Waddock. 1993. "Institutional Owners and Corporate Social Performance." *IABS Proceedings 1993,* 557–62.

Heald, Morrell. 1970. *The Social Responsibility of Business: Company and Community, 1900–1960.* Cleveland: Case Western Reserve University Press.

Heinze, D. C. 1976. "Financial Correlates of a Social Measure." *Akron Business and Economic Review* 7:1: 48–51.

Hill, Charles W. L., Patricia C. Kelley, and Bradley R. Agle. 1990. "An Empirical Examination of the Determinants of OSHA Violations." *IABS Proceedings 1990,* 402–12.

Hoffer, George E., Stephen W. Pruitt, and Robert J. Reilly. 1988. "The Impact of Product Recalls on the Wealth of Sellers: A Reexamination." *Journal of Political Economy* 96:3, 663–70.

Holman, Walter R., J. Randolph New, and Daniel Singer. 1985. "The Impact of Corporate Social Responsiveness on Shareholder Wealth." In *Research in Corporate Social Performance and Policy,* ed. L. E. Preston. Vol. 7. Greenwich, CT: JAI Press. Pp. 136–52.

Holmes, Sandra L. 1977. "Corporate Social Performance: Past and Present Areas of Commitment." *Academy of Management Journal* 20:3 (September), 433–38.

———. 1978. "Adapting Corporate Structure for Social Responsiveness." *California Management Review* 21:1 (Fall), 47–54.

Ingram, Robert W. 1978. "An Investigation of the Information Content of (Certain) Social Responsibility Disclosures." *Journal of Accounting Research* 16:2 (Autumn), 270–85.

Ingram, Robert W., and K. B. Frazier. 1980. "Environmental Performance and Corporate Disclosure." *Journal of Accounting Research* 18, 614–22.

———. 1983. "Narrative Disclosures in Annual Reports." *Journal of Business Research* 11, 49–60.

Jarrell, Gregg, and Sam Peltzman. 1985. "The Impact of Product Recalls on the Wealth of Sellers." *Journal of Political Economy* 93:3, 663–70.

Jones, Thomas M. 1980. "Corporate Social Responsibility Revisited, Redefined." *California Management Review* 22, 59–67.

Kedia, Banwari L., and Edwin C. Kuntz. 1981. "The Context of Social Performance: An Empirical Study of Texas Banks." In *Research in Corporate Social Performance and Policy,* ed. L. E. Preston. Vol. 3. Greenwich, CT: JAI Press. Pp. 133–54.

Keim, Gerald. 1978a. "Corporate Social Responsibility: An Assessment of the Enlightened Self-Interest Model." *Academy of Management Review* 3 , 32–39.

———. 1978b. "Managerial Behavior and the Social Responsibility Debate: Goals vs. Constraints." *Academy of Management Journal* 21, 57–68.

Kinder, Peter D., Steven D. Lydenberg, and Amy L. Domini. 1993. *Investing for Good: Making Money While Being Socially Responsible.* New York: HarperBusiness.

Kohls, John. 1985. "Corporate Board Structure, Social Reporting and Social Performance." In *Research in Corporate Social Performance and Policy,* ed. L. E. Preston. Vol. 7. Greenwich, CT: JAI Press. Pp. 165–89.

Levy, Ferdinand K., and Gloria M. Shatto. 1980. "Social Responsibility in Large Electric Utility Firms: The Case for Philanthropy." In *Research in Corporate Social Performance and Policy,* ed. L. E. Preston. Vol. 2. Greenwich, CT: JAI Press. Pp. 237–49.

Mahon, John F., and Patti N. Andrews. 1987. "Social Issues in Management Literature: A Preliminary Citation Analysis." *Academy of Management Best Papers Proceedings,* 344–48.

Mallott, Mary J. 1993. *Operationalizing Corporate Social Performance.* Doctoral thesis, University of Pittsburgh.

McGuire, Jean B., Alison Sundgren, and Thomas Schneeweis. 1988. "Corporate Social Responsibility and Firm Financial Performance." *Academy of Management Journal* 31:4, 854–72.

Miles, Robert A. 1987. *Managing the Corporate Social Environment: A Grounded Theory.* Englewood Cliffs, NJ: Prentice-Hall.

Mitchell, Neil. 1983. "Ownership, Control, and Social Policy." In *Research in Corporate Social Performance and Policy.* Vol. 5. Greenwich, CT: JAI Press. Pp. 205–30.

Mitnick, Barry M. 1993. "Organizing Research in Corporate Social Performance: The CSP System as Core Paradigm." *IABS Proceedings 1993,* 2–15.

———. 1994. "Systematics and CSP." *IABS Proceedings 1994.*

Morris, Sara A., Robert L. Armacost, J. C. Hosseini, and Kathleen A. Rehbein. 1991. "Organizational Misconduct: A Test of Three Competing Explanations." *IABS Proceedings,* 367–81.

Morris, Sara A., Kathleen A. Rehbein, Jamsheed C. Hosseini, and Robert L. Armacost. 1990. "Building a Current Profile of Socially Responsive Firms." *IABS Proceedings 1990,* 297–303.

Moskowitz, Milton. 1972. "Choosing Socially Responsible Stocks." *Business and Society Review* 1 (Spring), 71–75.

Newgren, Kenneth E., A. A. Rasher, M. E. LaRoe, and M. R. Szabo. 1985. "Environmental Assessment and Corporate Performance: A Longitudinal Analysis Using a Market-determined Performance Measure." In *Research in Corporate Social Performance and Policy,* ed. L. E. Preston. Vol. 7. Greenwich, CT: JAI Press. Pp. 153–64.

Parket, Robert, and Henry Eilbirt. 1975. "Social Responsibility: The Underlying Factors." *Business Horizons* (August), 5–10.

Pinkston, Tammie S., and Archie B. Carroll. 1993. "An Investigation of the Relationship between Organizational Size and Corporate Social Performance." *IABS Proceedings 1993,* 109–14.

Preston, Lee E. 1978. "Analyzing Corporate Social Performance: Methods and Results." *Journal of Contemporary Business* 7:1, 135–49.

Preston, Lee E., and J. E. Post. 1975. *Private Management and Public Policy: The Principle of Public Responsibility.* Englewood Cliffs, NJ: Prentice-Hall.

Pruitt, Stephen W., and David R. Peterson. 1986. "Security Price Reactions around Product Recall Announcements." *Journal of Financial Research* 9:2, 113–22.

Randall, N. H., and W. L. Neuman. 1979. "The Impact of Government Sanctions on the Large Corporation: The Cost of Antitrust Law Violation." Unpublished paper. (Cited in Baucus 1989.)

Reilly, Robert J., and George E. Hoffer. 1983. "Will Retarding the Information Flow on Automobile Recalls Affect Consumer Demand?" *Economic Inquiry* 21, 444–47.

Rockness, Joanne, Paul Schlachter, and Howard O. Rockness. 1986. "Hazardous Waste Disposal, Corporate Disclosure, and Financial Performance in the Chemical Industry." *Advances in Public Interest Accounting* 1, 167–91.

Roman, P. M., and T. C. Blum. 1987. "The Relation of Employee Assistance Programs to Corporate Social Responsibility Attitudes: An Empirical Study." In *Research in Corporate Social Performance and Policy*, ed. L. E. Preston. Vol. 7. Greenwich, CT: JAI Press. Pp. 213–35.

Sethi, S. Prakash. 1979. "A Conceptual Framework for Environmental Analysis of Social Issues and Evaluation of Business Response Patterns." *Academy of Management Review* 4, 63–74.

Shane, P. B., and B. H. Spicer. 1983. "Market Response to Environmental Information Produced Outside the Firm." *Accounting Review* 58, 521–38.

Sharfman, Mark. 1993. "A Concurrent Validity Study of the KLD Social Performance Ratings Data." *IABS Proceedings 1993*, 551–56.

Siegfried, J. J., K. M. McElroy, and D. Biernot-Fawkes. 1983. "The Management of Corporate Contributions." In *Research in Corporate Social Performance and Policy*, ed. L. E. Preston. Vol. 5. Greenwich, CT: JAI Press. Pp. 87–102.

Smith, S. M., and D. S. Alcorn. 1991. "Cause Marketing." *Journal of Consumer Marketing* 8:3, 19–35.

Sonnenfeld, Jeffrey A. 1982. "Structure, Culture and Performance in Public Affairs: A Study of the Forest Products Industry." In *Research in Corporate Social Performance and Policy*, ed. L. E. Preston. Vol. 4. Greenwich, CT: JAI Press. Pp. 105–27.

Spicer, B. H. 1978a. "Investors, Corporate Social Performance and Information Disclosure: An Empirical Study." *Accounting Review* 53, 94–111.

———. 1978b. "Market Risk, Accounting Data and Companies' Pollution Control Records." *Journal of Business, Finance and Accounting* 5, 67–83.

———. 1980. "The Relationship between Pollution Control Record and Financial Indicators Revisited: Further Comment." *Accounting Review* 55, 178–85.

Strachan, James L., David B. Smith, and William L. Beedles. 1983. "The Price Reaction to (Alleged) Corporate Crime." *Financial Review*, 121–32.

Sturdivant, Frederick D., and James L. Ginter. 1977. "Corporate Social Responsiveness: Management Attitudes and Economic Performance." *California Management Review* 19:3 (Spring), 30–39.

Swanson, Diane. 1994. "The CSP Field Divided: Irreconciled Economic and Deontological Perspectives." *IABS Proceedings 1994*.

"Toronto Conference: Reflections on Stakeholder Theory." 1994. *Business and Society* 33:1 (April), 82–131.

Trotman, K. T., and G. W. Bradley. 1981. "Associations between Social Responsibility Disclosure and Characteristics of Companies." *Accounting, Organizations, and Society* 6, 355–62.

Tuzzolino, Frank, and Barry R. Armandi. 1981. "A Need Hierarchy for Assessing Corporate Social Responsibility." *Academy of Management Review* 6, 21–28.

Ullmann, Arieh. 1985. "Data in Search of a Theory: A Critical Examination of the Relationships among Social Performance, Social Disclosure, and Economic Performance." *Academy of Management Review* 10, 540–77.

Vance, Stanley C. 1975. "Are Socially Responsible Corporations Good Investment Risks?" *Management Review* 64:8: 19–24.

Wartick, Steven L., and Philip L. Cochran. 1985. "The Evolution of the Corporate Social Performance Model." *Academy of Management Review* 10, 758-69.

Weir, P. 1983. "The Costs of Antimerger Lawsuits." *Journal of Financial Economics* 11, 207–24.

Wiseman, J. 1982. "An Evaluation of Environmental Disclosures Made in Corporate Annual Reports." *Accounting, Organizations, and Society* 7, 53–63.

Wokutch, Richard E., and Barbara A. Spencer. 1987. "Corporate Saints and Sinners: The Effects of Philanthropic and Illegal Activity on Organizational Performance." *California Management Review* 29:2, 62–77.

Wood, Donna J. 1991a. "Corporate Social Performance Revisited." *Academy of Management Review* 16 (October), 691–718.

———. 1991b. "Social Issues in Management: Research and Theory in Corporate Social Performance." *Journal of Management* 17 (June), 383–406.

———. 1991c. "Toward Improving Corporate Social Performance." *Business Horizons* (July-August), 66–72.

Wynn, James A., and George E. Hoffer. 1976. "Auto Recalls: Do They Affect Market Share?" *Applied Economics* 8, 157–63.

5

How Does Firm Size Affect Corporate Philanthropy?

DWIGHT F. BURLINGAME AND PATRICIA A. FRISHKOFF

INTRODUCTION

It was recently reported that for the first time in 22 years corporate contributions to charitable organizations declined ("Corporate Giving," 1993). In addition, the Center for Corporate Community Relations at Boston College (Corporate Community Relations Letter, 1993) reported on a survey of community relations specialists of America's largest corporations, which found that requests for support from businesses by nonprofits are increasing while the ability to meet the need is declining. United Ways across the country are seeking ways to increase the base of their support among businesses—particularly among medium- and small-sized businesses. Community development initiative organizations, nonprofit agencies, and business civic groups are often heard making the cry for bringing small businesses into the "civic fold."

Small business owners and corporate executives play crucial roles in selecting beneficiaries, types, and amounts of gifts dedicated as their firms' charitable contributions (O'Connor, 1973, p. iii; Hall, 1989, pp. 229–30; Stendardi, 1992, p. 25). In past research, interview, survey, and case study methods helped researchers examine these roles usually in relation to one of several philosophies of giving (Galaskiewicz, 1989) or according to size of contributions, kinds of companies, or types of contributions (O'Connor, 1973).

Those organizations that are primarily responsible for providing information about corporate giving (the Council for Financial Aid to Education, the Conference Board, and the Council on Foundations) focus almost exclusively on large corporations (those with 500+ employees).

Cash contributions are most often studied for all sizes of firms, including small or family businesses (Wiltsek, 1990; Cronk, 1988). In-kind donations and volunteered time contributed by businesses rarely are reported in studies.

The primary organizational factor in corporate giving is firm size (Useem, 1987). Useem contends that larger firms are more generous (regardless of profits) because their programs are more formalized and professional. Neil Mitchell (1989) in *The Generous Corporation* offered a political perspective of corporate social responsibility which confirmed this premise. He stated that a corporation, as a political institution, retains power through legitimacy in order to meet its profit objective. Viewed in this light, corporate social responsibility is seen as one of many avenues for legitimation. Subsequently, larger firms are more likely to engage in socially responsible activities since they are more likely to encounter problems associated with legitimacy.

McElroy and Siegfried (1985) have perhaps done the most extensive research on the relationship of firm size and corporate contributions. Three interesting results emerged from their work. First, medium-sized firms (based on number of employees) contribute proportionately more than larger and smaller firms. Second, as the firm size increases, contributions to health and welfare organizations decrease because most giving is done through the United Way, which is considered a fixed rather than proportionate obligation. Third, larger firms are more apt to contribute to education and national organizations.

This chapter presents results which indicate that community service is significant from small businesses. These findings have important implications for business owners, beneficiaries, and development officers. Although these businesses represent only a small percentage of the total amount of corporate giving, that percentage is crucial to some beneficiaries, especially those in small communities. Moreover, the small-business share of total giving is likely to grow as the number of small businesses increases; businesses of under 100 employees are currently the fastest growing type of business. This is also expected in light of the fact that corporate contributions declined in 1992 for the first time in 22 years ("Corporate Giving," 1993).

Information about the contributions of small and medium-sized businesses cannot be extrapolated from information about the giving patterns of large corporations; in their giving practices, as in their business practices, these smaller businesses are not just miniature versions of big businesses.

The research in Indiana and Oregon was guided by five basic research questions:

- What are the types and size of contributions and how does size of the company affect contributions?
- Who decides to give?
- What motivates giving?
- How do cash contributions compare to in-kind donations and volunteer time on behalf of the business?
- Who are the beneficiaries, and how are they chosen?

METHODOLOGY

Business Contributions to Community Service (Frishkoff and Kostecka, 1991) examined and described community service activities of 182 firms of various sizes from four cities in Oregon. Data were gathered through customized, personal, on-site interviews with the president, CEO, or designee. The contributions occurred in the 1989 tax year of the businesses.

Burlingame and Kaufmann (1995) conducted a survey of over 1,200 businesses in the state of Indiana in the fall of 1993. A random sample of companies was drawn from across the state, and a survey instrument was administered during a prearranged conference call with company presidents and CEOs or their designees. Both studies inform the content of this chapter.

FINDINGS

TYPE AND SIZE OF CONTRIBUTION

In the Oregon study data on contributions were normalized on a per-employee basis to allow comparisons of levels among companies of different sizes; data were also presented in terms of relative magnitude of cash versus in-kind contributions (Figure 1).

Two important findings were apparent from this data: (1) Small businesses gave at least as much as larger companies, and (2) for small companies, noncash contributions matched cash gifts. Connors and Wise (1988) reported that "based on assets, U.S. corporations give on the average about 0.05 percent of domestic assets. Per employee, it is about $60 per employee" (p. 35.5). Only medium-size Oregonian companies tended to contribute a mean cash contribution under $100 per employee; the average cash donation exceeded $200 per employee. If in-

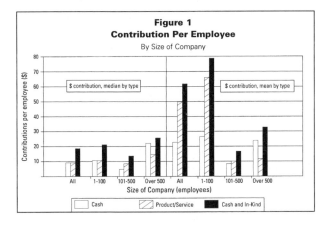

Figure 1
Contribution Per Employee
By Size of Company

kind contributions were valued, the overall average contribution donated by all Oregonian companies in 1989 exceeded $600, and in the
case of firms with 100 or less employees, that average contribution of
cash and in-kind gifts ranged upward to almost $800.

The Indiana study obtained similar results. When the percent of
company net income contributed to charitable causes was compared by
size of firm (number of employees) smaller firms were more apt to give
3 percent or more of their net income than were medium and large
companies (See Figure 2).

These findings tend to point to giving at significantly higher levels,
especially for small business, than previously documented.

When controlling for size, the larger the company the more likely it
was to give cash. Smaller companies were more likely to give in-kind
gifts and gifts of time than their larger counterparts.

In-kind donations covered a broad spectrum of gifts, and they
accounted for about one-third of business donations. These contributions were commonly deducted as business expenses, representing
expensive kinds of "superstructure" support recipients could not easily
purchase. Comprising mostly business products, property, facilities,
and services, these donations also represented creative and useful
contributions to beneficiaries. Connors and Wise (1989) present a list of
ways (pp. 35.12–35.17) nonprofits can take advantage of corporate in-
kind donations and also confirm our finding, stating that "corporations
frequently assist not-for-profit institutions through loans of employees,
donations or loans of equipment and space, volunteer programs, and
direct dollar investments in economic redevelopment efforts—all of
which may be accounted for as business expenses" (p. 35.4).

Figure 2

Contributions as a Percent of Net Income

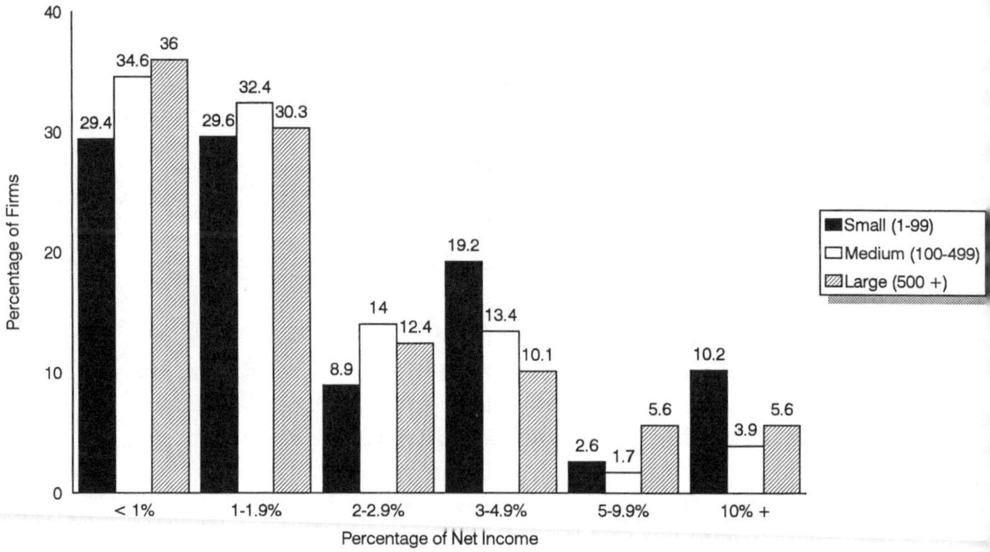

Of all the companies in the Indiana sample, 63 percent gave locally, 7 percent gave nationally and statewide, and only 2 percent gave internationally. It was rather surprising to find that smaller companies gave more often to international causes than medium and large companies. While McElroy and Siegfried (1985) discovered that larger firms tended to support national organizations, our findings revealed that a slightly higher proportion (1.4 percent) of small companies gave nationally than their larger counterparts. Medium-sized companies are most likely to give locally, although the difference among the groups is only 5 percent.

VOLUNTEER TIME

The proportion of employees who volunteer on behalf of their company can also be computed from the Oregon data, and it indicates the propensity for corporate volunteerism. A much larger proportion of employees in small companies volunteered on behalf of the business than in larger companies. Volunteered time represented, however, a major contributory cost for all firms, and for very small companies (1–

20 employees), the cost of volunteered time was about two-thirds of the total cost of contributions. The remaining third of the cost divided between cash and in-kind, with in-kind taking the bigger share. Cash clearly emerges as the least important type of contribution for small companies.

In *Philanthropic Giving*, Magat asserts that "the donation of time is intertwined with cash giving. A higher proportion of volunteers donate funds to charitable organizations than persons who do not volunteer" (1989, p. 7). Our results on types of gifts and on beneficiaries affirm that notion—an important observation for nonprofit agencies.

ACCOUNTING AND BUDGETING FOR CONTRIBUTIONS

Accounting treatment of donations varied by type of donation. Cash contributions were almost always categorized as contributions (for which there are specified limits according to tax law). In-kind donations of product were usually treated as operating expense; they were treated as goods used up and included in cost of goods sold. Few companies attempted to allocate the cost of volunteer time to contributions, meaning that these costs were included in administrative salaries. Therefore, it is impossible to review financial or tax records and compute the cost of contributions.

The likelihood that a company will have a formal contributions budget increases with the size of the company. In our studies, on average three out of every four large companies had a contributions budget, while only one out of five small companies had a formal budget for contributions.

WHO DECIDES TO GIVE?

One of the questions often asked is: "Does the type of owner-ship (family or nonfamily) affect contributions to the local commu-nity?" In the Indiana study, 63.3 percent of the businesses were family owned. That is, more than 50 percent of ownership was held by one family. As previously mentioned, the smaller the company the more likely it was to be family owned. However, what is interesting is that family-owned companies do not equate to greater involvement in the community. In fact, a larger but not statistically significant percentage of non-family-owned companies were involved with the community. This finding is consistent with earlier research by Atkinson and Galaskiewicz (1988). When comparing what family-owned businesses versus non-family-owned businesses contributed to, the Indiana study found that non-family-owned businesses were almost twice as likely to give to arts

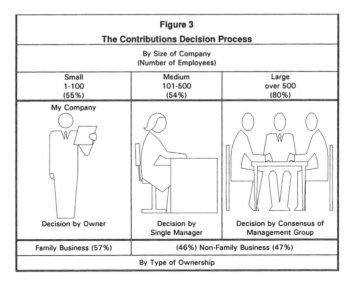

Figure 3
The Contributions Decision Process

By Size of Company (Number of Employees)		
Small 1-100 (55%)	Medium 101-500 (54%)	Large over 500 (80%)
Decision by Owner	Decision by Single Manager	Decision by Consensus of Management Group
Family Business (57%)	(46%) Non-Family Business (47%)	
By Type of Ownership		

and culture organizations as were family-owned businesses. Further analysis will need to be done to determine why this is so.

People who made decisions about contributions most often consisted of business owners and managers either acting alone or in small groups.

In one-half of the Indiana companies, the decision of whom to give to was made by the owner. In slightly more than one-third of the companies the decision was made by senior management. And in only 15 percent of the cases was the decision made by a designated contributions person or committee.

As might be expected, the decision maker was more likely to be the owner in small businesses, management in medium-sized firms, and a designated person or committee in large companies. Breaking out the small companies into three categories (<2, 3–10, 11–99 employees) yielded an interesting finding. There appeared to be a shift in decision making from the owner to management when the firm moved from the category of 3–10 employees to the category of 11–99 employees. When size was controlled, the personal values of the owner/CEO were given greater weight. The larger the company the more likely they considered their social responsibility as a factor. The general business condition was a more important factor for smaller companies. Tax considerations were given a slightly higher consideration in larger companies. In addition, employee considerations grew as company size became larger.

In addition, the decision process can be characterized as either a one-person decision, vote by committee, or one reached by consensus. As might be expected, the smaller the company the more likely a one-person decision is made. In Oregon, the shift away from one-person decisions to consensus reaching occurred between medium and large firms (Frishkoff and Kostecka, 1991). By comparison, the Indiana study depicted a more consistent yet substantial transition, and it reflected a larger proportion of medium-sized firms utilizing voting.

The data confirm findings from prior research that targets managers and top executives in medium and large firms as the decision makers on contributions (Hyland et al., 1990, p. 113; Logsdon et al., 1990, p. 105; Wiltsek, 1990, p. 64).

MOTIVATIONS

In order to determine what factors motivate giving, both studies asked a series of questions relating to what the company considers when deciding whom to contribute to. The strongest factors affecting giving by companies in both studies were personal values of the owner, the condition of the business, social responsibility, public relations, and the quality of the organization making the request. Lesser motivating factors were prior giving, tax regulations, other companies' giving, and the interest of employees.

Figure 4 displays the motivating factors in the Indiana study as a percentage of companies by size. When asked to identify the most important factor, the most frequent responses across all company sizes were business responsibility and the condition of business. Business responsibility was overwhelmingly in first position among large companies and also first among medium-sized companies. Business conditions was the next most cited factor in medium-sized firms, with soliciting organizations a close third. Values of the CEO and business conditions were the two most frequent responses for small companies.

It is interesting to compare the aforementioned motivations to the responses given regarding the benefits of contributing to community service. According to 37 percent of the respondents, the most important benefit to the company for making contributions is that it supports community and economic growth. The second most often cited reason was company obligation/responsibility (17 percent). The third and fourth most often cited responses (8 percent and 6 percent, respectively) clustered around supporting a good cause and meeting community needs. Company and community image combined represented about 7 percent of the responses.

Figure 4

Major Motivational Factors for Contributions to Community Service

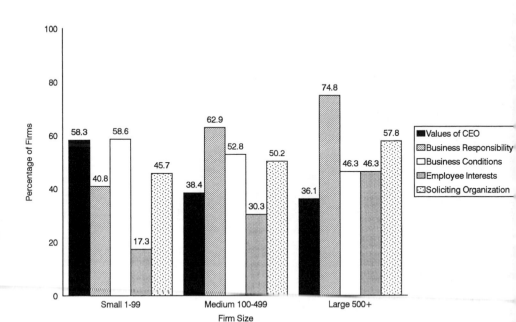

WHO ARE THE BENEFICIARIES?

Figure 5 shows the percentage of companies in the Indiana study (Burlingame and Kaufmann, 1994) that contributed to health and human services, education, arts and culture, civic and community organizations, and other. As expected, the most popular area for companies to contribute to was civic and community organizations (77.3 percent). Health and human service organizations were second (59.5 percent); education was third with 55.8 percent; and arts and culture was a distant fourth with 35.5 percent. In the category labeled "other" the most frequent response was the United Way (34 percent) followed by religious organizations with approximately 19 percent.

Information gathered on beneficiaries in the Oregon study (Frishkoff and Kostecka, 1991) indicated that firms donated 71 percent of their contributions to three top beneficiaries; the first-ranked beneficiary typically received 40 percent, the second received 20 percent, and the third received 11 percent of total contributions. Overall, four kinds of beneficiaries most often received the donations of the respondents.

Figure 5

Beneficiaries of Business Contributions

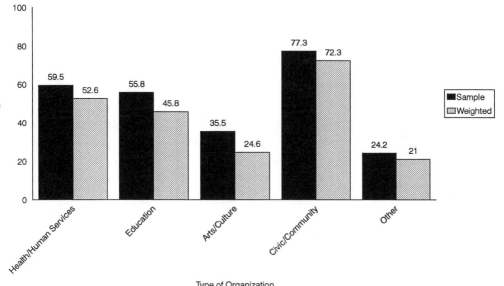

Type of Organization

Combined appeals, health and human services, higher education, and professional and trade associations consistently received ranking in the top three beneficiaries; furthermore, the percentages of contributions other than cash consistently amounted to over 70 percent of giving regardless of size of company or type of ownership. Smaller firms and family-owned firms targeted their giving to health and human services and associations; large firms preferred combined-appeal beneficiaries (like United Way) and education. Interestingly, in the Indiana study the larger the company the more likely it was to give to health and service organizations. Part of this is certainly explained by the fact that most United Way agencies are health and human services groups and United Way giving was not broken out in the Indiana study as it was in the Oregon one.

In both studies, when controlling for size, larger companies gave more often to education than smaller companies. This conclusion was also reached by McElroy and Siegfried (1985). Larger companies were also more likely to support arts and culture organizations. The Oregon study found this to be generally true with the exception of a slight dip in the medium-sized firms. Civic and community organizations represented the closest percentage of giving by all three size groups. Similar results were obtained in the Indiana study, when contributions per employee were analyzed.

Recipients of donations tended to be local. Our findings about beneficiaries basically supported that of prior studies both with respect to smaller companies and larger firms (O'Connor, 1973, pp. iii, 9; Wiltsek, 1990).

RECONCILIATIONS

The results of the Oregon and Indiana studies lead us to conclude that contributions patterns of small businesses differed from those of large businesses; that small businesses gave more than large businesses based on per-employee donations; that contributions consisted primarily of types other than cash, and that decisions were made through processes and for reasons different from those of large firms.

TERMINOLOGY

Concepts about business giving have progressed over time, moving through various developmental stages from "acts of charity" to the "social responsibility" role of corporations (Bock, 1980, pp. 5-17). To help managers and researchers discuss these notions, we propose a spectrum as a philosophical framework for business contributions, a continuum that extends from altruism to stewardship (Figure 6). Midway between these two extremes, we have placed enlightened self-interest, and we propose two additional concepts that describe giving based on two recent conceptual developments. Each philosophical position is illustrated beneath its description by examples from the literature on charitable contributions.

Between enlightened self-interest and stewardship we have placed a concept called "charitable investment." From an ethical perspective, Dienhart argues that charitable investment as a strategy captures the notion of "the giver and the recipient as engaged in a common project for their mutual benefit" (1988, *Journal of Business Ethics*, p. 69). Dienhart explains that charitable investing "gives back to the community some of the wealth the business has created and acquired, in a way that benefits all concerned (1988, *Business and Professional Ethics Journal*, p. 49). Dienhart tries to convince us that his definition of charitable investments focuses on the givers' concern for the "good of others" (1988, *Journal of Business Ethics*, p. 68). It seems that every-

Figure 6
Philosophical Framework--Charitable Business Contributions

< ------------------Continuum of Philosophical Positions------------------ >

Altruism[a]	Shared Benefits[b]	Enlightened Self-Interest[a]	Charitable Investment[c]	Stewardship[a]
Unselfish regard for the welfare of others. In its purest sense, altruism means that the donor has no knowledge of the beneficiary and receives no external recognition for contributing.	*Giving to common concerns with community recognition but without expectation of a particular gain.* Business, especially an owner or top manager, recognizes a desire or an obligation to help its community and expects several constituencies to share in the benefits.	*Giving with an aim to enhance or focus one's business advantage and well-being.* The business donor looks for specific, long-term gains to the business as a reciprocal payoff for contributions to community. Corporate philanthropy viewed as ultimately improving business climate and preserving capitalism.	*Targeting giving with the aim of short-term monetary or social gain, a return greater than the expenditure.* Charitable investments seek to integrate giving into the objectives of overall corporate goals--giving communicates a clear corporate mission about corporate products.	*Responsibility to direct business in a way that enhances the wealth of the owners.* In its strictest sense, stewardship entails the maximization of net income and return on the owners' investments.
Examples: Anonymous donations Pooled donations Endowments (Hall)	**Examples:** Volunteered time, skills Donated use of facilities In-kind giving Acknowledged donations (Frishkoff & Kostecka)	**Examples:** Cause Related Marketing (Dienhart, Galaskiewicz) Giving to Advertise (Dienhart, Galaskiewicz) Long-term, targeted gifts (Hall, Galaskiewicz)	**Examples:** Short-term targeted gifts (Dienhart) Strategic philanthropy (O'Hare, Logsdon, et al.) Status Giving (Galaskiewicz) Social Investing (Stendardi)	**Examples:** Giving as Tax Strategy (Galaskiewicz)

[a]Adapted from Frishkoff and Kostecka, p. 2--1.
[b]Adapted from Frishkoff and Kostecka, p. 2--6, 2--22.
[c]Developed from Dienhart.

where else in the literature, however, the meaning of "charitable" reflects on the recipient status of beneficiaries as a nonprofit, tax-exempt organization, a status specifically determined in a letter by the U.S. Internal Revenue Service under §501(c)(3) of the 1954 Internal Revenue Code, with its subsequent amendments in force (Mortensen, 1991, pp. 13-16). A reading of the *Taft Corporate Giving Directory* (1988) and *Corporate 500: The Directory of Corporate Philanthropy* (1988) supports our belief that "charitable" means "nonprofit" because virtually every contributory program description in these source books requires "proof of tax-exempt status" (*Taft)* or states "Must be tax-exempt under 501(c)3" (*Corporate 500*). Dienhart himself ties "charitable investments" to traditional descriptions of aligning gifts with

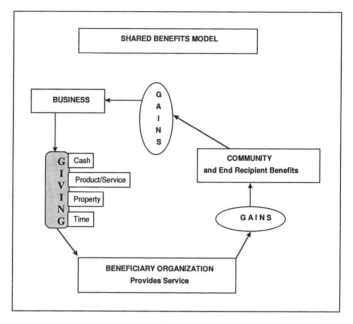

Figure 7

company products or goals (p. 48); therefore, we prefer to place the concept called charitable investments on the continuum where it emphasizes the focus of the business. Dienhart's ideas of undirected mutual benefits derived from corporate giving fits what we call "shared benefits."

The notion of "shared benefits" was introduced in the final report *Business Contributions to Community Service* (Frishkoff and Kostecka, 1991, pp. 2-7) as a model to examine the gains of businesses, beneficiaries, and communities from contributions by small businesses (Figure 7). "We reject the concept of pure altruism behind business contributions because this project demonstrates how—at the minimum—the owner or manager experienced personal gains, got to feel good, when the business made a difference in the community. This expected and important gain moves the corporation along the spectrum toward enlightened self-interest" (1991, pp. 2-6). We believe the key to a "shared benefits" concept is that while a business, especially a small business, selects a beneficiary and contributes specifically to it, direct and indirect unanticipated gains emerge for several constituencies. The motives we encountered as reasons for contributing to top recipients support this notion of shared benefits as a framework that grounds the giving of small businesses.

It is not our purpose to suggest a preferred ethical position along the continuum displayed in Figure 6. However, it is possible for managers and business owners to use this spectrum to explore their companies' philosophical basis for contributions with regard to purpose of the giver, type and value of gift, type of beneficiary, effect of gift on giver and on beneficiary, and effect of giving and gift on the wider community. The spectrum also provides insight on where certain giving activities can be located within a company.

EXHIBIT 1 Key Questions for Strategic Philanthropic Planning	
Personal values of the owner	What matters to you or your owners in terms of charitable contributions? Does your firm's community service achieve your wishes?
Business citizenship	Where does your company's philanthropy fit on the continuum of philosophic positions? Why does your business give? What, if anything, do you wish to achieve? Do your forms of giving and beneficiaries meet these goals? Does the company receive acknowledgment appropriate to your philosophy? Do the job descriptions and performance expectations for employees reflect these goals?
Condition of the business	How much do you want to give? Can the business afford that level of contributions, in dollars, products, and time? What proportion of management time should be budgeted to community service?

FOR CONTRIBUTORS

How should these findings affect the behavior of contributing businesses? Businesses operate to maximize return for the dollars invested. Given this premise, we translate the findings of the research—especially in terms of the magnitude of contributions and the reasons stated for giving—into the following strategic questions, asking owners and managers to incorporate a philanthropic posture into their business planning processes.

The goal of development in this context is no less "bottom line" than that of business. Nonprofit organizations must continually receive contributions in order to provide or enhance services; to do so they constantly seek increased contributions from the business community as one source of support.

The findings of this project invite redirection of efforts to cultivate and solicit contributions from small businesses:

- Small businesses give big dollars locally. Maximizing contributions means developing a plan to tap the potential of small business as well as big business.
- Decision-making approval regarding contributions often rests with one person, usually the owner in small businesses. Getting commitment from that one right person is a necessary condition for contributions. Involvement is relationships based and depends at least somewhat on the payoff to the business or the owner, who at least gets to feel good about giving. This finding suggests a targeted cultivation process based on relationships developed, over a long period of time, by staff or board members.
- Key executives, including owners in smaller and family-held firms, acted as principal volunteers in businesses. Top volunteers performed a variety of services but volunteered more than half the time for board service or as fund-raisers for beneficiaries. Top volunteers donated a significant amount of time—about 135 hours per year to their communities—a bargain bonus for top-level expertise at work in the nonprofits' interest. Getting owners involved is strategically important.
- The payoff can be big for nonprofits that nurture relationships with top executives and business owners—most of the dollar value of contributions goes to top beneficiaries. A concentrated approach to retain or move to one of these top beneficiary positions could be more tactically wise than an approach which attempts to hit all the bases and solicit, with minimum effort, a wider number of firms. Getting to know individuals and their wants and interests is vital. This obviously implies person-to-person calls and strategically directed involvement of the key prospects in program activities, a strategy not met by broad-based letter campaigns.
- Nonprofits which conduct special events should remember that

many small businesses usually give a token donation when approached. This bodes well for solicitation for auctions and the like. A first step could be developing a database of local small businesses and their owners. This can begin by gleaning from lists (Chamber, trade associations, board contacts) or by purchasing lists from commercial sources, especially ones which can screen based on ownership, location, and size and which can provide owner's names.

• Effort of the soliciting organization is a major factor determining the level of contributions. Nonprofits must "nurture" contributors and prospects from a "customer service" perspective, and they must publicize the contributions made by small businesses, unless the donors request no acclaim.

Community service is "big business" for small business. Their contributions are large, especially in relative comparison to those of large business, even though they may not fully realize the cost of contributions, especially in terms of volunteer time. Research to date has failed to recognize the importance of contributions by small businesses.

Business Contributions to Community Service provided data suggesting that businesses and development officers may want to examine philosophies of giving, consider the impact of noncash gifts as well as cash, and adjust management behaviors to maximize their efforts aimed at small business contributions.

ACKNOWLEDGMENTS

The Oregon research for this chapter was conducted under contract #SBA-4119-0A-89 for the Small Business Administration. The Indiana research was carried out with support from the Aspen Institute, Lilly Endowment, Mays Chemical Company, Associated Group, and Indiana Power and Light.

R E F E R E N C E S

Ackerman, R. W., and R. A. Bauer. *Corporate Social Responsiveness: The Modern Dilemma*. Reston, VA: Reston Publishing Company, 1976.
Americans Volunteer 1985. An Independent Sector Summary Report. Washington, D.C. 1986.
Atkinson, L., and J. Galaskiewicz. "Stock Ownership and Company Contributions to Charity." *Administrative Science Quarterly* 33 (1988), 82–100.

Bakal, C. *Charity U.S.A.* New York: Times Books. 1979.

Baumol, W. "Business Responsibility and Economic Behavior." In *Altruism, Morality and Economic Theory,* ed. E. S. Phelps. New York: Russell Sage Foundation, 1975. Pp. 45–56.

Blackford, M. G., and L. A. Kerr. *Business Enterprise in American History.* Boston: Houghton Mifflin Company, 1986.

Bock, R. H. "Modern Values and Corporate Social Responsibility." *MSU Business Topics* 28 (Spring 1980), 5–17.

Burke, L., J. M. Logsdon, W. Mitchell, M. Reiner, and D. Vogel. "Corporate Community Involvement in the San Francisco Bay Area." *California Management Review* 28 (1986), 122–41.

Burlingame, D. F., and D. A. Kaufmann. *Indiana Business Contributions to Community Service.* Indianapolis: Indiana University Center on Philanthropy, 1995.

Center for Corporate Community Relations at Boston College. *1993 Profile of the Community Relations Professions.* Chestnut Hill, MA, 1993.

Clotfelter, C. I. *Federal Tax Policy and Charitable Giving.* Chicago: National Bureau of Economic Research. 1985.

Commission on Private Philanthropy and Public Needs. *Giving in America: Toward a Stronger Voluntary Sector.* Report. N.p. 1975.

Connors, T. D., and S. R. Wise. "Seeking Revenue or Support from Corporations." In *The Nonprofit Organization Handbook,* ed. T. D. Connors. 2nd ed. New York: McGraw-Hill, 1988.

Corporate 500: The Directory of Corporate Philanthropy. 7th ed. San Francisco: Public Management Institute, 1988.

"Corporate Giving Declines for First Time since 1970." *Nonprofit Times* 7, no. 11 (1993), 51.

Cronk, V. M. *Small Business Philanthropy.* Ph.D. dissertation, University of Wisconsin, Milwaukee, 1988.

Danco, L. A., and J. L. Ward. "Beyond Success: The Continuing Contribution of the Family Foundation." *Family Business Review* 3 (Winter 1990), 347–56. Special issue on family foundations.

Dienhart, J. W. "Charitable Investments: A Strategy for Improving the Business Environment." *Journal of Business Ethics* 7 (1988), 63–71.

———. "Ethical and Conceptual Issues in Charitable Investment, Cause Related Marketing, and Advertising." 1988. *Business and Professional Ethics Journal* 7 (3 and 4), 47–59.

Duffy, M. N. *Survey of Corporate Contributions, 1990 Editions.* Report No. 942. New York: The Conference Board, 1990.

Emory, W. C. *Business Research Methods.* Illinois: Irwin Series, 1985.

Fenn, D. H., Jr. "Executives as Community Volunteers." *Harvard Business Review* (March-April 1971), 4–10, 12–16, 156–57.

Fremont-Smith, M. R. *Philanthropy and the Business Corporation.* New York: Russell Sage Foundation, 1972.

Frishkoff, P., and A. Kostecka. *Business Contributions to Community Service.* Corvallis, OR: Oregon State University. Prepared for the U.S. Small Business Administration. Contract #SBA-4119-OA-89, 1991.

Galaskiewicz, J. "Corporate Contributions to Charity: Nothing More than a Marketing Strategy?" In *Philanthropic Giving,* ed. R. Magat. New York: Oxford University Press, 1989. Pp. 246–60.

Hall, P. D. "Business Giving and Social Investment in the United States." In *Philanthropic Giving,* ed. R. Magat. New York: Oxford University Press, 1989. Pp. 221–45.

Hall, R. H. *Organizations: Structure and Process.* Englewood Cliffs, NJ: Prentice-Hall, 1977.

Harris, J. F., and A. Klepper. *Corporate Philanthropic Public Service Activities.* Report No. 976. New York: The Conference Board, 1976.

Harris, L. C. "Corporate Giving: Rationale, Issues, and Opportunities." In *Research Papers,* vol. 3: special behavioral studies, foundations, and corporations, 1789–1825. The Commission on Private Philanthropy and Public Needs, Dept. of Treasury. n.p., 1977.

Heald, M. *The Social Responsibility of Business, Company and Community 1900–1960.* Cleveland, OH: The Press of Case Western Reserve University, 1970.

Hougland, J. G., and J. M. Shepard. "Voluntarism and the Manager: The Impact of Structural Pressures and Personal Interest on Community Participation." *Journal of Voluntary Action Research* 14 (April-September 1985), 65–78.

Huffman, F. "The Gift of Giving." *Entrepreneur* (November 1990), 147–54.

Hyland, S. E., A. Russel, and F. Hebb. "Realigning Corporate Giving: Problems in the Nonprofit Sector for Community Development Corporations." *Nonprofit and Voluntary Sector Quarterly* 9 (Summer 1990), 111–19.

Internal Revenue Code Sec. 170 (b) (2); Reg. Sec. 1.170A-11 (Q).

Johnson, O. E. "Business Corporations and Philanthropy." *Journal of Business* 39 (1966), 496–504.

Logsdon, J. M., M. Reiner, and L. Burke. "Corporate Philanthropy: Strategic Responses to the Firm's Stakeholders." *Nonprofit and Voluntary Sector Quarterly* 19 (Summer 1990), 93–109.

Maddox [McElroy], K., J. J. Siegfried. "The Community Influence on Corporate Contributions." *Public Finance Quarterly* 14 (October 1986), 394–414.

———. "The Effect of Economic Structure on Corporate Philanthropy." In *The Economics of Firm Size, Market Structure and Social Performance,* ed. J. J. Siegfried. Proceedings of a Conference. U.S. Government Printing Office, Washington, D.C. (July), 1980. Pp. 202–25.

———. "The Effect of Firm Size on Corporate Philanthropy." *Quarterly Review of Economics and Business* 25 (Summer 1985), 18–26.

Magat, R., ed. *Philanthropic Giving: Studies in Varieties and Goals.* New York: Oxford University Press, 1989.

Maher, P. "What Corporations Get by Giving." *Business Marketing* (December 1984), 80, 84–89.

McElroy, K. M., and J. J. Siegfried. "The Effect of Firm Size and Mergers on Corporate Philanthropy." In *The Impact of the Modern Corporation,* ed. Betty Bock, Harvey J. Goldschmid, Ira M. Millstein, and F. M. Scherer. New York: Columbia University Press, 1985.

Milani, K., and J. L. Wittenbach, "A Charitable Contribution Deduction Flowchart for Corporations—An Update." *Taxes - The Tax Magazine* 61 (May 1983), 319–24.

Mitchell, N. J. *The Generous Corporation: A Political Analysis of Economic Power.* New Haven: Yale University, 1989.

Mortensen, A. L. *Section 403(b) Manual.* 8th ed. Chicago: Dearborn Financial Publishing, 1988 and 1991.

Navarro, P. "Why Do Corporations Give to Charity?" *Journal of Business* 61, no. 1 (1988), 65–93.

Nelson, R. L. *Economic Factors in the Growth of Corporation Giving.* New York: National Bureau of Economic Research, 1970.

O'Connor, R. *Corporate Contributions in Smaller Companies.* Report No. 603. New York: The Conference Board. 1973.

O'Hare, B. C. "Good Deeds Are Good Business." *American Demographics* (September 1991), 38–42.

Oregon Economic Development Department. *Small Business Survey*. Salem, OR (June), 1989.

Payton, R. L. "Giving Gets Unfashionable." *New York Times*, February 2, 1988, sec. 3.

———. "Philanthropic Values." In *Philanthropic Giving: Studies in Varieties and Goals*, ed. R. Magat, 1989. Pp. 29–45.

Platzer, L. C., and M. N. Duffy. *Survey of Corporate Contributions, 1989 Edition*. Report No. 924. New York: The Conference Board, 1989.

Schiffer, D. "Business Support of the Humanities: A Global Perspective." In *Philanthropy and Culture: The International Foundation Perspective*, ed. K. D. McCarthy. Philadelphia: University of Pennsylvania Press [for The Rockefeller Foundation], 1984. Pp. 55–64.

Sheehan, R. "Those Fund Raising Businessmen." *Fortune* (January 1966), 148–50, 180-83.

Smith, C. "Not Selfish, Sophisticated." *New York Times*, 21 February 2, 2, sec. 3, 1988.

Smith, G. C. "Corporations Turning Charity into Cash." *Business and Society Review* 69 (Spring 1989), 42–45.

Smith, L. "The Unsentimental Corporate Giver." *Fortune* (September 1981), 129, 132, 137, 140.

Stendardi, E. J., Jr. "Corporate Philanthropy: The Redefinition of Enlightened Self-Interest." *The Social Science Journal* 29, no. 1 (1992), 21–30.

Sturtz, P. "Community Service on Company Time Growing Trend." *The Business Journal* (April 15, 1991), 23, 26.

Taft Corporate Giving Directory. 9th ed. Washington, D.C.: The Taft Group. 1988.

Troy, K. L. *Public Affairs in Financial Services*. Report No. 899. New York: The Conference Board, 1987.

———. *The Corporate Contributions Functions*. Report No. 820. New York: The Conference Board, 1982.

Useem, M. "The Decision Making and Allocation Process in Corporate Philanthropy." *The Constitution and the Independent Sector: Working Papers Spring Research Forum*. Washington, D.C.: INDEPENDENT SECTOR. employee, 1987.

———. "Market and Institutional Factors in Corporate Contributions." *California Management Review* 30 (Winter 1988), 77–88.

Van Auken, P. M., and R. D. Ireland. "Plain Talk about Small Business Social Responsibility." *Journal of Small Business Management* (January 1982), 1–3.

Wiltsek, N. L. *Corporate Charitable Contributions, Motivation for Giving, and Variables that Influence Giving Behavior among Small, Privately Owned Businesses in San Francisco*. Master's Thesis. University of San Francisco, 1990.

6

Corporate Philanthropy and Business Performance

DAVID LEWIN AND J. M. SABATER

COMMUNITY INVOLVEMENT, EMPLOYEE MORALE AND BUSINESS PERFORMANCE

How, if at all, does a company's involvement in the community influence its performance as a business? How, if at all, does a company's employee morale influence its business performance? And, how, if at all, does the interaction of community involvement and employee morale influence a company's business performance? These questions are addressed in this chapter, both conceptually and empirically.

CONCEPTUAL FOUNDATIONS

To begin this inquiry, consider the relationship between employee morale (or satisfaction) and business performance. A voluminous literature exists on the subject of employee morale, and the vast bulk of this literature has been concerned with the determinants of morale (see, for example, Herzberg, 1966; Freund and Epstein, 1984; Lawler, 1986). Among the determinants of employee morale, employee participation or involvement in decision making has clearly received the most theoretical and empirical attention (Gershenfeld, 1987; Cotton et al., 1988; Lawler, Mohrman, and Ledford, 1992).

More recently, employee morale has been modeled and empirically studied in terms of its effects on organizational outcomes such as productivity, product quality, and financial performance (Wellins, Byham, and Wilson, 1991; Lawler, Mohrman, and Ledford, 1992; Gerhart, Milkovich, and Murray, 1992). In most of this work, employee morale is modeled as an intervening variable that links employee involvement/participation in decision making to measures of business performance (see, for example, Ichniowski, 1992).

By itself, employee morale (satisfaction) has not been consistently shown to be positively related to business performance. When treated as a consequence of employee involvement/participation in decision making—what may be labeled nonfinancial participation—or as a consequence of employee financial participation programs, however, morale has been shown in several recent studies to be significantly positively related to business performance and changes in business performance (Mitchell, Lewin, and Lawler, 1990; Levine and Tyson, 1990).

For the purposes of this chapter, we begin with the proposition that employee morale is a measure of *internal* employee involvement in decision making, and we model employee morale as being positively related to measures of business performance. Note that surveys of business executives and managers show that they strongly believe in a positive employee morale-business performance relationship (Lawler, Mohrman, and Ledford, 1992).

From this perspective, company community involvement can be conceptualized as a form of *external* involvement. Most of the literature on company involvement in the community places such involvement within the larger context of corporate social responsibility (CSR), and much of this literature is taken up with the question of whether or not companies should be so involved, the extent of such involvement, and the issue of "voluntary" versus government-mandated involvement (see, for example, Committee for Economic Development, 1971; "The Business Roundtable," 1981).

In addition, the CSR literature often features "values" debates between those who support and oppose company involvement in the community, respectively (Friedman, 1982; Marx, 1985; Chamberlain, 1975), while a portion of the business strategy literature focuses on the determination of a company's community involvement in the context of stakeholder analysis (Anshen, 1980; Scherer, 1982; Matthews, Goodpaster, and Nash, 1991).

When it comes to the relationship between company community involvement and business performance, very little of the academic literature focuses on this linkage, and few attempts have been made to examine this relationship statistically (for an exception, see Preston, 1978–1985). Moreover, business executives and managers rarely discuss company involvement in the community in terms of its relationship to business performance, and it appears that few executives and managers believe that company community involvement is positively related to company financial performance—especially when compared with executive and managerial views about the relationship between employee morale (internal involvement) and business performance (however, see McGuire, Sundgren, and Schneeweis, 1988).

For the purposes of this chapter, we treat company community involvement as a measure of external involvement and treat employee morale as a measure of internal involvement. We model company community involvement as being positively related to measures of business performance. Further, we hypothesize that company community involvement (external involvement) will be positively related to employee morale (internal involvement), and that the interaction of company community involvement and employee morale will be positively related to measures of business performance.

RESEARCH DESIGN AND DATA COLLECTION

A primary research design was used in this study and featured a series of mail survey questionnaires to gather data on company community involvement and employee morale. The financial performance data for this study were obtained from the COMPUSTAT financial performance file maintained by Standard and Poor's (which, in turn, obtains these data from its own survey of publicly held companies headquartered in the United States). The financial performance measures are for the business units (or, as Standard and Poor's labels them, business lines) of U.S.-based companies. While many measures of company financial performance are available (or may be calculated) from COMPUSTAT, we chose to use three such measures, namely, return on investment (ROI), return on assets (ROA), and productivity (PROD, calculated as net sales revenue divided by full-time equivalent employment). These are the main dependent variables used in this study.

The employee morale measure was originally constructed for a study of relationships between company human resource management policies/practices and business performance (Delaney, Lewin, and Ichniowski, 1989). Operationally, the measure of employee morale used here was the percentage of employees in a company who responded to the most recent employee opinion (morale) survey conducted by the company by indicating that they were "highly" or "completely" satisfied with the company. The scale used to elicit responses to this question was of the 1 = low, 5 = high type, and responses were gathered separately for four employee groups, namely, managerial, professional, clerical, and production. The overall employee morale measure for each company was weighted by the percentage of employees in each of these four categories and was constructed so as to range between an overall low of zero percent and an overall high of 100 percent.

The company community involvement measure took the form of an index ranging between zero and 18 points. The index score for each company was calculated based on responses to questions about the company's policies with respect to financial support for part-time employee involvement in the community; financial support for full-time employee involvement in the community (such as through "loaning" employees to community organizations for specified time periods); donations of equipment and supplies to community organizations; formal company programs to recognize employee voluntarism in the community; provision of financial grants and/or matching grants to community organizations; sponsorship of specific community programs, such as athletic programs, crime-fighting programs, rehabilitation programs, and drug prevention programs; and the presence of a specific business process for committing resources to community involvement programs and activities.

This company community involvement index and its components were developed through a review of the relevant literature, discussions with 12 executives, managers, and professional staff having community involvement/community relations responsibilities for their companies, a pretest of the index and component questions administered to this same group of executives, managers, and professional staff, a pretest of the community involvement survey among 30 companies not included in this study, and factor and cluster analyses to determine the independence of the constructs underlying the component questions of the index.

The employee morale and company community involvement variables served as the two key or "experimental" independent variables in this study. Other independent "control" variables included size of company, age of company, the company's primary industry classification, the company's capital/labor ratio, and the company's market share in its primary product group. Data for the dependent and independent (experimental and control) variables were collected at two points in time, namely, 1989 and 1991.

The sample of companies used in this study was a 10 percent sample drawn randomly from the business units included in the 1989 COMPUSTAT file stratified to reflect the industry composition of U.S.-based businesses in that year. The 1989 surveys of employee morale and community involvement yielded usable responses from 188 companies, or 61 percent of the original sample. Of these 188 companies, 156 fully responded to the 1991 surveys of employee morale and

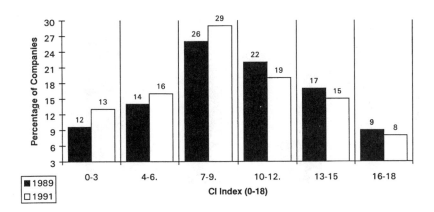

Figure 1
DISTRIBUTION OF COMPANIES
BY CI SCORES
1989 & 1991

community involvement, yielding an overall response rate of 51 percent (of the companies originally surveyed).

DATA ANALYSIS

Concerning what is perhaps the key variable of interest in this study, namely, company community involvement, Figure 1 shows the distribution of community involvement (CI) scores on the 0–18 point index. The 7–9 interval represents the modal score for companies included in this study, both in 1989 and 1991. Observe, however, that company community involvement, as measured by the index used here, declined between 1989 and 1991 (means of 9.4 and 8.5, respectively); this decline was statistically significant at the 5 percent level (that is, there is only one chance in twenty that the decline is not different from zero).

Figure 2 shows the distribution of companies by employee morale (scores) in 1989 and 1991. The modal interval of employee morale scores (on a 0 to 100 index) among the companies included in this study was 43–46 in 1989 and 39–41 in 1991. Observe that employee morale, as measured by the scaled survey questions used in this study, declined between 1989 and 1991 (means of 44.2 and 39.8, respectively); this decline was also significant at the 5 percent level (hereafter,

Figure 2
DISTRIBUTION OF COMPANIES
BY EMPLOYEE MORALE SCORES
1989 & 1991

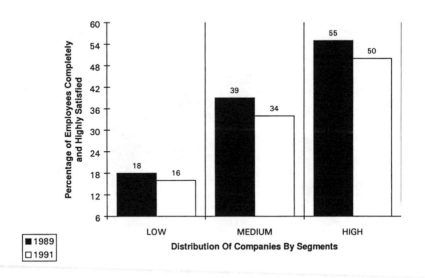

Figure 3
RETURN ON INVESTMENT (ROI) AND COMMUNITY INVOLVEMENT
1989 & 1991

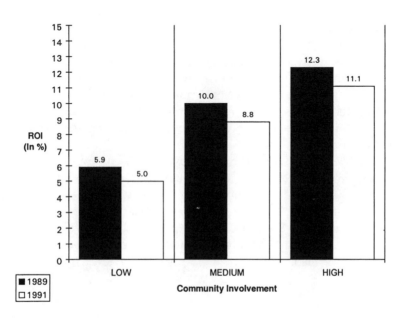

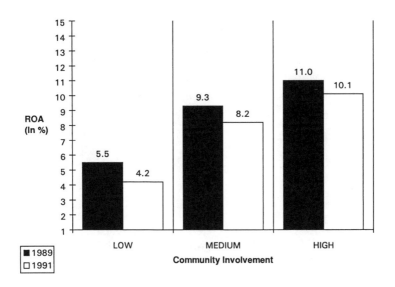

Figure 4
RETURN ON ASSETS (ROA) AND COMMUNITY INVOLVEMENT
1989 & 1991

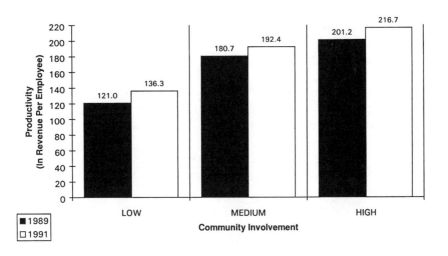

Figure 5
PRODUCTIVITY (REVENUE PER EMPLOYEE) AND COMMUNITY INVOLVEMENT
1989 & 1991

"statistical" significance will refer to the 5 percent level unless other-wise noted).

The simple cross-sectional relationships between community in-volvement and the three measures of business performance used in this study are summarized and presented in Figures 3, 4 and 5. Clearly, company community involvement and business performance were *positively* related, both in 1989 and 1991. The correlations between community involvement and the three measures of business perfor-mance are all positive, and five of six of these relationships are statisti-cally significant (the sixth correlation, between CI and PROD, was significant at the 7 percent level):

Year/Correlations Between:

	CI and ROI	CI and ROA	CI and PROD
1989	.31	.28	.26
1991	.33	.29	.28

These findings are important because, apparently for the first time, they were derived from a large database representative of companies and industries in the U.S. economy as a whole. Note further, however, that while the relationships between community involvement and re-turn on investment, return on assets, and productivity are positive and significant, they also appear (in Figures 3, 4, and 5) to be nonlinear; that is, movement from a low to a medium community involvement score is associated with larger increments in return on investment, return on assets, and productivity than is movement from a medium to a high community involvement score.

To more fully examine the relationships between community in-volvement and financial performance, a series of statistical (ordinary least squares [OLS]) regression analyses was performed in which return on investment, return on assets, and productivity, the dependent vari-ables, were estimated as functions of community involvement (the main independent variable) and the aforementioned control variables. The control variables were operationalized as follows:

- SIZE = company size, in dollar value of assets (in 1989 and 1991)
- AGE = company age, in years since founding (in 1989 and 1991)
- IND = the company's primary industry classification, with nonmanufacturing (NONMFG) = 1; manufacturing (MFG) = 0 (in 1989 and 1991) [note that other, finer industry classifications were used in some of the regression analyses but are not presented here

inasmuch as the results did not differ significantly from those obtained by using the NONMFG-MFG categories]

- CLR = capital/labor ratio, measured by investment in plant, equipment, and facilities divided by full-time equivalent employment (in 1989 and 1991)
- MKS = the company's market share in its primary product group, in percent of industry sales (in 1989 and 1991)
- e = an error term

TABLE 1

Ordinary Least Squares Regressions of Community Involvement (CI) and Other Variables on Business Performance Measures, 1989 & 1991 (standard errors in parentheses)

Independent Variable	Dependent Variable:					
	ROI		ROA		PROD	
	1989	1991	1989	1991	1989	1991
CONSTANT	4.08*	4.29*	4.63**	4.88*	17.2*	17.9**
	(1.93)	(2.02)	(1.96)	(2.16)	(8.3)	(7.7)
SIZE	-0.94	-0.89	-0.64	-0.48	-7.4	-6.5
	(0.71)	(0.69)	(0.48)	(0.39)	(5.5)	(4.6)
AGE	-2.05*	-2.07*	-1.89	-1.96*	-9.3	-10.7*
	(1.01)	(1.06)	(0.97)	(0.98)	(6.8)	(5.1)
NONMFG	-1.97	-1.99*	-2.04*	-2.08*	-10.6	-11.3*
	(1.03)	(0.97)	(1.01)	(1.02)	(6.1)	(5.5)
CLR	2.47*	2.54*	2.61*	2.58*	12.1*	12.4*
	(1.19)	(1.23)	(1.25)	(1.24)	(5.8)	(6.0)
MKS	2.07*	2.11*	2.19*	2.20*	11.8*	11.6*
	(1.02)	(1.04)	(1.08)	(1.17)	(5.7)	(5.2)
CI	2.38*	2.31*	2.09*	1.91	10.5	11.4*
	(1.14)	(1.11)	(1.02)	(0.99)	(6.1)	(5.9)
R-squared (n = 156)	.46	.43	.44	.42	.39	.37

* = Significant at $p = < .05$.
** = Significant at $p = < .01$.

The results from tests of three 1989 and three 1991 equations are presented in Table 1. To summarize, the capital/labor ratio and a company's market share are consistently and significantly positively related to return on investment, return on assets, and productivity in both 1989 and 1991. A company's place in the nonmanufacturing sector and company age are consistently negatively related to return on investment, return on assets, and productivity in both years. Company size is not significantly related to return on investment, return on assets, and productivity in both years. Community involvement is significantly positively related to return on investment in both years, to return on assets in 1989 (but not significantly related to return on assets in 1991), and to productivity in 1991 (but not significantly related to productivity in 1989).

Because the simple correlations between community involvement and the three measures of business performance suggested the presence of nonlinear relationships, an additional set of regression equations was specified and tested in which the entire sample of companies was split into two subsamples—"high" community involvement companies with scores above the mean, and "low" CI companies with

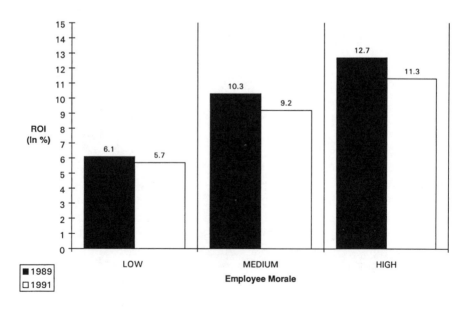

Figure 6
RETURN ON INVESTMENT (ROI) AND EMPLOYEE MORALE
1989 & 1991

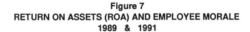

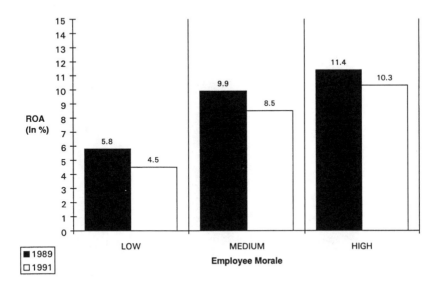

Figure 7
RETURN ON ASSETS (ROA) AND EMPLOYEE MORALE
1989 & 1991

scores below the mean. The 12 separate estimates that resulted from this procedure, for "high" and "low" community involvement companies in each of the three business performance measures in each year, consistently showed larger and more significant effects of community involvement in the "low" community involvement companies than in the "high" community involvement companies (coefficients were statistically significant in all six of the "low" community involvement equations and in three of the six "high" community involvement equations, and coefficients were larger for the "low" CI companies). These findings support those reported earlier, namely, that community involvement is related to return on investment, return on assets, and productivity in a nonlinear fashion.

Next, consider the correlations between employee morale (MORALE) and the three measures of business performance; these are summarized and presented graphically in Figures 6, 7, and 8. Clearly, employee morale and business performance were positively related, both in 1989 and 1991, but as in the case of community involvement the relationships appear to be nonlinear. The correlations between em-

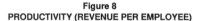

Figure 8
PRODUCTIVITY (REVENUE PER EMPLOYEE)

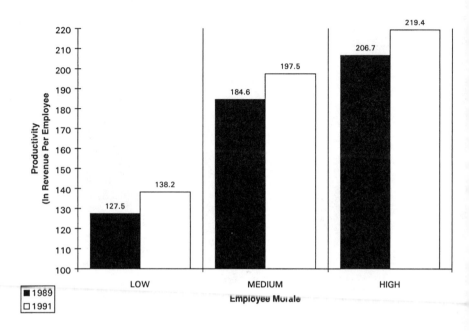

ployee morale and the three measures of business performance are all positive and statistically significant:

Year/Correlations Between:

	MORALE and ROI	*MORALE and ROA*	*MORALE and PROD*
1989	.29	.33	.29
1991	.31	.32	.33

For employee morale as well, we again carried out regression analyses in which return on investment, return on assets, and productivity served as the dependent variables, employee morale served as the main independent variable of interest, and the control variables were the same as those used previously. The results of these analyses are presented in Table 2.

To summarize, the capital/labor ratio and a company's market share are again consistently and significantly positively related to return on investment, return on assets, and productivity in both 1989 and 1991. A company's place in the nonmanufacturing sector and company age are again consistently negatively related to return on investment, return on assets, and productivity in both years. Company size is once more not significantly related to return on investment, return on assets, or productivity in both years. Employee morale is significantly positively related to return on investment in 1991 (and not significantly related to return on investment in 1989), significantly positively related to return on assets in both years, and significantly positively related to productivity in 1991 (and not significantly related to productivity in 1989).

TABLE 2

Ordinary Least Squares Regressions of Employee Morale (Morale) and Other Variables on Business Performance Measures, 1989 & 1991 (standard errors in parentheses)

Independent Variable	Dependent Variable:					
	ROI		ROA		PROD	
	1989	1991	1989	1991	1989	1991
CONSTANT	4.02*	4.16**	4.31*	4.36**	17.5**	17.1*
	(1.79)	(1.68)	(1.96)	(1.88)	(7.8)	(8.1)
SIZE	-0.87	-0.85	-0.61	-0.64	-6.9	-7.1
	(0.62)	(0.60)	(0.45)	(0.43)	(4.8)	(4.9)
AGE	-1.94*	-1.91*	-1.88*	-1.82	-10.4*	-9.9
	(0.92)	(0.88)	(0.86)	(0.93)	(5.1)	(5.4)
NONMFG	-1.84*	-1.86	-1.95*	-1.97*	-10.7*	-9.8
	(0.89)	(0.95)	(0.92)	(0.96)	(5.3)	(5.7)
CLR	2.37*	2.39*	2.44*	2.47*	11.8*	11.6*
	(1.14)	(1.17)	(1.19)	(1.20)	(5.8)	(5.6)
MKS	2.19*	2.23*	2.24*	2.26*	11.5*	11.3*
	(1.04)	(1.09)	(1.08)	(1.10)	(5.6)	(5.5)
MORALE	1.89	2.11*	2.18*	2.22*	9.8	10.6*
	(1.01)	(0.98)	(1.04)	(1.09)	(5.3)	(5.2)
R-squared (n = 156)	.34	.37	.42	.45	.40	.38

* = Significant at p = < .05.
** = Significant at p = < .01.

To explore the nonlinearity of relationships between employee morale and the three measures of business performance, we once again split the entire sample of companies, this time into "high" and "low" morale categories, using the mean employee morale score as the dividing line. Again, we estimated 12 separate regression equations for "high" and "low" employee morale companies on each of the three business performance measures in each year. These estimates consistently showed larger and more significant effects of employee morale in the "low" employee morale companies than in the "high" employee morale companies. (Coefficients were statistically significant in five of the six "low" employee morale equations and in three of the "high" employee morale equations.) These findings support the earlier findings that employee morale is nonlinearly related to return on investment, return on assets, and productivity.

We turn next to the relationship between community involvement and employee morale. As noted earlier, these measures were expected to be positively correlated, and they are. The correlations between CI and morale are significant and equal to 0.42 in 1989 and 0.44 in 1991 for the 156 companies included in the study.

In order to examine the combined effects of community involvement and employee morale on measures of business performance, we derived a community involvement–employee morale interaction measure and entered it into the regression equations. (This approach takes account of the fact that community involvement and employee morale are correlated with one another). The resulting effects of this variable on all measures of financial performance were positive and significant in both 1989 and 1991.

Year/Correlations With:

	ROI	ROA	PROD
1989	+0.37	+0.34	+0.35
1991	+0.36	+0.32	+0.33

These results indicate that company community involvement—external involvement—and employee morale—internal involvement—together are significantly positively associated with measures of business performance and, in conjunction with our previous findings, that the magnitude of the effects of the two variables taken together is larger than the effect of each considered separately.

Another possible interpretation of these results is that a company's business performance may influence community involvement and/or employee morale, rather than the other way around. Thus, we estimated an alternative series of (simultaneous) regression equations. In the first equation, community involvement served as the dependent variable and return on investment, return on assets, and productivity served as independent variables (together with the control variables previously mentioned). In the second equation, employee morale served as the dependent variable and return on investment, return on assets, and productivity served as the independent variables (again, with the control variables). Once the quantitative values of community involvement and employee morale were "estimated" in this way, those values of community involvement and employee morale were then entered as independent variables into the last of the regression equations in which return on investment, return on assets, and productivity served as the dependent variables, respectively; this was done for both the 1989 and 1991 data.

To summarize the results, community involvement and employee morale continued to be positively related to return on investment, return on assets, and productivity, though the magnitudes of the coefficients declined compared to the results from the original (ordinary least squares) regression analyses. Nevertheless, the coefficients on the community involvement and employee morale variables in the six business performance equations (three for 1989 and three for 1991) were statistically significant in four of the equations and nearly significant (10 percent level) in two of the equations. Thus, while business performance does "drive" some of a company's community involvement and employee morale, it does not drive all of it. Stated differently, community involvement and employee morale appear to positively and significantly influence a company's business performance even after the effects of business performance on community involvement and employee morale have been "netted" out.

To this point, we have been examining the data on community involvement, employee morale, and business performance strictly on a cross-sectional basis (that is, year by year). Our database also permits us to perform limited longitudinal analysis. For this purpose, we use the change in company return on investment, return on assets, and productivity between 1989 and 1991 as dependent variables, the change in community involvement and employee morale between 1989 and 1991 as the key independent variables of interest, and the changes in company size, age, industry, capital/labor ratio, and market share between 1989 and 1991 as the independent control variables.

First, it is notable that the changes in business performance between

1989 and 1991 for the 156 companies included in this study were significantly correlated with the changes in community involvement and employee morale during the same period. This is shown graphically in Figures 3–7, as follows:

Correlation between 1989–1991 Change in:

ROI and CI	*ROA and CI*	*PROD and CI*
.36	.33	.35

ROI and MORALE	*ROA and MORALE*	*PROD and MORALE*
.35	.37	.34

Further, the change in community involvement and the change in employee morale between 1989 and 1991 for the companies included in this study were also significantly positively related. (It was noted earlier that both community involvement and employee morale declined between 1989 and 1991 in the companies included in this study; so too did average return on investment and return on assets, while average productivity increased during this period.)

The findings from regression analysis of these change data are presented in Table 3. They show that change in community involvement was significantly positively associated with changes in return on investment and productivity between 1989 and 1991. The findings from testing the three business performance equations in which the change in employee morale was included are presented in Table 4. They show that change in employee morale was significantly positively associated with changes in return on investment, return on assets, and productivity between 1989 and 1991.

When a change-in-community-involvement–change-in-employee-morale interaction variable was included in the change-in-business-performance regression analyses, the effect of this variable on business performance was positive (ranging between .34 and .39) and statistically significant in all three equations. Finally, a simultaneous regression framework was again used in this longitudinal analysis of business performance, community involvement and employee morale. The results showed that changes in community involvement and employee morale continued to be statistically significant, though they had smaller effects on changes in the three measures of business performance once the effects of changes in business performance on changes in community involvement, and employee morale had been "netted" out.

TABLE 3

Ordinary Least Squares Regressions of Changes in Community Involvement (CI) and Other Variables on Changes in Business Performance Measures, 1989–1991 (standard errors in parentheses)

Independent Variable	Dependent Variable: Change in		
	ROI 1989-1991	ROA 1989-1991	PROD 1989-1991
CONSTANT	0.41* (0.19)	0.48** (0.20)	0.43** (0.18)
SIZE	-0.07 (0.05)	-0.09 (0.06)	-0.10 (0.07)
AGE	-0.09 (0.07)	-0.08 (0.06)	-0.06 (0.04)
NONMFG	-0.13 (0.07)	-0.16* (0.08)	-0.15* (0.07)
CLR	0.26* (0.12)	0.24* (0.11)	0.18* (0.08)
MKS	0.38* (0.17)	0.41** (0.16)	0.36* (0.17)
CI	0.32* (0.15)	0.29 (0.16)	0.30* (0.14)
R-squared	.35	.36	.35

(n = 156)

* = Significant at $p = < .05$.
** = Significant at $p = < .01$.

TABLE 4

Ordinary Least Squares Regressions of Changes in Employee Morale (Morale) and Other Variables on Changes in Business Performance Measures, 1989–1991 (standard errors in parentheses)

Independent Variable	Dependent Variable: Change in		
	ROI 1989–1991	ROA 1989–1991	PROD 1989–1991
CONSTANT	0.40* (0.18)	0.45** (0.18)	0.42** (0.17)
SIZE	-0.08 (0.05)	-0.09 (0.06)	-0.09 (0.06)
AGE	-0.10 (0.07)	-0.08 (0.05)	-0.07 (0.04)
NONMFG	-0.15* (0.07)	-0.14 (0.08)	-0.16* (0.08)
CLR	0.27* (0.13)	0.25* (0.12)	0.20* (0.09)
MKS	0.36* (0.17)	0.39** (0.16)	0.37* (0.18)
MORALE	0.30* (0.14)	0.34* (0.16)	0.33* (0.15)
R-squared (n = 156)	.33	.35	.34

* = Significant at $p = < .05$.
** = Significant at $p = < .01$.

Finally, in an attempt to probe more closely into the causal relationships among the key variables of interest included in this study, we performed several regression analyses which included certain "lagged variables." For example, one such analysis used the 1989 community involvement, employee morale, and control variables data with the 1991 (lagged) business performance data. Another such analysis used 1991 community involvement, employee morale, and control variables data with 1989 business performance data. The underlying question involved in such analyses is, "Can one or more variables, such as community involvement or employee morale, measured at one point in time (say, 1989) 'predict' the direction and/or magnitude of another variable, such as return on investment, return on assets, or productivity, measured at a later point in time (say, 1991)?"

What may be concluded from these analyses is that the business performance measures used here are slightly better able to "predict" company community involvement and employee morale than either community involvement or employee morale alone are able to "predict" business performance. However, the interaction of community involvement with employee morale is better able to "predict" company business performance than are any of the three measures of business performance able to "predict" community involvement, employee morale, or the interaction of community involvement with employee morale.

Thus, and in a practical vein, it is important to understand that the combination of a company's involvement in the community—external involvement—and the morale of its employees—internal involvement—can contribute to (raise or lower) the performance of business enterprises more than either community involvement or employee morale can alone. Our results also imply that the financial performance of a business can affect (raise or lower) its community involvement or its employee morale, or both. However, the combination of community involvement and employee morale has a larger effect on business performance than does business performance on the combination of community involvement and employee morale.

DISCUSSION AND CONCLUSIONS

A company's involvement (or lack of involvement) in the community is generally justified by appeals to social responsibility or ethical/value beliefs—that is, by the claim that it will be good (bad) for business. More often, perhaps, initiatives to raise a company's employee morale are undertaken in the belief that they will enhance business performance, though occasionally such initiatives are accompanied by appeals to social responsibility or ethics/values.

While beliefs about community involvement and employee morale can be (and are) strongly held by some executives and managers, there have been few systematic attempts to measure the effects of company community involvement on business performance (and vice versa), and also surprisingly few attempts to measure the effects of employee morale, per se, on business performance (and vice versa). When it comes to possible linkages, conceptual or empirical, between company community involvement and company employee morale, both the academic and practitioner landscapes are barren.

In this chapter, we have attempted to forge a conceptual link between company community involvement, or external involvement, and employee morale, or internal involvement. In other words, we ask the reader to consider whether or not there are two faces of involvement at work in a business enterprise, one external and community focused, the other internal and employee focused. While this conceptual link may seem strained to some and may be rejected out of hand by others, we have sought to explore this linkage empirically by examining recent data on business performance, community involvement, and employee morale drawn from 156 publicly held businesses headquartered in the United States.

Our findings, both cross-sectional and longitudinal, indicate that there are indeed systematic linkages among community involvement, employee morale, and business performance in business enterprises. To the best of our knowledge, this is the first time that such linkages have been demonstrated empirically. Moreover, the weight of the evidence produced here indicates that community involvement is positively associated with business performance, employee morale is positively associated with business performance, and the interaction of community involvement—external involvement—with employee morale—internal involvement—is even more strongly associated with business performance than is either "involvement" measure alone.

Our findings also shed some light on what might be labeled the "causality" or "feedback loop" issue in all of this. In particular, the longitudinal analysis and simultaneous regression analysis employed here lead us to conclude that business performance does to some extent "drive" or "leverage" both community involvement and employee morale. That is, businesses which experience increasing (decreasing) return on investment, return on assets, and/or productivity will also experience increasing (decreasing) involvement in the community and increasing (decreasing) employee morale—but not on a one-to-one basis. However, these same analyses also lead us to conclude that both community involvement and employee morale do to some extent drive or leverage business performance. That is, businesses which experience increasing (decreasing) involvement in the community and/or increasing (decreasing) employee morale will also experience increasing (decreasing) return on investment, return on assets, and/or productivity—

but, again, not on a one-to-one basis. Over time, then, each of these key variables has some causal or feedback effects on the other variables.

Rather than muddying the water, this conclusion seems to us to both enlighten us about the "business performance" argument for company community involvement, and to square with most social reality and social science research. Rarely in the real world of business or in the equally real world of social science are causal relationships proved conclusively. And, in those rare instances in which they seem to be proved, longer-term events, findings, and discoveries often wreak havoc with the "proof."

What we can perhaps best expect from the world of business enterprise and the world of social science research is a careful analytic "search for order" among social phenomena or, in our parlance, variables. Here, we have shown that systematic relationships exist among measures of business performance, community involvement, and employee morale in a relatively large, representative sample of U.S.-based companies; that these are positive rather than negative or indeterminate relationships; and that, finally, community involvement, employee morale, and business performance may have mutually reinforcing, causal, feedback effects on each other. This alone should spur other business executives and researchers to follow up and expand on this study to see if our findings are generalizable beyond the set of companies, time period, and geographical boundaries used here. In fact, and in the end, this too is one of the major reasons for our having undertaken this study of corporate philanthropy and business performance.

REFERENCES

Anshen, Melvin. 1980. *Corporate Strategies for Social Performance.* New York: Macmillan.
The Business Roundtable. 1981. *Statement on Corporate Responsibility.* New York: The Business Roundtable.
Chamberlain, Neil W. 1975. *The Limits of Corporate Responsibility.* New York: McGraw-Hill.
Committee for Economic Development. 1971. *The Social Responsibilities of Business Corporations.* New York: Committee for Economic Development.
Cotton, John L., David A. Vollrath, Kirk L. Froggatt, Mark L. Lengnick-Hall, and Kenneth R. Jennings. 1988. "Employee Participation: Diverse Forms and Diverse Outcomes," *Academy of Management Journal* 13, pp. 8-22.
Delaney, John Thomas, David Lewin, and Casey Ichniowski. 1989. *Human Resource Policies and Practices in American Firms.* Washington, D.C.: U.S. Department of Labor, Bureau of Labor-Management Relations and Cooperative Programs, BLMR #137.

Freund, William C., and Eugene Epstein. 1984. *People and Productivity.* Homewood, IL: Dow Jones-Irwin.

Friedman, Milton. 1982. *Capitalism and Freedom.* Chicago, IL: University of Chicago Press.

Gerhart, Barry, George T. Milkovich, and Brian Murray. 1992. "Pay, Performance, and Participation." In *Research Frontiers in Industrial Relations and Human Resources,* ed. David Lewin, Olivia S. Mitchell, and Peter D. Sherer. Madison, WI: Industrial Relations Research Association. Pp. 193-238.

Gershenfeld, Walter J. 1987. "Employee Participation in Firm Decisions." In *Human Resources and the Performance of the Firm,* ed. Morris M. Kleiner, Richard N. Block, Myron Roomkin, and Sidney W. Salsburg. Madison, WI: Industrial Relations Research Association. Pp. 123-58.

Herzberg, Frederick. 1966. *Work and the Nature of Man.* Cleveland, OH: World.

Ichniowski, Casey. 1992. "Human Resource Practices and Productive Labor-Management Relations." In *Research Frontiers in Industrial Relations and Human Resources,* ed. David Lewin, Olivia S. Mitchell, and Peter D. Sherer. Madison, WI: Industrial Relations Research Association. Pp. 239-71.

Lawler, Edward E., III. 1986. *High-involvement Management: Participative Strategies for Improving Organizational Performance.* San Francisco, CA: Jossey-Bass.

Lawler, Edward E., III, Susan A. Mohrman, and Gerald E. Ledford, Jr. 1992. *Employee Involvement and Total Quality Management.* San Francisco, CA: Jossey-Bass.

Lee, Lung-Fei. 1978. "Unionism and Wage Rates: A Simultaneous Equations Model with Qualitative and Limited Dependent Variables," *International Economic Review* 19, 415-33.

Levine, David I., and Laura D'Andrea Tyson. 1990. "Participation, Productivity, and the Firm's Environment." In *Paying for Productivity: A Look at the Evidence,* ed. Alan S. Blinder. Washington, D.C.: Brookings. Pp. 183-237.

Marx, Thomas G. 1985. *Business and Society: Economic, Moral, and Political Foundations.* Englewood-Cliffs, NJ: Prentice-Hall.

Matthews, J., Kenneth E. Goodpaster, and Laura L. Nash. 1991. *Policies and Persons: A Casebook in Business Ethics.* New York: McGraw-Hill.

McGuire, Jean B., Alison Sundgren, and Thomas Schneeweis. 1988. "Corporate Social Responsibility and Firm Financial Performance," *Academy of Management Journal* 31, 854-72.

Mitchell, Daniel J. B., David Lewin, and Edward E. Lawler, III. 1990. "Alternative Pay Systems, Firm Performance, and Productivity." In *Paying for Productivity: A Look at the Evidence,* ed. Alan S. Blinder. Washington, D.C.: Brookings. Pp. 15-88.

Preston, Lee E., ed. 1978-85. *Research in Corporate Social Performance and Policy,* vols. 1-8. Greenwich, CT: JAI Press.

Schmidt, Peter. 1978. "Estimation of a Simultaneous Equations Model with Jointly Dependent Continuous and Qualitative Variables: The Union-Earnings Equation Revisited," *International Economic Review* 19, 453-65.

Wellins, Richard S., William C. Byham, and John M. Wilson. 1991. *Empowered Teams: Creating Self-Directed Work Groups that Improve Quality, Productivity, and Participation.* San Francisco, CA: Jossey-Bass.

7

The Ethical Frame of Corporate Philanthropy

LANCE C. BUHL

THE CONTEXT

Corporate philanthropy is filled inherently with ethical challenges and opportunities. That does not say much about it. So, too, is the normal conduct of a company's business. In a sweeping and provocative survey of ethics and business, John R. Boatright (1993) implies that all business activities have an ethical dimension to them and that it is insufficient, logically and in fact, to think of business operations strictly from economic and legal perspectives. The moral or ethical perspective is also required, indeed, is built into both general and quite specific public expectations of corporate conduct. "[T]o think," he says, "that sound business decisions could be made solely from a perspective that excludes ethics is just as wrongheaded as it is to think that they could be made on the basis of ethical reasoning alone." Therefore, corporate decision making "should involve an integration of all three points of view: the economic, the legal, and the moral. Business ethics is simply the attempt to think clearly and deeply about ethical issues in business and to arrive at conclusions that are supported by the strongest possible arguments" (Boatright, p. 18). Tellingly, after laying out the major theoretical perspectives on ethics, Boatright's detailed analysis about how ethical theories might apply is focused on business activities and situations that have nothing to do with corporate philanthropy.

Considering corporate philanthropy in the larger context of corporate ethics is eminently sensible. Corporate philanthropy is too frail a reed to support the whole burden of ethical demands on business. I know of no one who thinks it can. The ethical requirements for a business are, as Boatright suggests, part of the social contract between society and the engines of economic production it sanctions. This is understood even by classical economists, the descendants of Adam Smith. Surely, they would argue, creating wealth and value for communities by producing goods and services that society needs and values is both the chief economic and, at base, ethical function of a business. And, they might add, the more efficiently such goods and services are provided, the more responsible and ethical. Most of Smith's heirs are also likely these days to concede that efficiency (defined as both a business and a social virtue) must take into due account quality, fair pricing, customer satisfaction, honest dealings with suppliers, environmental quality, and observance of pertinent laws.

A company which fails to honor these considerations actively and consistently can hardly establish a credible claim to ethical behavior no matter how generous it may be in support of its communities through charitable grant making, social investing, sponsorships, and encouragement of employee volunteering. Corporate grant making and associated activities do not and cannot substitute for the ethical conduct of a company's central economic functions.

This understanding of things explains why "corporate social responsibility" is not corporate philanthropy's exclusive domain. Ronald Litke (1994, p. 36) points out that "evaluating companies by 'socially responsible' measures is . . . rather difficult, because the term itself seems inclusive of anything beyond maximizing profit." While the notion that American corporations can play philanthropic roles is nearly as old as this century, it is only since the late 1950s or early 1960s that they have been projected not only as economic entities but "by virtue of their size, their resources and their impact on the society . . . important instruments to achieve a number of societal tasks" (Report of the Task Force on Corporate Social Performance, p. v). Boatright devotes only one chapter to the subject of corporate social responsibility. Following the categorization defined in an influential 1971 Committee on Economic Development (CED) report, he envisions corporate philanthropy as part of an "outer circle" of rather diffuse responsibilities for social problem solving that businesses are under some pressure increasingly to accept. These are differentiated from more clear-cut social responsibilities in directly business-relevant "inner" and "intermediate" circles of corporate activities (Boatright, p. 387). Similarly, in a largely forgotten but still highly relevant and important set of statements, contributors to the U.S. Department of Commerce's 1980 Report of the Task Force on Corporate Social Performance treat corporate social responsibility as a very broad concept.

Again, corporate grant making per se, is but one piece, briefly mentioned, of a much larger whole. Indeed, one contributor, former Aetna Casualty and Life CEO John Filer, argues that where, once, most corporations "viewed social responsibility as an important but separate pursuit, to be taken care of largely by charitable gifts and community services, now [w]e must bring social responsibility into our day-to-day operations and make it a part of business decisions" (Report, p. 80).

What can we draw from this broader context of corporate ethics and social responsibility? First, corporate grantmakers should take regular doses of humility. They operate in a tiny corner of the corporate universe. It is altogether arguable, for example, that a plant manager, by running an efficient, clean, safe, environmentally responsible shop, may contribute more social good to her community than the contributions officer can ever manage.

Second, it is nonetheless fair to conclude that a company can hardly establish full ethical credentials without also demonstrating its support for community problem solving *beyond* the normal course of business operations. If the word of CEOs is not enough, we can look to students of the subject, like Boatright (1993, pp. 390–401) and Robert C. Solomon and Kristine R. Hanson (1988, pp. 181, 192–98), for external confirmation. They go to great and convincing lengths, for example, to deflate the well-publicized thesis of Milton Friedman that the corporation's only true social responsibility is to make a profit for its owners. Here, despite the scant treatment it receives, corporate philanthropy and the role of the corporate grantmaker receive their legitimization, though by indirection.

Third, the scope for business involvement in a community's efforts to improve the quality of life for its citizens is broad. It extends to the need for a well-educated and trained citizenry, for a people's access to the range of competent medical and social services, for cultural recreation, for protecting and restoring the earth and its environment's capacity to sustain life, for repairing the social fabric torn by economic dysfunctions and social dislocations, and for institutions that bolster the capacity for civic virtue.

Fourth, Boatright and other corporate ethicists emphasize the importance of clear and deep thinking about corporate social responsibility and ethics. There is more to make of this later on, but for now it is enough to stress the importance of active, open moral reasoning by corporate grantmakers about what they do and why they do it.

Fifth, while it is necessary to understand the power of the corporation as a company of people with enormous resources, it is essential to disaggregate that company when fixing the locus of ethical responsibility.

Boatright and each of the four corporate CEOs who contributed to the U.S. Commerce's Report on Corporate Social Performance essentially place the responsibility for corporate ethics and social responsibility widely and, more importantly, at the individual level. Boatright talks about corporate decision making and illustrates his text with real and hypothetical decision makers, at all levels of a corporation. The four businessmen—then CEOs Reginald Jones of GE, John Filer of Aetna, Thornton Bradshaw of ARCO, and Walter Haas of Levi Strauss—describe, variously, the ways in which their companies assign expectations to employees and managers. It is not, after all, the business that acts ethically or unethically, despite the heft of the fiction that a corporation is a "person." It is the company of men and women who compose the business and who, collectively and individually, act or fail to act with due respect for ethical standards. I will have occasion, as well, to comment on the personal ethical responsibilities that fall on the shoulders of corporate contributions and/or foundation officers—again by virtue of the power to influence that comes with their jobs. Power—the ability to alter human events—is at the core of all moral and ethical issues.

Sixth, however well they establish the tone of debate, none of these considerations is much help to corporate grantmakers in coming to specific terms with their own job and associated ethical responsibilities. We need to look elsewhere, primarily to the words that seem to rule how current CEOs and fellow contributions officers justify and defend corporate grant making.

CLASH OF PARADIGMS

What concerns me is that today's dominant justification for corporate philanthropy, in fact, is likely to make the job and its possibilities something considerably smaller, more ethically cramped and less generative than, by the rights of power allotted to corporations, ought to be the case. This interpretation—a ruling paradigm, stated with increasing frequency and certitude at meeting after meeting of corporate grantmakers since the late 1980s—holds that corporate social responsibility is a very good thing, but its real and only purpose is self-interested. The company contributes time, talent, and treasury to community projects because these are means to advance the company's business purposes. If it cannot be demonstrated that there is a positive connection between these "investments," then there is no justification for maintaining them, much less increasing them.

My experience and study of the ethics of corporate grant making lead me to call for a reconsideration of this frame of reference. Were I a physicist, I'd argue for a paradigm shift. Almost clichéd these days, "paradigm" nonetheless is a handy, evocative word, sufficient to the purpose. The crucial shift involves no more than a subtle alteration in wording the way one justifies the corporate grant-making function: from "doing good for the community by doing well for the company" to "doing well for the company by doing good for the community." The first formulation is the chief tenet or explanatory assumption of what I will call the "reality" school. This idea is advanced by its adherents on grounds that this is how the corporate world "really" is. Its dominance of this paradigm in corporate America was established beginning in the late 1980s as a number of leading industries experienced severe bottom-line traumas. The second formulation is the basic tenet of what I call the "transformational" paradigm, transformational in its effect on the ways in which corporate grantmakers define the ethical content of their missions. Arguably, it held the dominant position pretty securely in the 1970s (perhaps somewhat earlier) and through the mid-1980s.

The critical point here is that this small shift in wording to describe how "good" is achieved drives the outcomes of basic definitional issues—whether and over how long a period of time the company will use the contributions and associated programs as a tool to help get at root social problems, how the program will be assessed, and what the role of the corporate grantmaker will be.

These two ways of justifying the contributions function may be seen, in one sense, as defining two poles of a continuum from, at its most constrained, corporate philanthropy as an extension pure and simple of unalloyed self-interest and image making toward grant making, at the mid-range, as a largely reactive charitable endeavor, to grant making, at its most generative, as active engagement in issues surrounding the relative absence of social and economic justice for millions of our fellow citizens.

My fearful impression is that corporations tend, these days, to fall in greatest number from most constrained to mid-range. Some, however, maintain programs that gravitate toward the generative pole; some have done so for a decade or longer. Moreover, they have discovered satisfactory links between doing good in this sense and doing well in the self-interested sense. But, what is important about their example is that they have moved beyond seeing options along a simple con-tinuum, one I've already denoted as superficial. Consciously or not, they seem to be working intellectual space described in theory by Charles Hampden-Turner in *Charting the Corporate Mind* (1990).

Hampden-Turner argues that, in most cases in organizations, con-flicts over values have to do with equally weighted options and that a productive way of coming to terms with them is to establish a dialogue between the adherents of both values. This dialogue aims, not at eliminating the rightful claims of either value, but at developing solutions which fully integrate both. In the context of corporate philanthropy, this means accepting the equal validity of the needs of the community and the interests of the company. Think of the task, Hampden-Turner suggests, as developing a 10/10 solution in an intellectual space of possibilities described by a matrix where community needs and corporate interests each define one of the two axes (from 0 "totally unsatisfied" to 10 "totally satisfied"). Think of it, also, as an ongoing dialogue in which the question of how to make this grant or that grant program of more utility to either company or community or to both is as germane as how to eliminate grants or programs which do not satisfy the interests of one or the other well.

What this exercise accomplishes, if done honestly and with some rigor, is to get corporate grantmakers and those they report to beyond the trap which both practitioners and scholars tend to fall into by thinking of the corporate contributions function within too narrow a framework of responsibilities, opportunities, and potential outcomes. The continuum of possibilities tends to become one of polarized thinking, pure self-interest or simple pursuit of the charitable impulse. The ruling paradigm, in not admitting the independent validity and claim on corporate resources of community need, has great difficulty in understanding that active engagement in serving the ends of a more just society might be a legitimate interest and set of behaviors for corporations. Those working within its tenets risk creating profiles of corporate social responsibility that, subordinated to the public relations concern for comparative advantage in the marketplace, are without substance, irrelevant to social problem solving and, ironically, do not contribute much over the long run to advancing the good names of their companies. Conversely, if the adherents of the transformational paradigm cannot admit the validity of corporate self-interest, they run the risk of developing plans and programs which do not take root in their corporate cultures, cannot take advantage of the full range of resources corporations can bring to bear on targeted social issues, and, ironically, are too short-lived to make a real impact on those issues.

THE CASE AGAINST AND FOR
A TRANSFORMATIONAL PARADIGM

To extend the range of possibilities and confront the practical and ethical territory defined by Hampden-Turner may be an unwelcome challenge to the corporate contributions officer. Why should he take on the arduous business of concerning himself with the potential of a transformational ethic? After all, she might argue, one can justify publicly the validity of any profile of corporate support. A little bit of PR does that trick. Besides, hasn't society already defined a kind of parity of "worthiness" among charitable causes and tax-exempt organizations, one that is codified, even sanctified, by federal and state tax code treatment? So, who is to tell him that fighting cystic fibrosis or maintaining a vibrant performing arts sector is any less important than reinvesting in low-income neighborhoods, assuring equity in primary and secondary education, or reforming the criminal justice system? There are, after all, truly deep needs across the spectrum of human challenges.

Moreover—and here's the crux of resistance and a central idea of the "reality" paradigm—corporate contributions officers might and usually do argue that we are dealing with a corporation, not a foundation in the true sense. (For all practical purposes the distinction between line-item corporate contributions functions and corporate foundations, the great majority of which are pass-through entities in any case, is meaningless. They are expected to serve the corporate interests and are managed accordingly. Even substantially endowed corporate foundations are subject to strong corporate pressures and expectations for some sort of corporate payback in goodwill or name enhancement.) These are corporate funds which might otherwise be paying for operating costs, or investments in new ventures and other profit-seeking vehicles, or for dividends to shareholders. So, let us not be naive. Corporate self-interest *is* the controlling dynamic. The contributions program must in the first and final instance be organized to satisfy corporate, not community and charitable, needs. Do the corporate thing first, then worry about what is right.

Finally, from this latter and quite prevalent line of argument as well as from a healthy respect for one's own security flows the argument that the job of the corporate contributions officer is that of corporate servant. She should work the community on behalf of the company. He should develop a grant-making program that is most sensitive to the political and public relations interests of the company. That is what he is paid for and what line managers, staff managers, and senior executives expect and understand. In the context of this formulation of the matter, thinking otherwise is arguably irresponsible, besides being onerous and personally risky.

Let me reply, first, by admitting that these arguments are not without validity. The expanse of charitable needs is vast. Companies do pay the freight and do so in a highly competitive environment for internal funds. At one level, in fact, one need not challenge the paradigm, but could be content worrying less about the absolute profile of giving than the nature and consistency of the process companies use to struggle with what their respective corporate grant-making programs ought to stand for and accomplish in a world of need.

But against all this I persist in believing that problem solving out of the new paradigm is necessary. The contributions function should be thought of in different terms, which are, incidentally, both serviceable and have at least as much grounding in reality, even in hardheaded thinking about corporate self-interest, as the opposing paradigm I have tried to capture above. The reason for a paradigm that is more inclusive, which in its simplest form might be stated as "do the right thing first, then worry about the corporate interest," has to do with power and privilege. Because of that, the mind-set one begins with when exploring the Hampden-Turner matrix is critical.

Here I will recapitulate arguments I made as a corporate contributions officer for BP America in the previously cited "Ethics at the Margins" (1989), in "Leadership Opportunities for Grants Officers" (1991), and "Ethical Considerations in Corporate Support for Communities," penned for an international conference in 1992 on the Ethics of Business in a Global Economy.

First, it hardly needs saying that corporations are powerful institutions, whose potential for massive harm as well as great good is awesome. There exists a huge discrepancy, perceived and real, between the abilities of corporations to influence public policy and those of ordinary citizens to do so. The capacity of corporate figures to influence is well understood by the public and by corporate decision makers to be roughly proportional to their economic might. Business executives enjoy relatively open access to and influence at the table of public decision making affecting the distribution of social goods. The noted Yale political scientist Charles E. Lindblom was deeply impressed by this form of power and of the privileged position businessmen are granted in free-market economies. He argued that the corporate CEO becomes "a kind of public official and exercise[s] what . . . are public functions" (Lindblom, 1977, p. 172). The uses of power, particularly when discrepancies in its ownership are broad and pervasive, are richly productive of moral and ethical dilemmas. Thus, at its very core, the work of corporate contributions officers is saturated with ethical meaning just by virtue of representing powerful institutions and advising powerful people.

Second, to recapitulate the discussion of corporate social responsibility developed at the beginning of this chapter, one piece of the social contract between society and corporations in America is related to the exercise of corporate might—and the constrained role of government, compared to other nations—and involves the social role of companies. In return for a fairly unconstrained marketplace and the license to hold on to the lion's share of their earnings, corporations are expected to help support the civic problem-solving and service-providing capacity of their communities, as expressed through nonprofit, tax-exempt organizations. This understanding has been validated by corporate practice across the twentieth century and encouraged by tax law.

Third, corporate contributions officers are key players in working out the details of this aspect of the social contract. This is so even in terms of the ruling paradigm. While not the only players here, they are the ones which community representatives often know best, the ones who manage the contributions process internally, and who insist on grantee responsibility externally. Very often, they greatly influence who in the community benefits from corporate contributions and an even broader array of corporate resources (credibility, volunteer assistance, access to other power brokers and sources of capital, in-kind goods, and services). Corporate contributions officers, therefore, represent the corporate power to the community in special ways. In this sense, if in no other, they are privileged power players. This fact underscores and reinforces the ethical and accountable dimensions of their positions and work.

There are, then, sufficient grounds in discrepant social and political power, the social contract regarding corporate social responsibility, and the privileged position of the corporate grantmaker to justify building an alternative framework for thinking about the contributions function. In working through the Hampden-Turner matrix, it is important from this perspective to observe a self-restraining ordinance, based on the fundamental ethical injunction to do no harm. That is, corporate officers and grantmakers should conduct the exercise (within the terms of the second or transformational paradigm) by assuming from the outset that satisfying the—or some specified—social good is the task to accomplish before satisfying the corporate interest. Alternatively, if the dialogue on the self-restraining ordinance is not productive, then they should hold out as the proper test of the sufficiency of the 10/10 solution whether the social good in question has standing on its own merits (in the eyes of corporately disinterested, but knowledgeable representatives of the community). In the latter case, the rule would be, not to sacrifice the corporate interest, but to work at the problem with the recognition that corporations carry disproportionate power to affect (for ill as well as good) the fate of communities and that community interests have equal standing.

But, the rationale is not complete. Needed is an argument—and like the justifications for the ruling paradigm, it is no more than an unprovable assertion—about the self-interests of corporations in affirmatively contributing to creating a more just social order. Here I will only sketch it out.

The argument begins with the already well-rehearsed thesis that corporations, as legal instruments of society, are intimately connected to the welfare of their communities—through market exchanges, employees, taxes, and uses of society's multiple natural and human resources. The argument proceeds to the thesis that corporations owe something more to society than high-quality, cleanly produced, fairly priced goods and services. They owe, as part of the social contract mentioned above, investments in those nonprofit mechanisms which produce "social goods" that society needs but should not produce through the public sector.

These two theses are not foreign to the prevailing "reality" paradigm. The third is new and undoubtedly controversial. It holds that corporate self-interest is bound to social justice if, for no other reason, than that the costs to it in conditions of the many and profound dislocations associated with injustice are becoming intolerable. Indeed, one may plausibly reason that such costs—through increased taxes, decreased security for its employees and property, and the greatly increased costs of doing business—are always the price of injustice to any society's citizens and organizations. To turn this notion around, corporate social investments in programs and processes which ameliorate (and, more optimistically, reduce or resolve) poverty and inequality (even peace) benefit not only society but corporations, at least as much as, if not more than, social investments in the "safe" nonprofit enterprises—hospitals, colleges, and universities, the leading performing and visual arts organizations, and the normal range of social service providers. Understand, this is not an argument against the latter causes, but for extending the range of legitimate objects for corporate attention and support. On this extension rides the alternative paradigm.

ETHICAL RESPONSIBILITIES
OF THE CORPORATE GRANTMAKER

What matters, ultimately, is the corporate grantmaker's ability to reduce all this to her own situation. They must, as Boatright and other ethicists put it, think clearly and deeply about their ethical situations. What worries me most about the ruling paradigm is that it tends to muddy thinking about roles and responsibilities. If the bottom line for corporate grantmakers is truly whether and how much grants and related activities contribute to the corporation's bottom line, then how one defines the integrity of the function, the nature of one's position, the nature and quality of one's relationships to the community and its many spokespersons is greatly circumscribed. I would argue that working out the transforming paradigm and using the self-restraining rule in working through the matrix of values opens up far more possibilities for creative and productive definitions of the function, one's role and one's dealings with the community, definitions which ultimately better serve both company and community.

These thoughts suggest that corporate grantmakers engage in a two-step process as they construct guidelines for ethical and accountable behavior.

1. *Define the "essential integrity" of the contributions function.* It is crucial, as in any paradigm shift, to begin by believing as a matter of faith that something is other than you've been led to believe. In this case, it is that the contributions function is not a business function. Like many other staff functions, it does not have bottom-line accountability; its work cannot be measured by revenue-production measures. In this respect, the corporate philanthropy function may be more akin to the basic research function of the company. Both are clearly cost centers; neither are likely to have quick payoffs; both require long-term commitment. Unlike basic research, however, contributions' payoffs will probably always have inferred rather than direct measures. There may be intermediate, image-related measures that are relevant, but they are "soft" and sum more by argumentation than by verifiable results. The function may—should—be run in a business-like manner, but that is an issue of how, not what.

The problem with the "reality" paradigm is that it skews the terms of evaluation almost impossibly by setting up unachievable expectations. I have yet to find convincing arguments from any source that there is a provable relationship between corporate philanthropy and a corporation's bottom line. It is important here to observe the distinction between grant making (giving funds away) and corporate social investing (committing dollars to community-building but profit-generating ventures, such as the purchase of federal low-income-housing tax credits). Clearly in the latter case, one can calculate the specific return (or loss) to the company. How does one do that, except by highly stretched inferences about grants to this or that nonprofit? And even when you mix the two forms of community support together, how do you credibly calculate the nature and value of increased goodwill, when both forms together account for a very small part of the full corporate budget or its profile in the community? Is it even thinkable that a contributions officer can legitimately document that her company's sales are higher because of grant-making activities? Or that this or that public policy maker listens more carefully to our petition for relief or redress? or solely because of that grant making?

Probably the closest a company has been able to document some relationship between a positive profile of community support and a payoff in specific public policy making relates to Dayton-Hudson's popular and successful appeal to the Minnesota legislature and governor for special legislation to protect it from a hostile take-over by a foreign company. However, none of the documentation that I am aware of supports the case that corporate grant making was anything but one of the many threads that composed Dayton-Hudson's total profile and reputation in its communities. Contributions by the Dayton-Hudson Foundation were consistent with and part of the company's total commitment to solid corporate citizenship, but not measurably so (Goodpasture, 1990). If anything, this case proves the rules, first, that corporate social responsibility is much larger than contributions and, second, that quantifying the impact on the company of grants and social investments is not a productive way of measuring the importance of those activities. A literal host of conceptual and methodological puzzles having to do with isolating and measuring supposed relationships with any certainty stand in the way of tying contributions even to reputation, much less the bottom line. Where does that leave the corporate grantmaker and the philanthropic program if relationship to corporate profitability has been the basic assessment measure?

More pertinent to the essential integrity of the function is to understand that its fundamental and unique nature is to operate in the borderland between the corporation and the community. As a key agency for defining a significant part of the social contract for corporate social responsibility, its program officers act as intermediaries between the interests of the company and those of the community. Working properly, they translate company and community to one another and work to find common ground and interests each has for a healthier, more just social order.

Corporate grantmakers, operating in this sense, must assume that the interests of the company and the community are at least coequal, as well as codependent. And this, as we have seen, is the core of the new paradigm. Thinking of community and corporate interests of equal validity also translates, it seems to me, to the level of personal ethics. At issue is the personal bearing of the corporate grantmaker toward community members, some of whom are prospective grantseekers and, in lesser number, even grantees. They must create an environment in the corporation where spokespersons of those parts of the community most at risk get, at a minimum, a respectful hearing from time to time, and perhaps support in one form or another. Certainly, fair treatment of community representatives is a basic test of the adequacy of the ethical stance of grantmakers.

Truth be told, discussion of "essential integrity" and its implications undoubtedly seems like splitting hairs to John Q. Public. Neither he nor more than a few of his cocitizens is much interested in whether the corporate grantmaker is working out of the current "reality" paradigm or the one I'm arguing for. Who really cares whether a donation is logged as a corporate expense or a charitable contribution? So long as the money flows to the community in one form or another, what's the point? The point is the ability to maintain the integrity of the contributions' function over time. If the chief or sole criterion in deciding the corporate profile for grant making and social investing is how the company is benefited, then the ability to consider society's well-being, to think about and plan for the long-term health of corporate programs, and to act with full awareness of both the company's and the community's interests in the borderland between the two are deeply compromised. The range of ethical action and accountability is attenuated.

2. *Once a corporate grantmaker has defined the integrity of the function, the essence of what gives it ethical standing, the remaining task is to develop or rewrite her job description and job "contract" accordingly.* To the traditional catalogue of effective management responsibilities that he must do and do well (planning, budgeting, policy making, personnel administration, networking, public and political relations), he needs to add responsibilities which reflect new roles as broker, educator, and ethicist or truthteller. Since she and her staff are the only people in the company who are paid to worry about the health of society and how to improve it—a duty which automatically sets them apart, making them living contradictions to the company's chief ethos of building profits—these additional roles are necessary tools of the trade.

Brokering stems directly from the fact that the contributions function works at the margins—between company and community. To make communities better places to live and thrive for everyone calls for much more than grants. Required are partnerships to leverage dollars to best effect. Corporations can play important roles in identifying the need for partnerships, building them, supporting them, and ensuring that they produce intended results. These are all brokering functions, and the wise contributions officer learns (or finds) associated skills in mediation, negotiation, and needs assessment.

Educating comes with the territory. The corporate grantmaker should learn to be an effective teacher for the company's management and employees about parts of the community that they may not know, about aspects of corporate social responsibility that fall within your competence, about the mission of the contributions function and how it works. As with any decent educational process, the communication needs to be two-way. Corporate grantmakers should educate themselves and their staffs about their companies, their respective cultures, their quite legitimate interests, and the range of human and other resources it can put at the disposal of community problem solving.

The educational process should also be interactive, and here I am reminded of the possibilities for productive organizational learning that Peter M. Senge describes in his seminal study on systems. For instance, Senge reminds us of the difference defined by David Bohm between dialogue, the open-ended interchange between people in which all assumptions may be challenged, and discussion, where interchange is directed toward decision (Senge, 1990, pp. 239–49). By fostering dialogue as well as discussion about grant making within the company, the corporate contributions staff, as a logical extension of networking, increases the probabilities of building a constituency and a culture which will support the new contributions paradigm beyond a generational half-life (approximately 5 years).

Being an ethicist is a piece of the educator's role. As Robert Dunn and Judith Babbitts (1991) suggest, the role means, minimally, including in ethical and accountability guidelines a section on how contributions staff should behave as human beings when dealing with grantseekers and other people from the community; and training and evaluating for compatible results. More important, being a truthteller means saying things to senior managers that they're unlikely to hear from anyone else about community problems, their and the corporation's stake in them, and some unpleasant truths about what is and what is not a corporate interest. As an example, it's important from time to time to state the distinction between values central to a company's well-being (in both the short and the long run) and those that are merely expedient. More specifically, a grants officer may be called upon to resist the peculiar and hollow penchant—as part of what the social and political essayist Robert Hughes calls the "culture of complaint"—to cast corporations as "victims" of today's social and political order.

On a more positive note, the ethicist's role suggests fostering a sense of stewardship in self, staff, and others in corporation. Here the challenge is to stimulate and reinforce active moral and ethical reasoning about the conflicts between values choices. Learning—or hiring—the skills associated with working through the values dilemmas is handy, whether one uses the Hampden-Turner matrix exercise discussed earlier or some other approach.

The stakes here are higher than producing a heady set of discussions or training exercises. Where, for instance, is the line which separates a grant made for which the interests of the community predominate and one made primarily to satisfy the self-interests of the CEO's wife, the company's government relations function, or an operating unit which faces stiff community opposition to expanding one of its plants? The grantmaker as ethicist should actively identify and work through such real ethical dilemmas that almost inevitably arise in one form or another over the course of any year. If he or she does not, the essential integrity of the contributions function is eroded. Doing well for the company by doing good in the community sounds easier than it is.

Finally, truthtelling compels the corporate grantmaker to guard against letting all this transformational stuff go to her head. She's not better than, more special than, or morally superior to, other corporate players. The point is not to denigrate either actor, but to underscore the fact that the corporate contributions officer has a privileged position from which to view and help ameliorate the company's power to influence its communities.

In any event, one should approach the job with an understanding that the employment contract may not last long. Working at the margins, against the natural grain of a corporation's predominant revenue-producing culture, is inherently uncertain, especially at a time when corporate cultures are notoriously unstable. In this sense, there's no more job security in operating out of the more traditional contributions paradigm than in opting for the transformational one.

What I've explored is the rationale for an alternative paradigm for corporate philanthropy, a paradigm of active engagement in addressing society's worst dislocations. Acting out of that paradigm, in my judgment, offers great potential for enlivening the contributions function, making it a center for corporate learning about the community, a productive extension of the company in social problem solving, and a place in which, at the end of the day, one can claim the integrity of one's calling as a special kind of broker between diverse corporate and community interests.

POSTSCRIPT ON A RESEARCH AGENDA

By establishing a fuller view of social accountability, the new paradigm opens up new possibilities for a more relevant scholarship about corporate citizenship than I've seen to date. It is a scholarship that, while interested in probing for connections between corporate contributions and company reputation and/or in identifying a logic in the supposed relationship between grant making and corporate performance, devotes most of its efforts to helping corporate decision makers in any number of other, more prosaic but also more practical ways.

An agenda along these lines might take up such questions as (1) What tend to be the patterns in relationships between definitions of corporate social responsibility and various profiles of corporate philanthropy? How do these relationships affect the terms of the paradigms ruling the latter and the range of program options which corporate grantmakers are allowed to pursue? What can be learned from mismatches between definitions of corporate social responsibility (or citizenship) and corporate philanthropy?

(2) What are the relationships between intracompany justifications of corporate philanthropy (paradigms) and size, type, and scope of actual grant-making programs? How are competing claims of the needs of community and the interests of the corporation worked out? As level, type, and scope of engagement with the community change, do paradigms also change and in what ways? Do explanatory paradigms for grant making affect risk taking in grant making and social investments? If so, how?

(3) What are effective forms of engagement by corporate contributions and corporate social investment programs in society's most critical challenges—public K–12 urban and rural education, poverty, criminal justice, community disinvestment, AIDS, and so on? How long do such programs tend to last? Who in the corporation gets involved in them and in what capacities? How are the programs evaluated and how is evaluative information used? How are these programs regarded within corporations by influential decision makers? How are these beliefs and associated commitments related to corporate reputation—passively, programmatically?

(4) What roles do managers of corporate philanthropy tend to play in the dynamics described in the preceding set of questions? What do "careers" in corporate philanthropy look like and how do they correlate with different explanatory styles and levels of social engagement? Who are the "successful" grantmakers—tenures longer than seven or eight years, reputations for active engagement in critical social problems—in American corporations? What strategies and tactics have these leaders used to gain the kinds of support necessary to build and maintain their programs? To what extent, if any, are they brokers, educators, ethicists? What other roles have been useful in building credibility?

(5) Specifically as to the ethics of corporate grant making, are there describable relationships, and patterns of those relationships, between explanatory styles (paradigms) for corporate philanthropy and styles of engagement with the community, its representatives, grantseekers, or other petitioners, other corporate and noncorporate grantmakers and investors? How do differing paradigms affect definitions of social need, social justice, and the responsibilities of companies to address them? How do corporate grantmakers approach ethical issues that affect their programs, their decisions, and their staffs? How do these approaches relate to the broader ethical environments of corporations? How prevalent is the truthtelling function in practice? What forms of it are most and least successful? What risks to the program and the careers of its staff are and are not involved and under which sets of circumstances?

R E F E R E N C E S

Boatright, John R. *Ethics and the Conduct of Business.* Englewood Cliffs, NJ: Prentice Hall, 1993.
Buhl, Lance C. "Ethical Considerations in Corporate Support for Communities." Paper presented at a conference on the Ethics of Business in a Global Economy, Columbus, OH, March 26, 1992.
———. "Ethics at the Margins." *Foundation News* 30, no. 4 (July-August 1989), 53-55.
———. "Leadership Opportunities for Grants Officers." In *The Corporate Contributions Handbook,* ed. James P. Shannon. San Francisco: Jossey-Bass, 1991.
Dunn, Robert H., and Judith Babbitts. "Being Ethical and Accountable in the Grantmaking Process." In *The Corporate Contributions Handbook,* ed. James P. Shannon. San Francisco: Jossey-Bass, 1991.
Goodpasture, Kenneth. *Dayton-Hudson: Conscience and Control.* Council on Foundations, 1990.
Hampden-Turner, Charles. *Charting the Corporate Mind: Graphic Solutions to Business Conflicts.* New York: The Free Press, 1990.
Lindblom, Charles E. *Politics and Markets: The World's Political-Economic Systems.* New York: Basic Books, 1977.
Litke, Ronald. "Shifting Standards." *Foundation News & Commentary* 35, no. 4 (July-August 1994), 36-37.
Report of the Task Force on Corporate Social Performance. *Business and Society: Strategies for the 1980's.* U.S. Department of Commerce, 1980.
Senge, Peter. *The Fifth Discipline: The Art and Practice of the Learning Organization.* New York: Doubleday/Currency, 1990.
Solomon, Robert C., and Kristine R. Hanson. *It's Good Business.* New York: Harper & Row, 1988.

8

Corporate Philanthropy and Business Power

JEROME L. HIMMELSTEIN

INTRODUCTION

Although corporate giving programs in a real sense are both apolitical and highly individualized, they still have a broader political meaning for the corporate world as a whole. This chapter explores this meaning by (1) examining how these programs are embedded in intercorporate networks and share a common understanding of what they do, (2) analyzing the broad political rationale for corporate giving that is part of this common understanding, and (3) showing how normally taken-for-granted political assumptions become explicit when giving programs face criticism from groups like the Capital Research Center.

How is corporate philanthropy related to business power? In contrast to most of the other chapters in this book, my research focuses on the culture and politics of corporate giving. My topic is more of the "What does it all mean?" or "What are the broader implications?" variety. This is not to say that it ignores the everyday reality of corporate giving, but that it places this reality into a broader context.

"Business politics," however, may seem a strange context into which to place corporate philanthropy, at least to those who practice it. "Politics" seems to imply power, partisanship, and conflicts of interests. "Business" implies corporations acting as a cohesive collectivity. Neither term at first glance fits the everyday realities of corporate giving very well.

Although corporations obviously act politically in many ways, for example, by contributing to political candidates or lobbying legislators, most corporate giving officers would not regard their giving programs as simple adjuncts of the corporate PAC or lobbying operation. They see their mission very differently: They seek to do well for the corporation not in a directly self-interested way, but by doing good for society, by identifying those areas of concern in which the public interest and the corporate interest overlap. Far from being a collective business enterprise, furthermore, everyday corporate giving is resolutely individualistic. Corporate giving officers seek to tailor their giving programs closely to the strategic interests of their particular companies.

So, what do I mean by placing corporate philanthropy in the context of business politics? First of all, I mean that although resolutely individualistic, corporate giving programs nonetheless have a collective shape. They are embedded in intercorporate networks and as a result share a common culture, a common understanding of what corporate philanthropy is and ought to be. Second, corporate giving has a political frame: The common culture provides a political rationale for corporate giving.

I shall discuss the collective shape and political frame of corporate giving generally. I shall then look at how the specific political assumptions underlying corporate philanthropy become explicit when corporate giving officers confront a right-wing critic, the Capital Research Center, which does not share those assumptions. My discussion uses a variety of materials, including in-depth interviews conducted between June 1992 and June 1993 with representatives of 55 of the largest corporate giving programs in the United States.

THE COLLECTIVE SHAPE

No corporate giving program is an island. To varying degrees, each participates in a network of relationships with programs at other corporations. These ties help shape patterns of giving.

In a study of corporate giving in the Minneapolis/St. Paul area, for example, sociologist Joe Galaskiewicz found that the more ties that a CEO has to those corporate leaders central to the local philanthropic culture, the more money his corporation gives away (Galaskiewicz, 1985a). More generally, local business leaders have a powerful impact on giving by corporations and by affluent individuals. A recent study done by *The Chronicle of Philanthropy* found that in communities such as Minneapolis or Atlanta, where philanthropy thrives out of proportion to per-capita income, business leaders "set a pervasive tone" that encourages "people with financial resources" to "use them for the good of the whole." In such communities, "involvement with charity is practically a prerequisite to becoming a powerful figure in the business life of the city" (1994, p. 24).

In related work, Galaskiewicz also found that corporate giving officers (CGOs) themselves have ties to peers in other corporations, whom they consult when they are uncertain about a particular grant, and that peer opinion influences their evaluations of nonprofit organizations (Galaskiewicz, 1985b; Galaskiewicz and Burt, 1991).

Similarly, another sociologist, Michael Useem, using both a national sample of corporations and a sample from Massachusetts, concluded that intercorporate ties tend to create a degree of uniformity in corporate giving (Useem and Kutner, 1986; Useem, 1991). Because large corporations, for example, are more likely to share information about giving with each other, they tend to be more like each other in level and type of giving to the arts than are smaller corporations. Similarly, the more professionalized a corporation's giving program the closer its pattern of funding lies to the average for all businesses, again because professional corporate giving officers frequently interact with their peers in other corporations through professional associations. Finally, those corporations most influenced by other corporations in their giving decisions and headquartered in areas with a higher overall rate of corporate giving to the arts are more likely themselves to support the arts.

The implications of findings like these is that intercorporate ties promote the application of what Useem calls "generalized business norms and procedures" to corporate giving (p. 67). Put somewhat differently, these ties sustain a shared culture, a common set of assumptions about how much corporations should give, to whom, and through what kind of procedures. This culture in turn shapes the giving practices of individual corporations.

Thus, while each corporate giving officer thinks his or her own thoughts, each does so in a common language. This culture is sustained not only by informal ties with peers but also through more formal gatherings sponsored by the Council on Foundations and the Conference Board. The heads of America's largest corporate giving programs frequently mention these organizations as places where they discuss giving outside their own corporations. The shared culture of corporate giving has also been sustained and articulated in a growing body of published writing over the last few decades, much of it in recent years from the Council on Foundations.

One consequence of having a shared language is that major CGOs understand what they do in remarkably similar ways, regardless of whether they work for electronics firms or banks, retailers or oil companies, pharmaceutical manufacturers or computer producers. Asked why their corporations give money away, they reply with rationales from the shared lexicon of enlightened self-interest. Asked about recent positive developments in their field, they routinely refer to the various elements of professionalization and the promise of strategic giving. Corporations serving competitive consumer markets might be expected to approach philanthropy differently from those that don't, or labor-intensive firms from capital-intensive ones. While they may differ in the details of what they support, however, they think about what they do in quite similar ways.

POLITICAL FRAME

The culture that CGOs share not only provides a common sense about the everyday management of corporate giving programs but also contains an implicit political understanding about how business should best position itself in American society and about the role of corporate philanthropy in doing this. The core of this understanding is that nonprofit organizations are potential allies with whom corporations should build durable ties.

The notion of a special relationship between business and the nonprofit sector long predates corporate philanthropy. As historian Peter Dobkin Hall has argued at length, from the earliest days of the American Republic, elites generally and business elites in particular have constructed and supported nonprofit organizations of various kinds as alternatives to a state that they saw as too susceptible to unpredictable popular control. In other words, they have used nonprofits as a way of pursuing public goals through private action. Hall traces this vision from the late eighteenth century right through to the 1920s and Herbert Hoover's vision of the "associative state." In full-blown form, it pictures a "private-sector alternative to socialism," a network of nonprofit organizations, closely tied to for-profit organizations, which would provide many of the services delivered elsewhere by the emerging welfare state (Hall, 1982, 1992).

The subsequent development of government social welfare programs from the New Deal on has undoubtedly rendered this idea obsolete as a grand vision of society, but a similar outlook found a more limited expression in corporate philanthropy, as this became a serious business activity in the years following World War II. The development of this idea was integral to the diversification and expansion of corporate philanthropy from the early 1950s.

The idea that corporations have a collective interest in supporting the nonprofit sector, quite apart from the benefits that they might individually gain, was first articulated in the late 1940s and early 1950s by a group of leading businessmen concerned about the fate of America's private universities. They included Frank Abrams of Standard Oil of New Jersey, Alfred P. Sloan of General Motors, Irving Olds of U.S. Steel, and Arthur W. Page of AT&T. These men provided the rationale for expanded corporate support for higher education and helped found the Council For Aid to Education to encourage such support. They urged corporations not only to increase their funding of higher education, but to provide general support rather than merely aid for specific programs that might fit their immediate interests. Their central argument was that only by supporting private universities and colleges might business stem the growth of government-supported public education and the expansion of big government generally that had resulted from both the New Deal and the war. Olds stated the position this way:

> Capitalism and free enterprise owe their survival in no small degree to the existence of our private, independent universities. Both are not only important to each other—they are dependent upon each other. . . . I want to say emphatically that . . . every American business has a direct obligation to support the free, independent, privately-endowed colleges and universities of this country to the limit of its financial ability and legal authority.
>
> If the day ever comes when our tax-supported competitors can offer the youth of America a better education than we can—and at a lower price—we are through. (Curti and Nash, 1965, p. 251)

Olds's argument was echoed a few years later in the landmark case, *A.P. Smith Manufacturing Company v. Barlow,* which for the first time gave broad legal sanction to corporate philanthropy. It was also restated in the mid-1950s as a rationale for corporate giving in general by Richard Eells in his classic *Corporation Giving in a Free Society* (1956). The justification for corporate philanthropy, Eells wrote, was not simply to garner short-term "good will for the donor," but more profoundly to "protect and preserve the donor's autonomy by protecting and preserving the conditions within the greater society which ensure the continuity of a system of free, competitive enterprise" (1956, p. 136).

The key to doing this, he argued, lies in protecting the principle of "voluntary association" and the various "private sectors" of society, including the nonprofit sector. The fate of business and the nonprofit sector are intertwined. Business enterprise has a direct interest in promoting the strength of private sectors because it is itself a private sector.

For this reason, business must maintain the barriers against the progressive absorption of these sectors into state-controlled areas (Eells, 1956, p. 104).

The idea that business has a general interest in supporting the nonprofit sector to stem the growth of government has echoed through statements on corporate philanthropy ever since. In the early 1980s, the Business Roundtable linked its support for the Reagan tax and spending cuts to increases in corporate philanthropy. If business was serious "in seeking to stem over-dependence on government," the Roundtable argued, it had to "increase its level of commitment" to the private nonprofit sector (O'Connell, 1983, p. 386).

Just a few years ago, Brian O'Connell, head of Independent Sector, sounded a similar theme in James Shannon's *Corporate Contributions Handbook*. The for-profit and nonprofit sectors share a commitment to "the freedom of individuals to pursue their own ideas" and thus are equally threatened by the growth of the state:

> Both the for-profit and the nonprofit sides of private enterprise are faced with growing domination by government. . . . If this so-called third sector becomes further dominated by government, we will in fact have only two sectors and, inevitably, one sector. (Shannon, 1991, p. 48)

Reynold Levy of AT&T has made a similar point on a more concrete level. His central argument is that "philanthropy should be approached as a long-term investment that stimulates and reinforces the overall [corporate] relationship with nonprofit institutions." It is a way to build "stable and mutually beneficial relationships between the corporation and its nonprofit allies" (Levy and Oviatt, 1989, p. 133).

These ties are important for several reasons, Levy argues. First, "the more services nonprofits provide, the less government is required." Second, the nonprofit sector is a major economic force to which no business "can afford to pay less than full attention." Third, nonprofit organizations and their leaders command the "power of public respect" and constitute "a set of highly influential shapers of public opinion." Fourth, the nonprofit sector broadly defined has been the source of the great social movements of American society. Corporations either can deal with these movements after they have crystallized as problems or "can interact with these organizations and their issues before they become forces to be reckoned with on their own terms" (Levy and Oviatt, 1989, p. 131).

In summary, Levy strongly recommends that recipients of corporate largesse be seen as "potential partners, consultants, and allies" and that philanthropy be seen as "an open door for access, one route by which this constituency can be reached and meaningfully engaged" (p. 131).

CORPORATE PHILANTHROPY
AND THE CAPITAL RESEARCH CENTER

From this perspective, corporate philanthropy appears as part of a political strategy to promote the general interest of business in limited government by strengthening the nonprofit sector and corporate ties to it. This strategy usually remains tacit and taken for granted in the everyday world of corporate philanthropy. It finds a voice, however, in response to certain kinds of external criticism. Corporate philanthropy has come under fire in recent years for supporting Planned Parenthood, the Boy Scouts, Hispanic groups, and certain kinds of art. One of its most persistent critics has been the Capital Research Center, which condemns corporate givers for supporting allegedly liberal public policy groups. The response of CGOs to that criticism articulates their tacit political assumptions.

The Capital Research Center (CRC) was founded in 1984 by Willa Johnson, who had been a senior vice president at the Heritage Foundation and had served briefly as associate director of personnel in the Reagan White House. Its annual budget rose from $69,000 in 1984 to $380,000 in 1988 and $864,000 in 1991. About 60 percent of that comes from right-wing foundations, principally the Sarah Scaife Foundation, the John M. Olin Foundation, and the Adolph Coors Foundation, which have played a central role in building conservative think tanks generally. In virtually every other respect it is well integrated into the right: Its executive committee reads like a list of conservative luminaries; and its major books, which boast introductions from the likes of William Simon and Pete du Pont, receive attention in *The Wall Street Journal*, *National Review*, and *Human Events*, as well as from conservative columnists.

The CRC takes a dim view of the contemporary nonprofit sector and the philanthropic culture that dominates it. Under this culture, the third sector, far from being a natural ally of business, is all too cozily tied to government.

> Today, a unified sophisticated, and well-funded philanthropic elite is dedicated to imposing on us the doctrines of "progressive" philanthropy, doctrines that would reorder our political, economic, and cultural priorities. This movement, driven by a bankrupt ideology long since disproved by history, would impose its own standards of "social justice," based on more involvement of government in philan-

thropy and more involvement by charities in politics. It has lost faith in traditional American values of individual responsibility and free choice, to say nothing of diversity in the marketplace of ideas. (Capital Research Center, 1990, p. 3)

In other words, in Johnson's view, the philanthropic and nonprofit world is dominated by "a culture informed largely by those who would use the resources of the nonprofit world to expand the power of government" (Capital Research Center, 1991, p. 4).

The publications of the CRC have found fault with any number of specific elements of philanthropy and the nonprofit world. It has aimed its most visible and persistent criticism, however, specifically at corporate philanthropy in a series of annual volumes entitled *Patterns of Corporate Philanthropy*, which have appeared yearly since 1987 (e.g., Meiners and Laband, 1988; Bennett, 1989; DiLorenzo, 1990; Olasky, 1992). These books argue, in the words of the 1990 edition, that "American businesses are helping finance public policies that erode the American free-market economy and its underlying normative system of individualism, self-reliance, and self-responsibility" (DiLorenzo, 1990, p. 3). Or, as the 1988 edition put it, "the fruits of free enterprise" are going to those "whose purpose is the replacement of capitalism by a utopian collectivism" (Meiners and Laband, 1988, p. 2).

In other words, American corporations tend to support liberal public policy groups, which favor a bigger government role in the economy and "increased restraint on . . . private sector activities," rather than conservative groups, which are skeptical of government's ability to address social problems and encourage more reliance on the market (DiLorenzo, 1990, p. 89).

To document their claims, the CRC annually solicits information on corporate giving from the *Forbes* 250 corporations (receiving usable information from 146 of those companies for their 1990 volume). It then identifies all grants going to organizations who engage in public policy advocacy (225 organizations in 1990). The CRC classifies each of these organizations on a scale from 1 to 9, with 1 to 4 designating various degrees of liberalism (from radical left to center left), 6 to 9 designating various levels of conservatism (from center right to radical right), and 5 being middle of the road. Finally, it places corporations on the same scale based on the average ranking of the organizations that receive their dollars. Since 1991, it has also translated numerical rankings into grades ranging from A (6.5 or higher) to F (below 3.0).

The results vary little from year to year: Typically, the corporations in the study give about $30,000,000 a year to public affairs groups, with about 60 to 65 percent going to left-of-center groups and about 30 percent to right-of-center groups. No corporation has yet gotten an A. Only 10 to 15 percent get a grade of B (scores of 5.5 to 6.4), while 60 to 65 percent get Ds or Fs (scores of 4.4 or below). In addition, each report provides numerous specific examples of individual corporations supporting groups that are alleged to be its enemies.

The CRC does not systematically explain why corporations are so stupid or so perfidious as to support those who seek to undermine capitalism, but several of its authors suggest that corporate contributions programs have been captured by outsiders from the nonprofit world. CEOs, corporate directors, and top management fail to play an active role in corporate giving, thus leaving it, in the words of William Simon's introduction to the 1988 volume, to "the foundation world's professional managerial elite to define for them what is 'right'" (Meiners and Laband, 1988, p. v). In the 1992 volume, Olasky asks the dark question: "What if top executives (often politically conservative) and contributions managers (often politically liberal) are unevenly yoked? What if contributions managers are working not in the corporate or public interest, but in their own ideological interest?" (p. 14). He talks of "philanthropic trade groups" and "contributions officers who come from government or nonprofit groups" taking over corporate giving (Olasky, 1992, p. 1).

The CRC directs its message to top corporate management, whom it sees as potential allies in the battle against the philanthropic elite and their culture. It has routinely sent copies of its yearly study to CEOs; initially at least, these copies were accompanied by letters from prominent conservatives, including William Simon and Donald Rumsfeld.

The Capital Research Center clearly means its work to awaken slumbering CEOs and send them rushing to rein in their errant giving programs, or failing that, to get stockholders to issue a loud wake-up call. In fact, nothing of the sort has happened. Corporate giving programs have not changed their public policy funding, and CGOs have not even come under serious fire from the top.

Indeed, in its annual reports, the CRC does not claim to have had an impact on corporate giving, emphasizing instead only the attention the media pays to their studies of corporate giving. Data presented in their 1992 study, moreover, show no change over the previous five or six years in the grades corporations have received for their giving. The CRC's lack of impact led William Simon to lament in the preface to the 1992 study: "Nothing would make me happier than to be able to say that the last four years have witnessed a reversal of this sorry picture. I cannot" (Olasky, 1992, pp. 8, iii).

One of the few top executives to speak out on the subject, J. Richard Munro, chair of the executive committee of Time-Warner, criticized the Capital Research Center for giving low ratings to "companies most would regard as having exemplary public service programs such as AT&T, American Express, Mobil, and General Motors" and cautioned corporate executives to "analyze criticism of their giving carefully before reacting" (Munro, 1991, p. 1).

CGOs themselves dismiss the CRC with a casualness and humor that conveys no sense of feeling threatened. "They are a joke," said one corporate giving executive; others dismissed the CRC as "ridiculous," "pathetic," "pretty bizarre," and "nonsense." The director of corporate giving at a company that received a relatively good (i.e., conservative) rating from the CRC said he was "pretty embarrassed" by that fact. Several executives from companies who perennially received bad ratings termed themselves proud, one of these expressing "great pride" in recently making CRC's list of the top ten corporate "misgivers."

All but one of these corporate giving directors denied getting any serious heat from senior management about a too liberal rating from the CRC, nor did any know of other giving programs that had been brought to heel. A few reported casual inquiries from their CEOs, in response to which a simple memo sufficed. One mentioned with pleasure that senior management sent a note of praise for her foundation's especially low rating. The only exception was at a corporation whose "liberal" giving record had been mentioned first by Paul Harvey on his national radio show and then by a local conservative talk show host. "Everybody in the company" seemed concerned, the CGO said. Again, however, a memo noting that the rating was based on less than 1 percent of the corporation's grants and pointing out that many of the allegedly left-wing recipients were really not so radical sufficed to quiet the internal fuss.

Why didn't the CRC make a bigger impression on top corporate management? One senior CGO with over ten years' experience running contributions programs expressed considerable puzzlement that it had failed to "crack" that audience. After all, he noted ruefully, top management often mistrust people like himself:

> There are a lot people, including corporate directors . . . and shareholders, and, yes, including a lot of senior operating executives who think, "those fools over there [in contributions] are giving away the company's money. They don't really know what our corporate interests are, and they're not looking after our corporate interests. . . ." They think we are a bunch of do-gooder, probably left-of-center people. . . .

Others, in contrast, felt that the CRC failed for a very obvious reason:

Its data were shoddy and obviously so. They noted that the CRC ranks corporations on the basis of a very few grants, that it judges the politics of these grants in terms of the group receiving it, not the program being funded, and above all, that it defines liberal or left in impossibly broad terms. In regard to the last of these, several CGOs recounted with obvious glee how they turned aside inquiries from top management by noting simply that the CEO or chairman of the company sat on the board of one of the allegedly "liberal" groups that the contributions program had supported. In one case, it was the Aspen Institute; in another, the Foreign Policy Association:

> Our president has been a member of the board of the Foreign Policy Association and his predecessor had been a member . . . and he might call them a lot of things, but left of center wouldn't have been one of them.

The reason for the CRC's failure to crack its corporate audience in reality is neither thoroughly obscure nor thoroughly obvious. The CRC failed because it did not take into account that the fundamental political assumptions of corporate leaders bring to bear on corporate philanthropy differ dramatically from its own, even if they may see eye to eye on other matters. The CRC's argument makes sense only if one assumes the following:

- (1) The political world is sharply polarized between those who support a pristine, market-oriented capitalism and those who are utopian collectivists.
- (2) Virtually any government regulation of the economy or social welfare program puts society on a slippery slope to total collectivism.
- (3) Consequently, business in American society is surrounded by enemies who wish to destroy it and with whom, as a result, no compromise is possible.
- (4) The nonprofit sector is full of these enemies of business.

Given these assumptions, any group that sees government programs or regulation as a solution to a social problem is indeed anticapitalist and deserves to be labeled left-wing; any corporation that gave even a small percent of its giving budget to such groups would be suicidal indeed; and drawing a distinction between supporting a specific program and supporting a group would certainly be disingenuous.

Although top corporate executives and the CGOs who work for them may feel embattled at some times and over some issues, by and large they do not see the nonprofit sector as part of the problem. To the contrary, as we have seen, historically corporations have viewed the nonprofit sector as a special ally and corporate philanthropy as a way of strengthening their relationship with that ally.

Consequently, faced with nonprofit organizations with which business may not wholly agree politically, corporations see not enemies to be subdued, but differences of perspective to be discussed. The differences between business interests and these other interests can be reconciled on terms friendly to business, if business acts in a cooperative rather than a confrontational way. That is, while the CRC sees politics as a Manichean struggle between business and its enemies, business leaders often see a kind of *benign pluralism*. The key to success in this benignly pluralist world is *access*, cultivating ties with a broad range of other important political and social actors. Through these ties, businesses can communicate their positions on various issues and in the best case build alliances.

One CGO put it this way, drawing an analogy to lobbying:

> What we have found is even for moderate to liberal kinds of groups you're probably better off working on the inside than you are on the outside. When I was lobbying I went before many legislators . . . that I knew weren't going to vote my way. But all I wanted them to do is listen to me. And down the road it might just trigger a little doubt in their minds. . . . If I got my facts on the floor . . . I had to affect their reasoning somewhere down the road, and that's why I think it's important even where we think the group's position is in opposition to ours that we at least get a voice in.

Later in the interview, he gave a specific example of how philanthropic ties to environmental organizations might benefit a corporation by leading to business-friendly solutions to environmental problems:

> I think one of the best developments [in corporate philanthropy] has been the recognition that we really do have to look beyond ourselves. Many of the companies that impair the environment—oil companies, paper product companies—have become very socially responsible and . . . are working with environmental groups to see what they can do to prevent damage that is economically feasible. The argument that they're able to bring is, "Look, this costs a lot of money." And so it has brought some sanity to everything.

Another CGO spoke more broadly:

> I think from a strategic point of view in a pluralistic society like ours that no company can afford to paint itself into some ideological corner. And you need wide understanding and you need communication with a lot of people.

Others enunciated similar themes. A philanthropy executive at a major insurance company justified her program's support for projects of the Children's Defense Fund, a major CRC target, despite their differences on national health insurance, with a paradigmatic statement of benign pluralism. The company, she said, supported worthy specific projects with no concern for the recipient's broader politics. It believed in a "healthy pluralism" in politics, in which people could disagree about issues and still work together.

Another corporate giving director, working for a company often at odds with environmental groups, defended her foundation's selective support for some of those groups. "It is important to partner with environmental organizations," she said, "so we can arrive at win-win solutions to the problems we face." She distinguished in this respect "balanced" environmental groups, worthy of funding, from "polarizing" ones, who presumably are not.

Speaking more generally, another director said that "it is healthy to have a dialogue" with groups with which one disagrees, even groups that have taken (or may take) the corporation to court. Her company, she noted wryly, was always involved in litigation with someone or other anyway. Still another maintained that one of the most important things about corporate philanthropy is "its ability to build bridges" with people with whom you disagree.

CONCLUSION

The collision of corporate philanthropy with the Capital Research Center is intriguing precisely because it highlights the shared political assumptions underlying corporate giving that otherwise might be overlooked. It shows that the historical rationale for corporate giving is not "just history," but informs day-to-day thinking about the activity.

More important, the contrast underlines the distinctiveness of these assumptions. The CRC's conservative worldview is hardly alien to the business world; indeed, it has resonated with business leaders at other times and places, notably in the early 1980s with regard to the Reagan agenda. That it has failed to make any headway with regard to corporate philanthropy in the late 1980s and early 1990s testifies to the strength of the alternative political assumptions already in place there.

REFERENCES

Bennett, James T. *Patterns of Corporate Philanthropy: Ideas, Advocacy, and the Corporation*. Washington, D.C.: Capital Research Center, 1989.

Capital Research Center. *Annual Report*, 1990, 1991.

Chronicle of Philanthropy. "The Midwest's Charitable Advantage" (February 22, 1994), 1, 22-26.

Curti, Merle, and Roderick Nash. *Philanthropy in the Shaping of American Higher Education*. New Brunswick, NJ: Rutgers University Press, 1965.

DiLorenzo, Thomas J. *Patterns of Corporate Philanthropy: The Suicidal Impulse*. Washington, D.C.: Capital Research Center, 1990.

Eells, Richard. *Corporation Giving in a Free Society*. New York: Harper and Row, 1956.

Galaskiewicz, Joseph. *Social Organization of an Urban Grants Economy: A Study of Business Philanthropy and Nonprofit Organizations*. Orlando: Academic Press, 1985a.

———. "Professional Networks and the Institutionalization of a Single Mind Set." *American Sociological Review* 50: 639-58, 1985b.

Galaskiewicz, Joseph, and Ronald S. Burt. "Interorganizational Contagion in Corporate Philanthropy." *Administrative Science Quarterly* 36: 88-105, 1991.

Hall, Peter Dobkin. *The Organization of American Culture, 1700-1900*. New York: New York University, 1982.

———. "A Historical Overview of the Private Nonprofit Sector." In *The Nonprofit Sector: A Research Handbook*, ed. Walter W. Powell. New Haven: Yale University Press, 1987. Pp. 3-26.

———. *Inventing the Nonprofit Sector*. Baltimore: Johns Hopkins University Press, 1992.

Levy, Reynold, and Frank Oviatt, Jr. "Corporate Philanthropy." In *Experts in Action: Inside Public Relations*, ed. Bill Cantor. New York: Longman, 1989. Pp. 126-38.

Meiners, Roger E., and David N. Laband. *Patterns of Corporate Philanthropy: Public Affairs Giving and the Forbes 250*. Washington, D.C.: Capital Research Center, 1988.

Montague, William. "A Conservative Study Center Stirs Heated Controversy by Attacking Corporate Grant Makers' 'Liberal Bias,'" *Chronicle of Philanthropy* (May 15, 1990), 1ff.

Munro, J. Richard. "When Corporate Grantmaking Is Attacked as Too Liberal or Conservative." Washington, D.C.: Independent Sector, 1991.

O'Connell, Brian. *America's Voluntary Spirit: A Book of Readings*. New York: Foundation Center, 1983.

Olasky, Marvin. *Patterns of Corporate Philanthropy: The Progressive Deception*. Washington, D.C.: Capital Research Center, 1992.

Shannon, James, ed. *The Corporate Contributions Handbook*. San Francisco: Jossey-Bass, 1991.

Useem, Michael. "Organizational and Managerial Factors in the Shaping of Corporate Social and Political Action." *Research in Corporate Social Performance and Policy* 12 (1991), 63-92.

Useem, Michael, and Stephen I. Kutner. "Corporate Contributions to Culture and the Arts." In *Nonprofit Enterprise in the Arts: Studies in Mission and Constraint*, ed. Paul J. DiMaggio. New York: Oxford University Press, 1986. Pp. 93-112.

9

Paradigm Lost

Research toward a New Understanding of Corporate Philanthropy

DENNIS R. YOUNG AND DWIGHT F. BURLINGAME

INTRODUCTION

John Maynard Keynes is thought to have said, "There's nothing as practical as a good theory." Such an observation applies well to the current state of corporate philanthropy, a field that is in flux as a result of major upheavals in the corporate and social environments. As the authors and conference participants who have contributed to this volume variously attest, our thinking about corporate philanthropy is also in flux. As a result, there is a clear and desperate need for better information and analyses of the issues in this field. At the root of the problem, however, is the fact that we have no common way of thinking about corporate philanthropy: In particular, although thoughtful practitioners and scholars have made important headway, we still have trouble answering the question—Why *do* businesses engage in giving and volunteering?

If we knew how to respond to this question, much else would follow. We would know what to measure and what information to collect; we could identify promising alternative giving strategies; we would be guided by a common theory in analyzing our strategies with the information we collected; and we would know the audiences for our analyses—all in the cause of trying to make corporate philanthropy more effective. Indeed, we would know what we meant by the effectiveness of corporate philanthropy!

It is both the strength and the frustrating nature of this book that its contributors do not unambiguously define a single conceptual framework for thinking about corporate philanthropy. They do, however, suggest several fundamentally different theoretical frames of reference, each of which has claims to legitimacy and utility for corporate and nonprofit sector managers, policy makers, researchers, and scholars. The value of these alternative frames is twofold: First, they provide competing theories of corporate philanthropy. If we are ever to reach a general understanding of corporate philanthropy, the merits of these alternative frameworks will have to be debated and evaluated empirically. Some refinement or combination of the alternatives may eventually be found to be most powerful. Whatever the ultimate result, having the alternative theories in hand is step one in this process, and a real contribution of the authors of this work.

Second, each of the frameworks contains different implications both for the practice of corporate philanthropy and for the research agenda required to advance this field in the future. By sketching out these implications, we can begin to formulate a provocative and useful agenda, even before any consensus is reached on a "grand theory" of corporate philanthropy. In this chapter, by way of bringing together the thinking of our authors and contributors, we will first describe the alternative conceptual frameworks and then identify some of the research questions and issues that flow from each of them.

ALTERNATIVE CONCEPTS
OF CORPORATE PHILANTHROPY

The contributors here develop at least four essentially different ways of understanding corporate philanthropy, deriving from alternative ways of thinking about how corporations themselves actually work—different "theories of the firm" as economists would put it. Thus, although corporate philanthropy appears at first glance to be a specialized, even peripheral, function of corporations, its understanding actually cuts to the core of what the corporation is all about. We will label the four alternative frameworks or "models" as follows: the neoclassical or corporate productivity model; the ethical or altruistic model; the political model; and the stakeholder model.

THE NEOCLASSICAL/CORPORATE PRODUCTIVITY MODEL

In this conception, the basic purpose of, and motivation for, corporate philanthropy is to contribute to the ability of the firm to make profits. The ultimate measure of success is increased corporate productivity and enhancement of the financial bottom line. In some cases, the connection between corporate giving and the bottom line may be fairly clear, as when a cereal company gives its surplus product away free, hoping to influence people's tastes so that they will ultimately buy the product themselves. However, the processes through which corporate philanthropy achieves a corporation's financial goals may also be long term and indirect—for example, by improving employee morale or community relations as investigated by David Lewin and Jack Sabater in chapter 6, by improving public image through cause-related marketing as discussed by John Yankey in chapter 2, or by investing in the health and educational status of the future labor force or in technological research in the universities. The notion of "enlightened self-interest" is consistent with the neoclassical model as long as the focus remains on the long-run profitability of the corporation. But, as Craig Smith suggests in chapter 1, the implication of this model, which bears a striking resemblance to his "new paradigm," is that corporate philanthropy must prove itself in the same way as any other business function within the corporate setting. Thus, there are many that view the term "corporate philanthropy" as an oxymoron, since it implies action motivated by factors other than self-interest.

THE ETHICAL/ALTRUISTIC MODEL

This model, implied most strongly by Lance Buhl in chapter 7, is based on the assumption that corporations generate financial surpluses that are used by corporate leaders to do what is right for society. It is based on a concept and a culture of social responsibility and ethical behavior that comes with the power over resources granted to corporations in our society. It is based on an understanding that corporations and the societies they operate within are extremely interdependent. It presumes a certain level of discretion on the part of corporate giving officials and a certain aloofness from the operational pressures of making profits in the marketplace so that, within certain limits, managers can pursue a set of charitable goals not directly related to corporate interests. In this sense it resembles the "managerial discretion" branch of the economic theory of the firm. It conceives of corporations as citizens and corporate executives as societal leaders who, having run their businesses in a responsible and profitable manner (possibly by incorporating some philanthropic activity into corporate strategy), are free to switch hats and allocate some of their surpluses according to criteria of social value and ethical and moral precepts not tied to bottom-line considerations.

THE POLITICAL MODEL

This model has both an internal and an external face. Externally, as discussed in chapter 8 by Jerry Himmelstein, the political model postulates that corporate philanthropy may be understood as an exercise by corporations to advance their general long-term interests in society by building relationships and coalitions with nonprofit organizations and with the giving programs of other corporations and foundations. The basic motivation is to preserve corporate power and autonomy by building private initiatives as an alternative to the growth of governmental authority and by limiting government interference in the free enterprise system. Another take on the external political model is that corporations engage in philanthropy in order to legitimize or protect their economic power. Thus, corporations such as tobacco companies that have the most to lose from adverse public policy decisions or an irate public, give more, and build stronger relationships with nonprofit organizations, in order to prove themselves as good public citizens (Mitchell, 1989). In this interpretation, the political and neoclassical models converge, as political grant making may be interpreted as good long-term business strategy to protect the bottom line.

The internal version of the political model views the corporate giving officer as a player in a company game. Within the confines of the corporation, he or she seeks to build relationships with other departments and groups in order to survive in a stringent environment and increase leverage over corporate resources.

In both the external and internal versions, the political model emphasizes the preservation and enhancement of power and freedom of action, the building of relationships, and the principle of compromise and mutual interest in reaching negotiated or implicit agreements. In this view, corporate philanthropy is not driven by profits or by social good per se, but by desire of the corporate giving community to bolster its position in the environments in which it operates.

THE STAKEHOLDER MODEL

Stakeholder theory posits that the corporation is a complex entity that affects, and is affected by, various significant groups—stockholders, managers, workers, customers, suppliers, community groups, and so on. Each of these groups has different interests, is impacted by the corporation in different ways, and exerts different forms of leverage over the corporation. In this view, managing a corporation is an exercise in managing the stakeholders. As implied by Donna Wood and Raymond Jones in chapter 4, corporate philanthropy and corporate social behavior, broadly speaking, are guided by the desire of corporate leadership to steer a clear path through the shoals of stakeholder interests.

In some ways, the stakeholder model is the most comprehensive, but also the most amorphous conceptual framework for understanding corporate philanthropy. By acknowledging the multiple interest groups impinging on corporate activity, it resembles the political model. And by including both the financial objectives of corporate owners and the social interests and values of community groups, it encompasses some of the tenets of the neoclassical and ethical models. However, in its present state of development, the stakeholder model does not make clear exactly how the various stakeholders interact to determine corporate policy or how the various economic and social objectives are reconciled with one another.

It is possible to argue a reductionist approach to the four models— for example, that the stakeholder model is just a more generalized form of the political model or that the political model is a subset of the neoclassical model, which explicitly recognizes the need for political support of corporate goals. However, each model does bring a unique dimension to the study of corporate philanthropy. The neoclassical model focuses on corporate productivity and profits. The ethical model substitutes social criteria as the prime consideration. The political model focuses on corporate power as the prime issue and the positioning of corporate giving in the wider realms of corporate politics. The stakeholder model recognizes that there are many players in corporate life, each with different objectives and each pushing and pulling on the corporation to achieve them. If all this can be unified into a single helpful model, it will require the craftsmanship of some fine theoreticians.

In some ways, the four alternative models roughly reflect alternative historical periods in the development of the corporation and its role in society. The neoclassical model grows out of an era of American business domination of the economy through the 1950s. The ethical/altruistic model offers a 1960s flavor of social responsibility in which corporations began to be questioned about their impacts on society and their obligations to help with social problems. The political model reflects a growing sense of societal participation by corporations in the world of the 1970s and 1980s which required that business build allies in other sectors in order to minimize government encroachment and to promulgate its own ideas about social welfare. And stakeholder theory integrates the notion of empowerment, a growing societal force since the 1960s, wherein corporate owners and directors must acknowledge and demonstrate sensitivity to other groups that now hold considerable power and influence both within the corporation and in its environment.

The sequential flow of the four paradigms is also reflected in the longer-term legal history of corporate giving in the United States (see Karl, 1991). While nineteenth-century business tycoons gave some of their profits to causes they personally considered worthy, it was their own money uncomplicated by the constraints of the modern corporation. Much of the early twentieth century was characterized by "judicial and legislative debate over the benefits managers could offer employees without incurring the wrath of stockholders who considered benefits an assault on their rights to received dividends fully reflecting the company's profits" (Karl, 1991, p. 26). While in 1921, the IRS accepted the idea that corporations could contribute to charitable institutions that served their employees, this represented only a limited expansion of the accepted principle that corporate philanthropy was justified only where it directly benefited the company. Indeed, in 1919 Congress and the Supreme Court precluded corporate income tax deductions for charitable contributions. While the IRS code was broadened in 1936 to permit deduction of such contributions (for contributions benefiting the company), it was not until 1953 that the principle of direct corporate benefit was overturned in the case of *Smith vs. Barlow* in New Jersey, and a more general rationale of public responsibility allowed. Since that time, corporations have struggled with mixtures of self-interest and community benefit that drive their corporate contributions programs.

In the historical progression of models suggested above, corporations may be viewed as learning to recognize their social obligations and also answering critics who argued that corporations helped to create many social problems themselves, by externalizing some of their costs onto society. Thus, corporations sought to redress these problems, and to preempt possible government regulation, by undertaking voluntary, philanthropic initiatives.

What makes the present moment in time especially interesting is that all four paradigms now seem operant. The corporate world has become sensitized to the social obligations of business and to the legitimate needs and interests of multiple groups, and there is no going back on these fronts. Moreover, globalization of economic activity has made the political environment more complex, and the networks of corporate stakeholders more diverse. Yet changes in both the international and domestic economies make financial competitiveness more important than ever. Thus, corporate philanthropy must now be understood from the viewpoints of all four models.

RESEARCH IMPLICATIONS OF ALTERNATIVE MODELS

The four models serve usefully as alternative filters for screening and interpreting the research questions that flow from the chapters of this book and from the discussion of (earlier versions) of those chapters during the 1994 Conference on Corporate Philanthropy in Cleveland. The following text is based largely on an amalgam of ideas presented in the free flow of discussion during that event. Note that the framing of these research questions does not reflect consensus that corporate philanthropy can be studied as an exact science. While research can systematize our understanding, much of this "art form" will always remain outside the purview of precise analysis.

In the discussion that follows, many different research questions are raised. The purpose is not to give the impression that nothing is known about corporate philanthropy. Indeed, the authors of chapters here and in other literature, have made very substantial contributions to our understanding of this field. As the second and third parts of this book attest, substantial factual knowledge on corporate giving has been accumulated, and some rigorous empirical and theoretical work has been done. And, of course, there is a wealth of practitioner wisdom in this field that is only partially documented. Thus, the present purpose is to identify those issues whose study will advance knowledge and practice beyond the current state.

RESEARCH BASED ON THE NEOCLASSICAL MODEL

In this model, the focus is clearly on the impact of corporate philanthropy on the financial performance of the corporation. Given this focus, research can contribute to the understanding of corporate philanthropy by addressing a variety of critical measurement, effectiveness, and organizational questions.

Measurement Questions

Certainly the overall question here is whether corporate philanthropy has a bottom-line impact on corporate profits. Before that global question can be broached, however, more basic measurement and accounting issues must be addressed, including the following:

- How much does corporate philanthropy really cost? How should volunteer hours and in-kind gifts, as well as financial contributions, be measured?
- What expenses should be charged to Corporate Contributions versus other departments or functions of the corporation?
- On what elements of overall corporate financial performance does corporate philanthropy impact? Costs? Revenues? Market share? Labor productivity? What measures of financial effectiveness can best demonstrate the value of corporate philanthropy on corporate financial performance?

- How can corporate philanthropy be framed in terms of corporate investments? What measures can be used to demonstrate the value of corporate philanthropy over time?

Effectiveness

The questions of measurement and accounting reflect the more basic issues of *how* exactly corporate philanthropy influences corporate productivity and profitability, that is, through what processes and means, both within the corporation and in its interaction with the corporate environment? In particular:

- How does corporate philanthropy impact or intersect other business functions, such as marketing, governmental affairs, research and development, or human resources, in terms of costs, revenues, and productivity measures? Indeed, where such functions are highly interwoven with corporate philanthropy, how are the impacts of the latter to be distinguished?
- What are the intermediary effects of corporate philanthropy that lead to impacts on corporate financial performance? Does corporate philanthropy lead to better employee morale? Improved community relations? Wider company recognition in the marketplace? A better corporate reputation? How do these in turn improve corporate financial performance?
- What are the intermediate and ultimate financial impacts of alternative modes of corporate philanthropy, such as cause-related marketing, sponsorships, gifts-in-kind, corporate volunteerism, partnership arrangements, and United Way participation?

Organizational and Strategic Questions

Given that corporate philanthropy may work through a variety of channels to impact on corporate financial performance, the framing of this function in strategic terms, and its organizational form and place within the corporation, become important considerations in understanding the circumstances under which corporate philanthropy is most effective. Thus, the following kinds of research questions arise:

- Where does corporate philanthropy fit within a corporation's overall business strategy, quality management, or continuous improvement protocols?
- How should corporate philanthropy be organized as a unit within the corporation? For example, under what circumstances is the establishment of a separate corporate foundation most effective?

- How can corporate philanthropy programs become more closely integrated with other departments and functions of the corporation? What are the different models for accomplishing such integration?
- How important is it for the CEO to be directly involved in corporate philanthropy? What is the most effective way to structure the relationship between the CEO and the head of Corporate Giving?
- In the long run, is corporate philanthropy best thought of as a business specialization in itself or should it be subsumed or diffused within other corporate functions? What are the implications of answers to this question for the education of business executives and for business school curricula?

Overall, it is interesting that many of the questions that derive from applying the neoclassical model are ones that are uppermost on the minds of corporate giving officers themselves. This observation applies especially to research information that would allow corporate giving staff to make a case that their function contributes significantly to the bottom line of the organization and is not just a peripheral function or luxury that can be ignored or neglected when the corporation comes under pressure. Whether or not the neoclassical model best explains corporate giving or indeed should serve as its ultimate justification, the fact that it leads to lines of inquiry of use to corporate giving officers recommends it as a helpful framework for formulating a research agenda of interest to both practitioners and scholars.

RESEARCH BASED ON THE ETHICAL/ALTRUISTIC MODEL

In this model, the issue is how corporate philanthropy can work best in terms of the good it does for society. The research agenda implied in this perspective again involves considerations of measurement, internal organization, and effectiveness, but in addition must include examination of concepts of the public good, the social contract between corporations and society, the moral standards by which corporations themselves operate, and the role of corporate philanthropy in influencing socially relevant behavior of the corporation as a whole.

Criteria and Measurement

The altruistic model suggests the investigation of both global questions on criteria of social benefit and particular issues of measurement. For example:

- What is a sensible way of characterizing the social contract between corporations and society? What are the concepts of a "just society" or the "quality of life" issues to which such a contract is addressed?

- What are the measures of a just society or the quality of life dimensions by which the impacts of corporate philanthropy may be gauged?
- How useful is benchmarking, that is, setting target levels for corporate giving (e.g., percentages of pretax earnings), in measuring corporate contributions to society or in motivating corporations to give?
- How useful are social audits in gauging the societal contributions of corporations?
- What are the societal impacts of different forms of corporate philanthropy, such as cause-related marketing, corporate volunteerism, and so on? How are these impacts best measured?

Ethics of Corporate Grant Making

If corporate philanthropy is driven by a paradigm of ethics and altruism, it must itself be guided by values that reflect these motivations. However, the art of corporate grant making is still primitive in this sense because standards have not yet been clearly articulated or codified. Thus, the following research issues arise:

- What standards can be applied to assure fairness and avoid parochial favoritism in corporate grant making?
- What is appropriate disclosure policy in corporate grant making? What data should be reported and how much explanation should be given for why certain grants are made and others are not?
- How should controversial issues or potential grantees be dealt with? Should grants be given to causes around which there are serious societal divisions or which threaten the economic viability of the corporation?

Impacts of Corporate Philanthropy on
the Ethical and Social Performance of the Corporation

Students and practitioners of corporate philanthropy such as Lance Buhl (chapter 7) believe that effective corporate giving programs operate not only through their own direct programming but also by their influence on the social responsibility and ethics practiced by other parts of the corporation. This perspective raises a number of additional research issues associated with the strategic focus, organization, and role of corporate giving programs within the corporation. Specifically:

- What other business functions impact directly or indirectly on the societal goals of interest to corporate philanthropy? How can corporate giving programs influence and work together with other business functions in a manner that contributes positively to social goals and minimizes social harm?

- How are basic American business values changing? What is the role of corporate philanthropy in influencing overall business values and ethical standards within the corporation?
- What is the best way to organize corporate philanthropy within the corporation so as to maximize its effectiveness in implementing overall standards of corporate responsibility and ethical behavior and addressing its agenda of social issues?

The research agenda that derives from the ethical model will, of course, be of considerable interest to social policy makers and theorists concerned with the role of business in society. But it will also be of interest to business decision makers with a social conscience and to corporate giving officers who conceptualize their own roles as social agents within the corporation rather than simply officials responsible for carrying out corporate strategy in the community.

RESEARCH BASED ON THE POLITICAL MODEL

The political model brings our attention to the strategic relationships between corporate philanthropy and other business functions within the company, as well as to the external relationships of the corporation with other businesses, with nonprofit organizations, and with government. Here, too, measurement issues are important because information represents power in the politics of these relationships. The status and location of corporate philanthropy within the formal organizational structure of the firm also potentially affects internal politics. Finally, the political model brings into full view questions about the relationships between the corporation, its competitors and collaborators in the business world, the nonprofit recipients of its largesse, and government. Moreover, it highlights the intricate nature of multisector cooperative arrangements. Thus, a rich array of research questions is suggested by this model.

Measurement Issues

The political model suggests some new areas of measurement development as well as additional aspects of measuring some of the phenomena indicated by the other models. In particular:

- How does corporate philanthropy contribute to other business functions, such as marketing, government relations, human resources, and so on, and how can those contributions be measured in ways that reflect the value of those contributions to the particular departments *on their own terms*. That is, what are the measures of impact of corporate philanthropy that are relevant to the particular interests of the Marketing Department, the Human Resources Department, and so on? How does a corporate philanthropy program turn these measures of impact into "credits" in the context of the internal politics of the corporation?

- How do impact measurement, evaluation, and accounting practices per se affect the politics of corporate giving within the firm and in terms of who receives the benefits of corporate philanthropy?
- What measures of corporate philanthropy do CEOs find useful, for their own purposes, in their relationships with stockholders, customers, managers, employees, and others? Do these measures differ if the CEO is a principal owner versus a minor shareholder or a salaried executive?
- What data on nonprofit organization recipients are useful for informing the politics of giving within the corporation? For example, is it useful to know nonprofit executive salaries? The cost/effectiveness of contributions in achieving stipulated social goals? Where recipient nonprofits get the remainder of their funding? Other aspects of the nonprofit's operations or track record of accomplishments?

Internal Organizational Relations

The political model asks how corporate philanthropy interacts with other corporate functions and how these relationships in turn affect corporate philanthropy. This gives us another angle on research concerning strategic and organizational issues:

- How do different modes of corporate philanthropy, such as cause-related marketing versus United Way participation, affect political relationships within the corporation?
- What are the recommended norms of behavior for corporate contributions programs within the corporation? Should corporate contributions people be political deal makers, the moral conscience of the corporation, or social entrepreneurs? To what degree must the corporate philanthropy program reflect the particular corporate culture in order to be viable and effective? Are corporate giving officers most effective when they are mavericks or conformists?
- What are the organizational dynamics between the corporation's philanthropy program and the rest of the corporation? Under what circumstances do corporate contributions officers become "insiders" within top management circles, and when are they left out?
- Does organizing corporate philanthropy as a separate business unit or as a foundation tend to marginalize this function within the corporation, or does it empower it?

- How does the location of corporate philanthropy within the structure of the corporation affect its politics? How does the particular relationship between the corporate giving officer and the CEO influence the internal political process?

External Relationships

The external politics of corporate philanthropy requires understanding of a complex web of interactions between the corporation and its business, nonprofit, and governmental partners and antagonists. Research could productively assess this subject both from the viewpoint of corporations themselves and the recipients of corporate philanthropy in the nonprofit world:

- How do corporations receive social "credit" for the benefits they offer through corporate philanthropy? How does this help them in their relationships with government and community groups?
- How do corporations behave collectively with respect to social issues and philanthropic giving? Do they tend to collaborate, compete, or simply operate independently in separate, nonoverlapping spheres of influence? And what are the reasons for these observed patterns? Where they collaborate, what forms of cooperation are manifest, how do they work, and how effective are they? Where they operate separately, how does each corporation choose its social niche? Where they compete, what form does competition take?
- What is the nature of interaction between corporations, nonprofit organizations, and government? In what areas do the sectors collaborate, compete, or operate independently of one another? What explains these patterns? What are the different workable models of multisector partnerships? When multisector arrangements emerge, whose standards for evaluating effectiveness are used? Is the concept of the "seamless state," which melds corporations, the government, and private, nonprofit organizations into a continuous web of interactive relationships, a viable concept and sensible ideal, or just a naive notion? What does the "seamless state" look like in practical terms?
- Is there a strong ideological motivation for corporations to develop their giving programs, to collaborate in philanthropic endeavors, and to form partnerships with nonprofits? In particular, are corporations, as Jerry Himmelstein questions in chapter 8, motivated by the desire to limit government? Are other ideological motives at work, such as the promotion of free enterprise and individual effort?
- What are the effects of corporate partnerships and other forms of corporate giving on nonprofit organization recipients? Do

nonprofits lose their autonomy under these arrangements? Do they lose their senses of mission as the boundaries between nonprofits and business blur?

- What is the impact of nonprofit involvement on the corporation? Does involvement with nonprofits influence the corporate culture and modify the corporation's approach to business in general?

Research based on the political model will clearly be of interest to corporate giving officers wishing to understand how best to position themselves within the corporation. Executives of nonprofit organizations will also want to better understand the politics of corporate giving in order to ally themselves more effectively with corporate giving programs. Most importantly, this research agenda should also be of clear interest to corporate chief executives who must understand where philanthropy fits into the internal workings of the corporation, its overall approach to community relations, and its relationships with government. Social scientists wishing to better understand the politics of business and society, and management theorists studying the internal workings of the corporation, will also be drawn to this agenda.

RESEARCH BASED ON THE STAKEHOLDER MODEL

In one sense, the stakeholder model requires both a wider examination of the questions raised by the political model and a reassessment of the criteria suggested by the neoclassical and altruistic models. This model forces us to ask who the stakeholders in the corporation are, what they want, whether they are affected by how the corporation is organized and gauges its own performance, and how the corporation accounts for, and responds to, its various stakeholders. Some of the key research issues are:

- Who are the stakeholders in the modern business corporation? What are the particular interests and objectives of each group? How is each affected by, and how does each influence, the function of corporate philanthropy?
- How does the corporation as a whole balance and respond to the interests of its different stakeholder groups as it sets corporate direction and policy? What role and influence does corporate philanthropy have in these deliberations?
- Which internal stakeholders (major stockholders? corporate officers?) have important roles in corporate philanthropy? Which business units and departments (marketing? government relations? human resources?) see themselves as having important interests in this function? What are the particular concerns of each? How does each influence corporate philanthropic decision making?

- How do external stakeholders (stockholders, employees, citizen groups) each define their interests and influence the process of corporate giving?
- How do alternative strategies of corporate giving (cause-related marketing, volunteerism, United Way, etc.) differentially impact on stakeholder groups? Do particular groups favor some strategies over others?
- How do particular stakeholder groups influence the choice and character of corporate giving strategies? For example, how do institutional investors or organized consumer groups with political agendas affect corporate giving behavior?
- How does the location and organization of philanthropy within the corporate structure affect which stakeholder groups receive attention or which ones are neglected?
- How does the use of particular accounting and evaluation systems by the corporation as a whole, or by the corporate philanthropy program, affect the responsiveness of corporate philanthropy to alternative stakeholders?
- How do external conditions such as the state of the economy, social conditions such as crime, lagging educational levels, or health problems, or the extant political mood, affect the responsiveness of corporations to its various stakeholders? What social indicators would make good predictors of the "climate" for corporate response to different groups?

The research agenda stemming from the stakeholder model will certainly be of interest to social scientists and policy makers concerned with developing theory and designing policies related to the nature of the corporation, who benefits from it, how it is governed, and how corporate philanthropy serves its various constituents. Top corporate executives will be interested in how various stakeholder groups are best managed, and how different corporate policies and practices, including philanthropy, contribute to effective stakeholder relations under different environmental conditions. And, corporate giving officers will want answers to enable them to design their programs to respond effectively to relevant stakeholder interests important to the corporation, or to advocate for, or otherwise serve, particular stakeholders groups not well represented elsewhere in corporate decision making.

CORE ISSUES

While the four research models/paradigms generate an almost overwhelming panoply of important, specific research issues, these sets of issues are not entirely divergent. A few common themes run throughout the foregoing lists, suggesting a common core to the research agenda around which practitioners and researchers can coalesce. Four such themes clearly emerge:

- 1. *The Theory of Corporate Philanthropy*. This theme is implied in the construction of the paradigms themselves. More thinking is needed on what core values actually drive corporate philanthropy and what the rationale for this activity is, from the viewpoint of the corporation and from that of society. Where does corporate philanthropy fit into a theory of the firm, a theory of social welfare, or a normative theory of human behavior and social conduct?

While this core issue seems esoteric and theoretical, it touches on the most critical of societal concerns. If corporate philanthropy is just a cost of doing business and simply driven by corporations' quests to maintain their political legitimacy and achieve greater profits by preserving the status quo, then how effective can it be in achieving real reforms of social conditions? But if corporate philanthropy is driven by ethics and altruism and is grounded in a social contract between business and the rest of society to improve social conditions, can it be sustained in the increasingly competitive business climate of today's global economy? These are some of the real dilemmas that emerge in strong relief by grappling with the implications of alternative theories of corporate philanthropy.

- 2. *The Impact of Corporate Philanthropy*. This theme laces all of the measurement issues associated with the four paradigms. What are the effects of corporate philanthropy within the corporation, on recipient groups and social problems, on the various stakeholders in the corporation, and on society as a whole? How do we measure these impacts, and what do the data have to say about their significance?
- 3. *The Strategy of Corporate Philanthropy*. Given a theory and means of measuring impacts, the four paradigms still ask in their various ways how corporate philanthropy is best implemented in terms of different program approaches, and where it fits into the larger scheme of policy and management choices. How does it fit within the corporation and intersect with other corporate functions? Where does it fit in terms of the corporation's overall strategic relationships with customers, stockholders, communities, governments, and other countries? And what particular modes of corporate philanthropy are most effective in these terms?

- 4. *The Political Economy of Corporate Philanthropy.* Three of the four paradigms specifically recognize that the corporation is not the only important actor in the world of corporate philanthropy, and in some cases perhaps not even the most important one. Hence, they suggest the study of corporate philanthropy in a societal framework, not just as a matter of concern to business and its immediate constituents. These paradigms specifically ask what other elements in society influence and are affected by corporate philanthropic activity. They also ask how the corporation itself is influenced, and perhaps even fundamentally changed, by its participation in philanthropic activity and by its philanthropic relationships with the other parts of society. Carrying this view further, the paradigms raise research questions about blurring of the very boundaries separating the corporate world from government and the nonprofit sector.

In short, while the various paradigms offer substantially different cuts at our understanding of corporate philanthropy and substantially varied research agendas, they also make clear that, addressed from whatever angle, we need to know a lot more about why corporate philanthropy is undertaken, how its impacts can be measured, where it fits into the larger strategic decisions of corporations, and what its significance is in the greater political economy in which corporations are embedded.

PARADIGMS FOUND?

As this chapter suggests, one use of the alternative models is to identify different ways of thinking about corporate philanthropy, each of them useful for generating research questions that will further the understanding of scholars and put powerful information in the hands of corporate giving officers, advocates, and perhaps critics. A second use is to help dig into the basic question—What does motivate corporate philanthropy in the 1990s, and what are the likely forces that will drive and shape it in the future? The four paradigms, combinations thereof, or perhaps other paradigms not explored here, constitute alternative answers to this question. As such they suggest some additions to our research agenda, as follows:

- What other ways of thinking about corporate philanthropy may be helpful to guide future action and study? What academic disciplines not yet engaged have something to contribute to this field? And how can the four paradigms suggested here be usefully refined? This in itself can constitute a fertile ongoing area for research.

- What are the paradigms actually in use in corporate philanthropy? How do these paradigms play themselves out in terms of the explicit or implicit assumptions used by corporate officials in making philanthropic decisions? What are the factors that discriminate between the uses of one paradigm versus another? For example, do small businesses use one paradigm and large corporations another? Are there differences in use by industry? Are there regional differences? Are there differences between domestic and international corporations?

In addition, we might ask:

- Why do some corporations give while others do not? And why do some corporations active in philanthropy give more than others? Are such differences explained simply by objective factors such as size, profitability, or type of industry, or do differences in thinking about corporate giving, as captured by alternative paradigms, mediate the relationship between objective economic reality and the propensity to give? According to what paradigm do nongivers operate, and can that thinking be influenced through processes of education or research to turn nongivers into givers?

Jerry Himmelstein (personal correspondence) has suggested a related research agenda that asks why programs of corporate philanthropy are stable in some companies and not in others. He offers four possibilities, each of which tends to reflect a different one of our paradigms. Specifically, he theorizes that stability may be related to: (a) the ability of a corporate giving program to marshal hard data showing that the program contributes to the bottom line (neoclassical); (b) the strength of relationships between corporations and nonprofit organizations in their communities (external political); (c) the level of support from corporate employees (internal political and stakeholder); and (d) a culture of social responsiveness within the corporation as a whole (the ethical/altruism). Alan Senger of TRW (personal correspondence) suggests another factor—that stability is related to the method selected by the corporation to fund its corporate giving program. He suggests that those programs funded through company foundations may be more stable and predictable than those programs funded through direct grants subject to annual budgetary vagaries, a notion consistent with the internal political paradigm.

Viewed in terms such as these, the search for a single, overriding, contemporary, "new paradigm" of corporate philanthropy is much less important than making maximum use of the alternative paradigms that we have in hand to help us understand the different sides and facets of corporate philanthropy, and to pursue a comprehensive research agenda that will advance the practice of corporate giving. Such a reduction may not only be very difficult, as we have previously suggested, but possibly inhibiting as well. The four paradigms vary in their ability to generate questions of interest to different groups of research consumers. Corporate giving officers and chief executives are more interested in information that applies at the (micro)level of the individual organization, while policy makers, social theorists, and industry, community, and nonprofit leaders may be more focused on the broader social (macro)impacts and implications of corporate philanthropy. To consolidate the four paradigms would lose much of the nuance that allows them to provide different "micro" and "macro" level insights. Thus, while the authors and conference participants who have participated in the development of this volume hope to have made a substantial contribution toward a broader understanding of corporate philanthropy and the identification of a research agenda that will significantly advance this understanding in the future, the development of a unified theory of corporate giving will have to await a more advanced and differently minded convocation of practitioners and scholars in the future.

ACKNOWLEDGMENTS

The authors would like to extend special thanks to the following people who contributed their substantive comments and suggestions to the writing of this chapter: Patricia Frishkoff, Jerome Himmelstein, David Introcaso, Vic Murray, Alan Senger, James Shannon, and Margaret Wyszomirski. The authors hope they will be forgiven for borrowing liberally on their ideas without specific attribution in most cases. All responsibility for errors remains with the authors.

REFERENCES

Karl, Barry D. "The Evolution of Corporate Grantmaking in America," chapter 2 in *The Corporate Contributions Handbook*, ed. James P. Shannon. San Francisco: Jossey-Bass, 1991.
Mitchell, Neil. *The Generous Corporation: A Political Analysis of Economic Power.* New Haven: Yale University Press, 1989.
Murray, Vic. *Improving Corporate Donations.* San Francisco: Jossey-Bass, 1991.

CONTRIBUTORS

Lance C. Buhl, former Director of Corporate Contributions for BP America, consults with corporations, foundations, and nonprofit organizations on strategic management and on building and evaluating programs and partnerships for community problem solving.

Dwight F. Burlingame is Director of Academic Programs and Research at the Indiana University Center on Philanthropy, Adjunct Professor in the School of Public and Environmental Affairs, Professor in the Graduate School, and Adjunct Professor of Philanthropic Studies at Indiana University. Among the books he has written and edited are *Responsibilities of Wealth* and *Taking Fund Raising Seriously*.

Patricia A. Frishkoff is Professor of Accounting and Director of the Austin Family Business Program in the College of Business at Oregon State University. Her research focuses on family business management and includes issues related to leadership development, succession, strategic direction, and philanthropy. Dr. Frishkoff is widely published in academic and business journals.

Jerome L. Himmelstein is Professor of Sociology at Amherst College. His books include *The Strange Career of Marihuana: Politics and Ideology of Drug Control in America* and *Doing Good and Looking Good: Corporate Philanthropy and Business Power*.

Raymond E. Jones is a graduate student at the Joseph M. Katz Graduate School of Business, University of Pittsburgh at the time of this writing. His main areas of interest are corporate social performance and corporate philanthropy.

Alice Korngold is Executive Director of the Business Volunteerism Council. BVC provides training and education, consulting and volunteer referral services to 450 nonprofit organizations and 85 corporations. For 20 years, Ms. Korngold has been a national consultant, speaker, and author in the areas of strategic community involvement, impact evaluation, and the governance of nonprofit organizations.

David Lewin is Professor, Vice Dean, and Faculty Director of the MBA Program in the Anderson Graduate School of Management and Chairman of the Human Resources Round Table (HARRT) at UCLA. A specialist in human resource management and employee relations, Dr. Lewin has published 12 books and more than 100 scholarly and professional articles. His recent books include *Research Frontiers in Industrial Relations and Human Resources, International Perspectives and Challenges in Human Resource Management*, and *Human Resource Management: An Economic Approach.*

J. M. Sabater retired at the end of 1993 from IBM as Vice President of the IBM International Foundation and IBM Director of Corporate Social Policy and Programs. He is currently on the boards of Jobs for America's Graduates and RSVP, International; is a Senior Consultant of the Council on Foundations; a consultant on international volunteerism to the Points of Light Education Foundation; and Executive Director of Reach & Teach USA, a nonprofit focused on education and training in South Africa.

Craig Smith is president of Corporate Citizen, a Seattle-based research institute.

Elizabeth Hosler Voudouris is Assistant Director of the Business Volunteerism Council, where she provides consulting and information services to assist more than 90 companies in planning and implementing strategies for community involvement.

Donna J. Wood is Professor of Business Administration at the Katz Graduate School of Business, University of Pittsburgh. She is founder of the International Association for Business and Society (IABS) and has served as Chair of the Social Issues in Management Division of the Academy of Management. Currently, she is editor of the IABS journal, *Business & Society.* Dr. Wood's research interests focus on corporate social performance and stakeholder theory, international dimensions of business and society relationships, collaborative social problem solving, business ethics, and business-governmental relations.

John A. Yankey is the Leonard W. Mayo Professor at the Mandel School of Applied Social Sciences, Case Western Reserve University. A member of the Program Faculty of the Mandel Center for Nonprofit Organizations, Dr. Yankey chairs the Center's Nonprofit Management Certification Program and codirects the Mandel School's Program for the Advancement of Public Human Services.

Dennis R. Young is Governing Director of the Mandel Center for Nonprofit Organizations and Mandel Professor of Nonprofit Management at Case Western Reserve University. He is editor of the journal *Nonprofit Management and Leadership*, and author and editor of several books including *Economics for Nonprofit Managers* (with Richard Steinberg), *Governing, Leading, and Managing Nonprofit Organizations* (with Robert M. Hollister and Virginia A. Hodgkinson), and *Nonprofit Organizations in a Market Economy* (with David C. Hammack).

INDEX

Abrams, Frank, 148
Accounting: and firm size, 91; in the neoclassical model, 164
Ackerman, Robert W., 43, 47-48, 51
Aetna Casualty and Life, 10, 129, 130
Agle, Bradley R., 59, 66, 79
Altruism, 9, 96-97. *See also* Ethics
American Express, 2, 16
Antal, Ariane Berthoin, 47
Arlow, Peter, 55
Armbrister, T., 16
Arts, contributions to, 91-92, 94
Aspen Institute, 154
Atkinson, L., 91
Aupperle, Kenneth E., 46, 49, 63, 64

Babitts, Judith, 140
Bailey, A. L., 11, 17
Baucus, Melissa S., 54, 65, 78
Bayless, Pamela, 27
Belkaoui, A., 75
Ben and Jerry's Ice Cream, 10
Berle, Adolph A., 47, 66
Boal, Kimberly B., 56-57
Boatright, John R., 127-28, 129, 130, 136
Bock, R. H., 96
Bohm, David, 140
Boston College Center for Corporate Community Relations, 2, 86
Bradshaw, Thornton, 130
Bragdon, Joseph H., 75
Brill, Jack, 54
Brilliant, E., 18, 19
Bromiley, Philip, 74
Brothers, T., 16
Buehler, V. M., 59, 72
Burlingame, D. F., 88, 94
Business in the Community (London), 3
Business Roundtable, 149
Business Volunteerism Council (BVC), 28-38
Byham, William C., 105

Calton, Jerry M., 44, 56
Canadian Centre on Philanthropy, 3
Capital Research Center, 144, 150-56

Carroll, Archie B., 43, 45-46, 50-51, 59, 64-65, 68-69, 73-76, 79
Case Western Reserve University Mandel Center for Nonprofit Organizations, ix, xiii, 3
Caudron, Shari, 27
Cause-related marketing (CRM), 12-13
CEOs: leadership of, 5, 6; personal values of, 92, 93; philanthropy culture of, 145-46; power of, 134; and social responsiveness, 46, 47; support for volunteerism, 30
Chamberlain, Neil W., 106
Charitable investment concept, 96-98
Charities. *See* Nonprofit organizations
Chen, K. H., 76
Civic organizations: frequency of giving to, 94, 96
Clark, Sylvia, 18
Clarkson, Max B. E., 49-50
Cochran, Philip L., 43, 49-50, 52, 77
Cohn, J., 59, 72
Collins, Denis, 51
Community involvement: and business performance, 106-108, 111-13, 120-21; ethical justification for, 129; measurement of, 109; and size of firm, 58, 101; of small businesses, 87, 101; and value beliefs, 123
COMPUSTAT financial performance file, 107, 108
Cone/Roper Study on volunteerism, 25
Conference Board, 24-25, 34, 35, 58, 86, 146
Connors, T. D., 88, 89
Contributions officers: Capital Research Center vs., 152-56; as community servants, 138-40; as corporate servants, 133; ethical responsibilities of, 136-41; networking among, 146-47; political frame of, 147-50; power of, 134-35; and size of firm, 92
Copperman, L. F., 59
Cornell, B., 56
Corporate Citizen, 1, 3
Corporate Citizenship Measurement Study, 3

Spencer, Barbara A., 58, 65, 73, 78
Spicer, B. H., 61, 75, 76
Sponsorships, 4, 13-14
Stakeholders, xi, 68-69, 161-62; and corporate social performance, 42, 47- 51, 55-68; customers as, 59-61; employees as, 59; government relations as, 64; information disclosure studies as, 63; laws/regulations as, 65-66, 78-79; management values as, 64-65; minorities as, 59; natural environment as, 61-62, 75-76; reputational ratings as, 62-63, 76-78; research based on, 171-72; responsiveness studies as, 63-64; stockholders as, 54-56
Steckel, R., 11, 12, 13, 15, 17
Steiner, George A., 59, 72, 75
Stendardi, E. J., Jr., 86
Stewardship, 96-97
Stockholders, 8; aversion to charitable giving, 163; and corporate social performance, 54, 55-56; returns related to charitable giving, 57
Strachan, James L., 78
Strategic giving, 9-10
Sturdivant, Frederick D., 77
Sullivan Principles compliance scale, 18, 52
Summers, William, 31, 32, 33
Sundgren, Alison, 77, 107
Swanson, Diane, 44

TAP Project (Atlanta), 69-70
Time Warner, 27
Total Quality Management (TQM), 3-4
Transformational paradigm, 131-36; and contributions officers, 137-41

Turner Broadcasting, 19

Ullmann, Arieh, 55, 56
United Ways, 18-20, 86, 87, 94, 95
Useem, Michael, 87, 146

Vance, Stanley C., 77
Volunteer Centers, 28, 34
Volunteerism, corporate, 12, 15-16, 21; advisory committees, 29; assessment of, 30; audits of community involvement, 29; benefits of, 26-27; Business Volunteerism Council (BVC), 28-38; companies conducive to, 34-35; evaluation phases, 35-38; and leadership, 23; and local government relations, 27; management involvement in, 30; McDonald & Company C.A.R.E.S., 30-33; media reports of, 26; and mission, 27, 29-30; obstacles to, 33-34; prevalence of, 24-27; program life cycles, 34; and size of firm, 90-91; in small businesses, 90-91; studies of, 25-26

Wartick, Steven L., 43, 49-50, 52
Weir, P., 55, 78
Wellins, Richard S., 105
Wiltsek, N. L., 93, 96
Wise, S. R., 88, 89
Wiseman, J., 76
Wokutch, Richard E., 58, 65, 73, 78
Wood, Donna J., 18, 43-44, 48, 50, 51, 77
Worrell, Dan L., 74, 78
Wynn, James A., 74

Zetlin, M., 9